The Essential
JAMES E.
TALMAGE

CLASSICS IN
MORMON THOUGHT SERIES
[to date]:

No. 1.
The Essential Parley P. Pratt

No. 2.
The Essential Orson Pratt

No. 3.
The Essential Brigham Young

No. 4.
The Essential Joseph Smith

No. 5.
The Essential James E. Talmage

The Essential

JAMES E.
TALMAGE

EDITED BY

JAMES HARRIS

SIGNATURE BOOKS
SALT LAKE CITY

To the memory of
James Edward Talmage,
1862-1933

Jacket Design: Randall Smith Associates

© 1997 Signature Books, Inc. All Rights Reserved.
Signature Books is a registered trademark of Signature Books, Inc.
Printed in the United States of America
∞ Printed on acid free paper
2001   2000   99   6   5   4   3   2

LIBRARY OF CONGRESS CATALOGING-IN-PUBLICATION DATA
Talmage, James Edward, 1862-1933.
    [Selections, 1996]
    The essential James E. Talmage / edited by James Harris.
        p.   cm.
    ISBN 1-56085-018-3
    1. Mormon Church—Doctrine. 2. Church of Jesus Christ of Latter
    -day Saints—Doctrines. I. Harris, James.   II. Title.
    BX8637.T292   1996
    230'.93—dc20
                                                96-21590
                                                    CIP

Contents

Acknowledgments

Many people deserve my heartfelt thanks. My wife, Diana, merits special mention for being patient and allowing me the time to work uninterrupted. Thanks to my stepchildren Amy, Melanie, and Matthew, who wondered why I spent so much time in the basement, and to James Jr., who kept me going, in his own inimitable way.

My mother, Alice Harris, helped make this project much easier. My father, Philip Harris, made sure I read *The House of the Lord* before I went to the temple. Both provided me with pocket-sized editions of *Jesus the Christ* and *The Articles of Faith* for my mission and have supported me in various ways. My mission president, Helio da Rocha Camargo, included these two books in our daily mission study plan.

Many friends in the Kingston Ward, Albany New York Stake, kept me on my toes, including Larry Kolts, Hamlet Montero, Rick Healy, Ken and Dawn Hill, Mary Ellen Bafumo, Lois Nichols, Alan and Kathryn Burgess, and Charles and Margie Seager-Olsen. Special thanks to David Avenius, for having faith in me and for opening windows of opportunity for so many. Chester and Beverly Hamilton provided a refuge for me and many others. They will always be remembered, as will members of the Lake Placid Branch and friends from the Glens Falls Ward.

My sister Renee spent considerable time and money at the Harold B. Lee Library, Brigham Young University, while her husband, Bill, and children Philip, Marie, and Garrett supported me on research trips to Provo, Utah. My brother Randy and his wife, Tami, and family kindly gave me a room for a week while in Utah. Thanks also to Ripsey Bandurian.

I am grateful for my other brother and sister, Brenda and Steven, and their families, for their prayers, support, and concern. The Emerick family, John, Anne, David, and Daniel, generously offered me transportation at a much needed time.

Special thanks to the James E. Talmage family, especially John R. Talmage, the last living son of James Talmage, as well as to Mary

Sanderson and James Talmage, grandchildren of James Talmage. Garrett Steenblik helped me locate members of the Talmage family.

Elder Carlos Asay, president of the Salt Lake temple and emeritus member of the First Quorum of the Seventy, allowed me and my brother and sister-in-law to visit the Talmage Room in the Salt Lake temple, where Elder Talmage wrote most of *Jesus the Christ*. Special mention to George I. Cannon, former president of the Salt Lake temple, for his kindness.

I am grateful to the Historical Department of the Church of Jesus Christ of Latter-day Saints, Salt Lake City, Utah; to Special Collections at the Harold B. Lee Library; to Special Collections at the Marriott Library, University of Utah, Salt Lake City; to the Kingston Area Library and the Saugerties Area Library, New York; and to Benchmark Books, Salt Lake City. Individual thanks to Thomas G. Alexander, Carol Bush, James D'Arc, Duane E. Jeffery, Stan Larson, Larry Skidmore, Susan G. Thompson, Thomas Wells, David Whittaker, and Dan Wotherspoon, for their encouragement.

The late Dennis Rowley, whose insightful research on James E. Talmage and whose patience, time, and support were particularly helpful, will be sorely missed by one who did not have the opportunity to meet him in person.

Finally, this work would not have been completed without Santo Benincasa.

Editor's Introduction

LDS church president Heber J. Grant was concerned over his colleague Elder James E. Talmage's workload and apparent lack of recreation. After much urging, Talmage agreed to accompany the president golfing on the condition that if he decided not to pursue the game, Grant would not insist that he play again.

Several church authorities who golfed joined the men at Nibley Park in south Salt Lake City. Grant and others demonstrated the proper strokes for their new student. Grant was especially confident that once Talmage played, he would embrace the game.

On his first and only shot, Talmage sent the ball close to 200 yards down the fairway, "a truly magnificent drive." The audience applauded eagerly.

"Congratulations," said Grant, rushing forward, with outstretched hand. "That was a fine shot you will remember for the rest of your life."

"You mean *that* was a fully satisfactory golf shot?" Talmage replied.

"It certainly was!" beamed Grant.

"Then I have fulfilled my part of the agreement?"

"You have—and don't you feel the thrill of excitement?"

Talmage hesitated, put on his jacket, then said, "If I have carried out my part of the agreement, then I shall call on you to live up to yours. You promised that if I hit a satisfactory drive and did not feel the spontaneous desire to play, you would stop urging me to do so. Now I should like to get back to the office, where I have a great deal of work waiting."[1]

Such was James E. Talmage, serious, bookish, always busy. Perhaps it was a sobering childhood that instilled such discipline in him. When Liberty Stake president Bryant S. Hinckley asked, "When and where did you receive a testimony of the gospel?" Talmage answered, "I do not know, I believe I was born with it as I belong to the third generation of Talmages in the Church. My paternal grandparents, James Talmage of Ramsbury, Wiltshire, England, and his wife, Mary Joyce of Hampshire, England, were the first, or among the first, to join the Church in that part of England. My father, James Joyce Talmage, and my mother, Susannah Praeter (Talmage) became members of the Church before I was born. They were active and devoted members." Continuing he said:

> Though I seem to have been born with a testimony yet in my early adolescence I was led to question whether that testimony was really my own or derived from my parents. I set about investigating the claims of the Church and pursued that investigation by prayer, fasting and research with all the ardor of an investigator on the outside. While such a one investigates with a view of coming into the Church if its claims be verified, I was seeking a way out of the Church if its claims should prove to me to be unsound. After months of such inquiry I found myself in possession of an assurance beyond all question that I was in solemn fact a member of the Church of Jesus Christ. I was convinced once and for all, and this knowledge is so fully an integral part of my being that without it I would not be myself.[2]

During a class examination at Brigham Young Academy, fifteen-year-old James Talmage wrote simply, "My testimony briefly expressed is, 'I know for myself, independent of the opinion of others, that the Church of Jesus Christ of Latter-day Saints is the true church of Christ,—restored by God's chosen prophet Joseph Smith, and I also claim to be a partaker and to hold a standing in that church.'"[3]

For those who have read Talmage's theological writings, there can be no doubt as to his belief in the restored gospel, in the LDS church, in the prophet Joseph Smith, and in Jesus the Christ. However, there is more to the man than this. He was devoted to his family, committed to education, scholarship, teaching, and to science and the scientific method as a means of arriving at truth. He was serious but not necessarily humorless. He was not a sports enthusiast, but enjoyed horseback riding and hiking. His interests were surprisingly varied, and whatever he pursued, he tried to do so to perfection.

James Edward Talmage was born on 21 September 1862 in Hungerford, Berkshire, England. The exact dates of the baptisms of his grandparents and parents are not known, but even though the LDS church was only thirty-two years old, James was a third-generation member.

His grandfather James was a herbal doctor, as was his father James Joyce, and this may have influenced young James's interest in science.[4] By the age of ten he had learned to plot the horoscope, an enterprise he would later dismiss as fraudulent.[5] Young James must have learned some rudimentary medicinal skills from his grandfather and father because at age seventeen, while touring LDS schools with Karl G. Maeser, he successfully extracted a bullet from a boy who had accidentally shot himself.[6]

At age eleven three events occurred that sobered the young boy. The first happened in the spring of 1873 when James became ill. His father blamed this on his not having yet been baptized. (His baptism had been postponed because of opposition to the church in the area.) When James had recovered, he and two friends were to enter the water the same evening, the baptism being held at night as not to arouse local hostilities. As James stepped to the water's edge, they reportedly heard a terrible shriek which James described as "A combination of every fiendish ejaculation I could think of." His father asked if he wanted to proceed; James said yes, and the noise stopped the moment he stepped into the water. Later James asked the other participants to sign an affidavit about what they remembered.[7]

The second incident was the accidental blinding of his younger brother Albert. Albert came up behind James who was working with a digging fork. James swung the fork around and punctured Albert's left eye. Albert later suffered from "sympathy blindness" in his right eye and was only able to discern bright colors at close range. Albert was only six years old at the time.[8] James was devastated by the tragedy. In later years he would become president of the Society for Aid of the Sightless and would meet Helen Keller. Albert actively promoted the use of braille and having church periodicals available for the blind.

The third event was the death of his grandfather. James had been close to his grandfather, spending time with him while his parents ran a hotel. The family migrated to Utah in 1876, about a year and a half after the death of Grandfather Talmage.

The Talmage family settled in Provo, Utah, where the newly founded Brigham Young Academy (BYA), with its venerable head, Karl G. Maeser, was just beginning. As Maeser's son Reinhard noted: "In this first year . . . came James E. Talmage, fresh from England and English schools. True to the customs of his native land he scattered his H's with a promiscuousness quite amusing. But from the beginning he gave evidence of a superior mind, thereby winning the admiration of his fellow students among whom he soon became a recognized leader."[9]

In England Talmage had distinguished himself as a scholar in the local diocese school system of the Church of England. In Provo, by age seventeen, Talmage was teaching courses such as physiology, Latin, and Pittman shorthand for $1.25 per week. In the classroom and in his evaluations of teaching accommodations, he noticed how light fell in the classroom, if there were adequate teaching supplies, and the like. He was very attentive to the needs and concerns of fellow teachers.[10]

During the 1880-81 academic year Talmage realized his need for further education. He consulted with church president John Taylor, who agreed and gave him a blessing of encouragement. Talmage's excursion to Lehigh University in South Bethlehem, Pennsylvania, became a mission of sorts. He was especially moved when the deacon's quorum of his Provo ward gave him a $2.00 donation for his trip east.[11]

Part of the admonition Talmage received when he left Utah was that he was "not to seek after personal honors or degrees" but bring this new knowledge back to Utah to serve the needs of BYA and the church. With limited resources he made the best of the facilities that were at his disposal in the East. In his year at Lehigh (1882-83) he completed freshman through senior classes with an emphasis on science. He attended lectures not on his schedule and took comprehensive and oral exams at the end of each semester. He also took many of his notes in Pittman shorthand and later translated them to longhand, thus giving him double exposure to classroom lectures.

He also visited the local steel works and other places of interest to a fledgling geologist, and spent considerable time in the well stocked campus laboratory. His only material indulgence was a walking cane, in vogue at the time. He taught a class in phonography (Pittman shorthand) to students who, at the end of the course, gave him an ebony, gold-headed walking cane with an engraved expression of appreciation.[12]

At that time there were no seminaries or institutes of religion for LDS students, neither was there a local Mormon congregation, so Talmage spent his Sundays at various denominations in the area.

After a year at Lehigh, Talmage decided to continue his studies at a university which offered courses unavailable at Lehigh. With encouragement and loans from friends in Utah, he enrolled at Johns Hopkins in Baltimore, Maryland. While at Johns Hopkins, he learned of the devastating fire that destroyed much of Brigham Young Academy. He thought that this might force him to return to Utah, but he was encouraged to stay. During this time he began outlining lectures that he would later deliver in Utah and would then find their way into his numerous articles.[13]

Talmage also spent as much time as possible in the Johns Hopkins laboratories, knowing that his scientific resources would be severely limited at BYA. One telling episode involved his research into the effects of narcotics, an incident which demonstrates his devotion to science and the scientific method. On 17 March 1884, as part of a class assignment, Talmage interviewed a man addicted to hashish. The man introduced the curious Talmage to others who had used hashish, all of whom described their experiences as being very different. Talmage and his associates decided "to try the effect of small dose upon ourselves." Talmage confessed that he "disliked the idea of doing such a thing, for as yet I have never known what it is to be narcotized by either tobacco, alcohol, or any drug . . ."

On 22 March he reported taking three doses of five grams each every hour. At midnight he had experienced no reaction. On Sunday, 6 April, he increased the dosage and reported "the effect was felt in a not very agreeable way."[14] Following his return to Utah, his lecture on "Stimulants and Narcotics" became one of the young scientist's most popular.[15]

Talmage returned to Provo in late June 1884, after first reporting to church authorities in Salt Lake City. He immediately resumed his old teaching posts at BYA, where he was also appointed acting principal. Additionally, he was called as a home missionary and spent many Sundays traveling to various wards and branches of the church.[16] On 29 September he was ordained a high priest and was named as an alternate to the high council (he had been ordained an elder on 28 June 1880).

Talmage had earlier been asked to run for political office, but could not because he was not an American citizen. He overcame that obstacle on 15 September 1884 when he was naturalized. Three years later he was made a deputy U.S. marshal and witnessed an execution, and in 1888 was nominated by the Mormon friendly People's Party to serve as a counselor from Provo's Third Ward. He went on to become an alderman and a justice of the peace. His personal papers describe many of the cases over which he presided.[17]

Talmage disagreed with the practice of mixing politics and religion. In a general conference address he spoke of political parties in general terms,[18] but never used the rostrum to encourage specific political sentiments.[19] In one instance in 1918 the Council of the

Twelve Apostles was engrossed in serious discussions concerning Woodrow Wilson's proposal for a League of Nations. Elder Reed Smoot, who also served as a U.S. senator, opposed the league, using the scriptures to defend his stand. Apostles who agreed with him included David O. McKay, Rudger Clawson, and Joseph Fielding Smith. Heber J. Grant believed that the league could help open doors for spreading Mormonism to other nations. Talmage concurred, as did Orson F. Whitney, Anthony W. Ivins, Stephen L Richards, and others. B. H. Roberts of the First Council of Seventy gave a talk the following March in the Tabernacle favoring the league. Although Talmage supported the premise of the talk, he objected to the Tabernacle being used for political purposes.[20]

Prior to Talmage taking on the responsibilities of his first political office in February 1888, he suffered a serious accident in his laboratory. "He was pouring molten slag from an assay crucible into a mould in the laboratory when some material inside the molten mass exploded, scattering the remainder and hurling some of it directly into [his] left eye."[21] Although the blindness was temporary, it caused him to reflect seriously on the part he had played in his younger brother's blindness.

On 14 June 1888 Talmage married Merry May Booth in the Manti temple. At her birth, the name Merry had been suggested by a sibling who had been singing a song which included the line "in the Merry, Merry Month of May." Talmage affectionately called her "Maia," after the Roman goddess of spring.[22] Maia was the youngest child in her family, Talmage the oldest in his. James and Maia became the parents of eight children: Sterling Booth, Paul Booth, Zella, Elsie, James Karl, Lucile, Helen May, and John Russell. All grew to maturity except Zella, who only lived eight months. Her death was a trying time in an otherwise happy household.[23]

Elsie later reported the following about her father:

> From the earliest memory of his children James E. Talmage was a man who "knew everything," and could explain most of it in a way to be at least partially understood by immature minds. Questions as to what thunder is made of, where water comes from, how high the sky is and why is it blue, and numerous others of similar character were never met with a weary "Do be quiet." Always there was a carefully worded explanation which helped to clear up the puzzle.
>
> To children this was a boon. Confidence in the clear understanding of their father and his ability to make things plain to them was

a strong part of the feeling which his sons and daughters held for him.

Strange and fascinating little bugs were shown to them through a microscope, queer things from strange lands and unfamiliar parts of their own, ore in which could be seen glints of precious metals, specimens of crystals, rocks, lime formations and other unusual, though natural peculiarities, all were regular parts of the hours which this man spent with his family.

Later the certainty that he could explain problems and make them simple carried over into fields other than the physical and geological. Questions of a more vital nature were propounded and clarified—questions of life and death, of where people came from and where they were going, of how to find the true values of life. Implicit faith in his answers helped them to take the ideas explained and weave [them] into their adolescent philosophy. Some of these children, now grown, feel that no problem can present itself which cannot be met satisfactorily by the man who has never failed them when they needed help [from] their father.[24]

When Elsie was only one year old, Talmage sent the following letter to her while he was in Russia. It not only shows his concern for his newborn daughter, but also his prose.

For Elsie, in Mamma's care.
Kychtym, Siberia, Russia-in-Asia.
August 16, 1897

Elsie, My Darling Daughter:

A father's fondest greeting to you on this the first recurrence of your natal day. Such I send to you from the plains of the far East, from the Steppes of Siberia. I write in the light of the early dawn, at an hour which to you on the opposite side of the earth is the same Sabbath hour at which one short year ago, you came to gladden our hearts, and to call forth our prayers of thankfulness; the hour at which your sweet mother reached the depths of the shadowy valley known as the Valley of Death, whither she had fearlessly gone to find you, my child. But the great Father, who is your parent as He is ours, guided and guarded her through the threatening darkness, and led her along the rough path of painful recovery, until she emerged from the pain and the travail, once more a sanctified mother, with you, my Darling, an added jewel to her crown.

May the one completed year of your life be the first of many, each bringing increasing wisdom and growing goodness in the service of our God. May the blessings pronounced upon you by the power of the eternal priesthood be realized in all your life and work. May you live to be a sisterly guide to your brothers' feet, and a comfort to the mother whom God has given to you and to me. And in the Lord's due time may you be crowned an honored mother in the House of Israel. Peace, happiness and the love that knoweth naught but good, be yours, my darling and my pride.

Affectionately,
Your Father.

> I send you blossoms, leaves and ferns, gathered for you on the slopes of Songomak.[25]

One exciting event that happened to the Talmages was in October 1912. The young family and recently appointed apostle moved into their new home at 304 First Avenue. They invited the other general authorities to a housewarming and had the house dedicated by President Joseph F. Smith.[26]

★ ★ ★

Throughout these years the church was struggling with problems occasioned by its practice of polygamy. Talmage never practiced plural marriage, though he was sealed polygamously to Zella Webb following her death in 1887. The Webb family were friends of the Talmages and James spoke of them frequently in his journals. Zella was burned in a fire and died as a result of her burns. Her mother asked that Zella be sealed to Talmage to help insure her a place in the Celestial Kingdom.[27] This was done with May's consent, and the sealing took place in 1891. The Talmages' first daughter was even named Zella after Zella Webb.[28]

In 1887 the Edmunds–Tucker Act authorized the federal government to confiscate the properties of any groups advocating and practicing polygamy. The act was aimed directly at the LDS church. The next year the government decided to enforce the Edmunds–Tucker Act and many church leaders fled into exile to avoid going to jail. On 24 March 1888 James noted:

> Attended the afternoon session of the District Court. This had been the day set by the Judge for sentencing brethren convicted under the infamous "Edmunds–Tucker Act" convicted of acknowledging and supporting their families! This is to the United States Government, a *crime!* Among the *prisoners* was my friend and fellow laborer Bro. [Karl G.] Maeser. He had pleaded guilty to the charge. His sentence was a fine of

$300.00 and the costs of prosecution. By special pressure brought to bear upon the judge through the gentile [non-Mormon] part of the community who entertained a respect for educational labor, he was spared imprisonment.[29]

Talmage was present at the general conference session which sustained the Wilford Woodruff Manifesto ostensibly banning plural marriage (at that same conference the Thirteen Articles of Faith were "readopted and sustained by the congregation"). Talmage recorded: "This manifesto has caused much comment among the Saints. Some regard this step as one of retrocession, others look wise and say, 'I told you so.' Since this document was issued I have prayed for light as to its true import; and see in it nothing but good for the people."[30]

Talmage also addressed the issue of plural marriage in his classic *The Articles of Faith*. The published book uses the topic to stress that Latter-day Saints observe the laws of the land.[31] In his papers is a seventeen-page section of notes titled "Items on Polygamy—Omitted from the published book." It is not clear if Talmage or a member of his reading committee decided not to include the document in the published book.[32]

During the Reed Smoot Hearings in early 1905, Talmage testified that the church was adhering to the Woodruff Manifesto. His testimony incurred the wrath of those members who continued to promote plural marriages secretly. On 21 March 1905 he wrote in his journal:

Interview with the First Presidency regarding cases of misrepresentation of the attitude of the Church Authorities in the matter of polygamous marriage. Some people claiming a standing in the church and many of them even officers in ward and stake capacities, unwisely and erroneously affirm lack of sincerity on the part of the General Authorities. My position as a witness in the recent proceedings in Washington places me before this class of people as a sort of target for their arrows of criticism; and I have referred several individuals to the First Presidency for investigation of their words and acts.

In 1924, as a member of the Council of the Twelve, Talmage was assigned to assist stakes in disciplining those who continued to practice plural marriage. He considered this a "very unwelcome appointment,"[33] and his journals are replete with references to his role in excommunicating members who refused to abandon polygamy.

★ ★ ★

Talmage played an important part in the development of education in the church and in Utah. He had the appropriate training as a teacher after receiving degrees at Lehigh University and Johns Hopkins, and in 1896 he received a Ph.D. from Wesleyan University for nonresident work. Honors also came for his scientific work, including membership as a Fellow of the Royal Society of Edinburgh, Fellow of the Royal Microscopical Society, and Fellow of the Royal Geological Society.

In 1888 Talmage was appointed president of Latter-day Saints College, a position he held until 1893. He then became president of the University of Utah, where he served until 1897 when he left to be a full-time mining and geological consultant. One of his final acts at the university was to have a seismograph installed.[34]

John Talmage tells of an incident that occurred while his father was president of the University of Utah. One evening Talmage came home bloodied, muddy, his clothes in tatters. Maia assumed the worse, fearing that he had been the victim of a robbery. However, James had been using a bicycle for transportation at the time. On his way home he would get off the bike to cross a single-plank footbridge across a small stream of water. That evening he decided that he would cross the plank without dismounting. He found the task more difficult than imagined. As John Talmage observed: "For the next hour, the president of the University of Utah might have been observed trundling his bicycle fifty yards or so down the road from the bridge, mounting and riding furiously toward the plank crossing, turning onto it with grimlipped determination—and plunging off it in a spectacular and bone shaking crash into the rough ditchbank."[35] Talmage repeated his attempts to cross the bridge until he finally mastered it.

★ ★ ★

In 1893, in connection with his work at LDS College, Talmage was asked by the church's First Presidency to undertake a series of public theological lectures. The first class had between 500 to 600 people in attendance; soon the classes were pushing close to over one thousand. The lectures were subsequently printed in the *Juvenile Instructor* and formed the basis for Talmage's classic work, *The Articles of Faith*. A "committee on criticism" was appointed consisting of Francis M. Lyman and Abraham H. Cannon of the Council of the Twelve, George H. Reynolds of the First Council of Seventy, John

Nicholson, and Karl Maeser. The book was "written by appointment; and published by the Church."[36]

Yet in spite of its official sanction, *The Articles of Faith* was not without controversy. Talmage introduced some ideas that conflicted with views held by others, including:

1. *The Spirit Body of the Holy Ghost.* Talmage's journals reveal that the subject of the Holy Ghost was of particular interest.[37] President George Q. Cannon was concerned about the ambiguity in some church literature over the nature of the Holy Ghost and felt there should be a consensus on the issue. For example, 1 Nephi 11:11 discusses the visit of "the Spirit of the Lord." Some wondered if this referred to the Holy Ghost or to the pre-existent Jesus Christ who visited the Brother of Jared in Ether 3.[38] Talmage's interpretation that the verse referred to the Holy Ghost prevailed. In 1920 when he added footnotes and chapter headings to the Book of Mormon, his one reference to 1 Nephi 11:11 directed readers to John 14:16, 17.

2. *Progression Among the Kingdoms.* On page 420 of the first edition of *The Articles of Faith* (1899) Talmage wrote:

It is reasonable to believe, in the absence of direct revelation by which alone absolute knowledge of the matter could be acquired, that, in accordance with God's plan of eternal progression, advancement from grade to grade within any kingdom, and from kingdom to kingdom, will be provided for. But if the recipients of a lower glory be enabled to advance, surely the intelligences of higher rank will not be stopped in their progress; and thus we may conclude, that degrees and grades will ever characterize the kingdoms of our God. Eternity is progressive; perfection is relative; the essential feature of God's living purpose is its associated power of eternal increase.[39]

Later, in October 1913, Talmage qualified his remarks by stating that we should not delay our repentance because we believe such matters can be dealt with in the next life.[40]

3. *The Change in Wording of the Fourth Article of Faith.* When the Fourth Article of Faith was written in 1842, it originally read: "We believe that these ordinances are: First, Faith in the Lord, Jesus Christ; second, repentance; third, Baptism by immersion for the remission of sins; fourth, Laying on of hands for the gift of the Holy Ghost." At Talmage's suggestion, the wording was changed to its current form: "We believe that the first principles and ordinances of the Gospel are: first, Faith in the Lord Jesus Christ; second, Repentance; third, Baptism

by immersion for the remission of sins; fourth, Laying on of hands for the gift of the Holy Ghost." He felt that faith and repentance were not ordinances. Also "these ordinances" did not introduce a new concept but referred back to the Third Article of Faith. The change was adopted by the First Presidency and accepted when the Pearl of Great Price was voted on in April 1902 general conference. Talmage was in charge of revising that book of scripture as well.[41]

J. Reuben Clark, a member of the First Presidency for twenty-eight years, was a student at Latter-day Saints College when Talmage was president. He assisted the busy president on *The Articles of Faith* and remembered: "I was blessed by being taken under the immediate tutelage of Dr. Talmage. I worked with him for several years. I came to know him rather well. I was with him when he prepared 'The Articles of Faith.' I often jokingly say that I wrote 'The Articles of Faith'—I did—on the typewriter."[42]

Talmage and Clark became friends. Talmage received special permission to solemnize Clark's marriage to Lucine A. Savage on 14 September 1898.[43] Clark was at Talmage's bedside when he passed away thirty-five years later on 27 July 1933.

★ ★ ★

During the years 1891 to 1905 Talmage traveled to Europe, Russia, and other places to lecture, accept awards, and do research. He wrote textbooks such as *First Book of Nature* (1888) and *Domestic Science* (1891), published his own research and observations in *Tables for Blowpipe Determinations of Minerals* (1898) and *The Great Salt Lake, Present and Past* (1900), as well as articles on scientific or theological topics.

He also became a mining consultant and prepared reports for his clients. He spent considerable time in courtrooms, observing the legal profession and how lawyers work. This prepared him for his testimony in the Reed Smoot case.

Reed Smoot was a member of the Quorum of the Twelve who was elected to the U.S. Senate from Utah in 1903.[44] The hearings held to determine if Smoot as a member of the LDS church should be allowed to join the Senate became more of a public inquiry into the LDS church than a referendum on Smoot. Talmage testified on 19 and 24 January 1905. He was regarded as an "expert" on Mormonism because of *The Articles of Faith* and his work on the new edition of The Pearl of Great Price. Talmage proved to be a difficult witness, making the committee work for each answer to their questions. At one point, while they were haggling over definitions for "edition" and "reissue," one committee member complained that the session "takes too long."[45]

Committee members reported that they had heard Talmage was to be brought up on charges of apostasy for something he had written in *The Articles of Faith*. Talmage answered, "No charge was actually made, though I was notified I would be so charged. But as one of the church officials had already expressed as holding the views set forth by myself in that work, and he being very much larger game, he was singled out first, and as the proceedings against him ended in a disappointing way, I was never brought to trial."[46] It is not clear what the charges were or who the "very much larger game" was.[47]

Talmage's primary vocations as teacher and mining consultant were supplemented by his behind-the-scenes work for the church. He consulted church leaders on ventilating the Salt Lake Tabernacle,[48] on *An Address: The Church of Jesus Christ of Latter-day Saints to the World* (a proclamation delivered at April 1907 general conference), on a 1909 First Presidency statement regarding evolution,[49] wrote a study guide for church youth entitled *The Great Apostasy,* and compiled a small booklet for the Bureau of Information on *The Story of Mormonism.*

★ ★ ★

Life continued as usual at this busy pace until at 4:00 p.m. on 7 December 1911, when Anthony W. Ivins of the Council of Twelve Apostles called on Talmage at his office to tell him he had been appointed to the apostleship. At 11:30 a.m. the next day, Talmage was ordained an apostle under the hands of President Joseph F. Smith, with counselors Anthon H. Lund and Charles W. Penrose, and apostles Francis M. Lyman, Hyrum M. Smith, George F. Richards, and Joseph Fielding Smith assisting.[50] Talmage, the fiftieth apostle of the church, filled the vacancy occasioned by the death of John Henry Smith.

Talmage's journal shows him humbled by his new calling. Referring to a patriarchal blessing, he wrote "May the Lord grant me His [support], and enable me to be a true witness of him. . . . I have looked upon myself as a lay member in the Church though I know that a patriarch Jesse Martin of Provo gave me to understand that, and I would be called and ordained one of the Twelve Apostles."[51] As part of his charge to the new apostle, Francis M. Lyman, President of the Quorum of the Twelve, instructed him as follows:

1. "The necessity of being in perfect accord with other brethren of the Twelve." He would be free to express his opinions, but once a decision was made, he was expected to join with the majority.

2. "Everything talked about and done in Council capacity should be held in strict confidence as matters sacred to the Council."

3. "His duties as an Apostle should take precedence over all others whether of a public, private or domestic nature."[52]

Just prior to Talmage's call, an attempt was made to extort money from the church. Some enterprising parties threatened to print pictures of the interior of the Salt Lake temple unless they were paid $100,000. At Talmage's suggestion, church leaders decided to publish a book about temples and temple ordinances, including pictures of the inside of the Salt Lake temple. By the time *The House of the Lord* appeared the next year, Talmage was an apostle.[53]

Talmage immersed himself in his calling, visiting stakes and occasionally investigating members who claimed revelations independent of official church protocol, including proponents of the so-called Dream Mine in Salem, Utah.[54] From September 1914 to April 1915, he fulfilled an assignment that would highlight his tenure as a member of the Twelve and produce one of the unquestioned classics in LDS literature. During these seven months he researched and wrote *Jesus the Christ*.

On 14 September 1914 he recorded:

During the school periods of 1904-1905, and 1905-1906, I delivered a series of lectures entitled "Jesus the Christ under the auspices of the University Sunday School. The sessions were held during Sunday forenoon's in Barratt Hall. I received written appointment from the First Presidency to embody the lectures in a book to be published for the use of the Church in general. Work on this appointment has been suspended from time to time owing to other duties being imposed upon me. Lately, however, I have been asked to prepare the matter for the book with as little delay as possible. Experiences demonstrated that neither in my comfortable office nor in the convenient study room at home can I be free from visits and telephone calls. The consequence of this condition and in view of the importance of the work, I had been directed to occupy a room in the temple where I will be free from interruption.[55]

(The Talmage Room remains a point of interest for those given tours of the Salt Lake temple).

When the First Presidency charged Talmage to undertake this

assignment in 1905, they made it clear they wanted "a valuable acquisition to our Church Literature." These words proved to be prophetic, for no other church book, except the scriptures, has surpassed the status of *Jesus the Christ*.[56] It was used as a Melchizedek priesthood course manual in 1916 and in 1963, is still required reading for missionaries, and continues to be a source of information and inspiration to church members worldwide.[57]

A particularly insightful analysis of *Jesus the Christ* is Malcolm Thorpe's "James E. Talmage and the Tradition of the Victorian Lives of Jesus."[58] Here Thorpe addresses "Victorian" approaches to Christ, in particular the influential writings of Frederick Farrar, J. Cunningham Geikie, and Alfred Edersheim. While the influence other writers had on Talmage's work cannot be overstated, Farrar's impact stands out with his own *Life of Christ*.[59] One need only scan the table of contents of Farrar's book to see how Talmage patterned *Jesus the Christ*. Yet Talmage's work cannot be branded plagiarism, for where Farrar accentuated his approach with a knowledge of biblical languages, Talmage supplemented the biblical narrative with modern revelation.[60]

Talmage and others were responding to what they understood to be the methodologies and conclusions of an emerging higher biblical criticism. There is some indication that this is why the First Presidency was anxious to have Talmage complete his work. Talmage was not a proponent of higher criticism, at least as he interpreted it, and on 5 April 1914 stated: "There be men who have arrogated to themselves the claim of superiority, who pronounce themselves higher critics of the scriptures of Almighty God, and proclaim that the scriptures mean not what they say. Right glad am I that my people are pleased with sound doctrine." He further noted: "I don't believe the Latter-day Saints are influenced by these vagaries of the so-called higher criticism of the scriptures." Fourteen years later he added: "There are those who forget what the Lord has said through the Book of Mormon, and who are led away into the jungle of error, much of which belongs to the marshy and uncertain ground preempted in the name of higher criticism."[61]

One important doctrinal matter to come to light during the writing of *Jesus the Christ* was the title "Son of Man" as applied to Jesus. Talmage's attention may have been drawn to this title by Frederick Farrar[62] and been accentuated by the frequent use of "Son of Man" in the Pearl of Great Price.[63] On pages 142-44 of *Jesus the Christ* Talmage discusses the significance of "Son of Man" and provides numerous scriptural references regarding it. He delivered a talk on the "Son of Man" at BYU on 15 November 1914, using students there as a test audience before giving the talk in April 1915 general conference. However, Charles W. Penrose of the First Presidency expressed "the opinion that the wide spread publicity of this doctrine would cause difficulty to the elders in the field, who he thinks would be confronted with the charge that we as a people worship a man." The official publication of this address contains significant omissions. Interestingly, the omitted portions have as much to do with Talmage's criticisms of higher biblical scholars as it does with the "Son of Man."[64]

★ ★ ★

In July 1915 the First Presidency assigned Talmage to represent the church at the World Congress of Religious Philosophies held in connection with the Panama-Pacific International Exposition in San Francisco.[65] From that experience came his classic address "The Philosophical Basis of Mormonism."

During World War I Talmage addressed the topic "Mormonism and the War," a speech that made headlines in a leading newspaper.[66] The Talmage family supported America's involvement, a commitment evident in an incident involving six-year-old John. During the early part of 1917, enlistment in the military was lagging and the government initiated a major recruitment drive. On 30 March young John coaxed his governess to take him downtown to buy a gift for a family member. While she was looking into a store window, he ran into a nearby National Guard office, where he declared himself ready for duty. The amused recruiters put John through the drill of attention and saluting. However, the boy was devastated when he was told he was too young, and John decided not to tell anyone of the humiliating experience. That afternoon the family received a call from Lieutenant Albert Meyers who related the incident and asked permission to report the story in the next day's newspaper.[67]

In 1919 Talmage began writing a newspaper column about the church titled "The Vitality of Mormonism." These articles appeared in major newspapers, such as the *Los Angeles Times* and the *Washington Herald,* and in lesser known papers, such as the *Alabama Weekly Times.* The articles were collected and published by Gorham Press in Boston under the title *The Vitality of Mormonism*. The book was widely used by missionaries.[68]

In 1916 Talmage and his colleague in the Twelve Joseph Fielding Smith were assigned to prepare "Ready References," a scripture index to be used by missionaries. For many years these "Ready References" were inserted between the Old and New Testaments in Bibles published for the church.[69]

On 31 October 1918 Talmage was one of the assembled apostles who sustained President Joseph F. Smith's Vision of the Redemption of the Dead. (Years later this vision would be incorporated as section 138 of the Doctrine and Covenants.[70]) Two years later he headed a committee to revise the Book of Mormon. The First Presidency had learned that there were some errors in the text. Years earlier Elder Orson Pratt had divided the Book of Mormon into chapters and verses, and Talmage was now given the assignment of adding chapter headings and footnotes. He was customarily meticulous, making sure there were no errors or omissions, and praised his secretary when she found an error he had missed.[71] One letter, dated 27 May 1920 and covering 1 Nephi to Alma 33, contains 90 recommended changes. In another letter, dated 19 September 1920, Talmage writes to his secretary, "I suggest that you announce these changes to no one."[72] Later Talmage revised the Doctrine and Covenants and suggested that the Book of Mormon, Doctrine and Covenants, and Pearl of Great Price be combined in one volume called a "triple combination."[73]

Talmage continued to speak and write. His journals outline exhausting schedules. In late 1924 he was called to replace Elder David O. McKay as the head of the church's European Mission. McKay had been ill and been advised to return home. Almost immediately he tried to visit with the editors of various newspapers to see if their anti-Mormon articles could be stopped. In one city he presented his calling card to a newspaper employee who gave it to his editor. At first the editor refused to see the Mormon apostle. But with the abbreviations F.R.S.E, F.R.M.S., F.R.G.S., representing the scientific societies of England of which he was a member, clearly visible, he could not be early ignored.[74]

While supervising the European Mission, Talmage injured his left knee. In later years he would suffer decreased mobility and be humiliated by an embarrassing fall in the crowded Tabernacle. After his return to Utah, he would experience serious health problems as well as problems for his sons Karl and Paul.

Talmage was enthralled with the radio and loved to listen to it. He was privileged to conduct a weekly series on the life of the Christ in 1928. He undertook another series in 1930 on various church doctrines, which were collected and printed as *Sunday Night Talks by Radio*. Just prior to his death he was doing a series on the priesthood each Sunday evening. In 1930 he was asked to assist *Webster's Dictionary* in preparing definitions for Mormon-related words.

Talmage was also largely responsible for a small work that came out in 1930 titled *Latter-day Revelation*. The work, an abridgement and condensation of certain sections of the Doctrine and Covenants, was prepared as an aid to missionaries and to facilitate translating the Doctrine and Covenants into other languages.[75]

★ ★ ★

In 1931 Talmage became entangled in a doctrinal dispute between B. H. Roberts of the First Council of the Seventy and Joseph Fielding Smith of the Council of the Twelve.[76] Roberts wanted to publish his "masterwork," titled "The Truth, The Way, The Life." In this book he suggested that there was life (and death) on the earth before Adam, "pre-Adamites" he called them.

Smith felt that Roberts was preaching false doctrine and had insinuated such publicly. Roberts queried the First Presidency to ask if Smith's pronouncements were official declarations. The two men were invited to present their cases to the Quorum of the Twelve. On 7 January 1931 Roberts argued his side, two weeks later Smith responded. Roberts may have lost the debate because he had spoken unkindly of Smith. President Heber J. Grant felt that both men were "dealing in the mysteries" and felt that such matters should be left alone.

As a scientist, Talmage was concerned that because of Smith's remarks, some might conclude that the church was anti-science. The result of this conflict was Talmage's talk "The Earth and Man," which was delivered at the Tabernacle on 9 August 1931. The speech eventually met with the approval of President Grant and was published in the *Deseret News* and as a pamphlet.[77] One unfortunate aftermath was that following Talmage's death, hard feelings lasted for several years between the Talmages and the Smiths.

Stan Larson, in his introduction to *The Truth, The Way, The Life,* outlines this controversy. He refers readers to a copy of Talmage's *The Earth and Man* upon which Smith had written, "False Doctrine."[78] Another copy of this pamphlet with Elder Smith's "False Doctrine" notation can be found at the Harold B. Lee Library archives, Brigham Young University.[79]

Talmage passed away at 8:45 a.m. on 27 July 1933 from "acute myocarditis, following a throat infection." With him were his beloved Maia, Paul, Elsie, and Helen and her husband, Harold Brandley, and J. Reuben Clark. The other children had been notified that he was failing but were unable to reach their father prior to his passing. His death made the front page headline of the evening *Deseret News:* "DOCTOR JAMES E. TALMAGE IS DEAD."[80]

★ ★ ★

To my mind, two things most distinguish the life of Elder James E. Talmage. First, he truly loved his family. In his journals he talked of his loneliness while traveling and of his deep concern when his children were sick or his wife was ill. John Talmage referred to him as "the most wonderful of fathers." The Talmage family made a great sacrifice to the church by approving of his absence on so many occasions.

Second, he willingly served others. This is probably best exemplified in the following story. In the spring of 1892 diphtheria ravaged Utah communities. Talmage had returned home on Memorial Day from ministering to people when he learned of the plight of the non-Mormon Martin family, who were afflicted with diphtheria. Local Relief Society leaders had been unable to get anyone to go to the house to help for fear of catching the disease. James immediately left for the Martin home. He recorded:

> One child, two and a half years old, lay dead on a bed, having been dead about four hours and still unwashed. Two other children, one a boy of ten and the other a girl of five, lay writhing in the agonies of the disease. A girl of 13 years is still feeble from a recent attack of diphtheria . . . The father, Mr. Abe Martin, and the mother, Marshia Martin, are dazed with grief and fatigue; and the only other occupant of the house, a man named Kelly who is a boarder in the family, is so ill and weak as hardly to be able to move about.

He cleaned the house and prepared the young child for burial. Food and clothing had been donated by the Relief Society. The soiled clothing and rugs had to be burned. A woman came by and offered to do the work for $5 a day, which she then lowered to $4.50, still a large sum for a family so destitute. Talmage dismissed her as a "vulture."

When he returned the next day, he found that the ten-year-old boy had died during the night. The five-year-old girl was now near death. Talmage took her in his arms. "She clung to my neck, ofttimes coughing bloody mucus on my face and clothing, and her throat had about it the stench of putrefaction, yet I could not put her from me. During the half hour immediately preceding her death, I walked the floor with the little creature in my arms. She died in agony at 10 a.m."

The three children were placed in wooden coffins and buried in a local cemetery. Talmage delivered the graveside blessing. After seeing to the well-being of the grieving family, he bathed in a zinc solution, burned his soiled clothing, and quarantined himself from his family for several days to prevent spread of the disease.[81]

★ ★ ★

In conclusion, a few questionable items concerning James Talmage should be cleared up. Many myths have circulated over the years regarding him. Perhaps the most prevalent is that noted physicist Albert Einstein said he was the smartest man in the world, or words to that effect. This is not true. Although the two scientists were contemporaries, neither crossed the other's path during his lifetime.[82] Although Talmage was a competent geologist, he was primarily an educator.

It has also been rumored that Talmage was a heavy smoker, that when he was writing *Jesus the Christ,* temple janitors had to dispose of barrels of cigar butts.[83] First, Talmage was a clear advocate of the Word of Wisdom, which prohibited smoking. In 1895 he was asked to speak in the Tabernacle on "The Tobacco Habit."[84] In his journal he spoke of his concern with young people smoking. He also wrote about the dangers of "Hot Drinks."[85] In the *Articles of Faith* he treated the Word of Wisdom and even mentioned it in *Jesus the Christ.*[86]

The rumors of his smoking originated in a remedy prescribed by a doctor, who believed that at one point Talmage was headed toward a nervous breakdown. He typically worked himself to exhaustion; in fact, one apocryphal story holds that he told a mission president that sometimes his head hurt so much from studying that he would wrap it in wet towels to relieve the pressure. In 1896 Talmage presided over Latter-day Saints College, worked on *The Articles of Faith,* taught a heavy course load, and delivered lectures and completed various other church assignments. He also suffered from insomnia and constipation. He noted in his journal that it had been reported to the First Presidency that "the moderate use of tobacco would have a good effect on me." They told him, "We give you this rather as an instruction than as counsel" to take up smoking. Talmage subsequently found "that a good cigar produced a marvelous quieting of my over-wrought nerves."[87] As medicine, this prescription was in keeping with the spirit of the Word of Wisdom, and Talmage did not prolong his use of it.

Another rumor pertains to the writing of *Jesus the Christ*. Reportedly, Talmage never left the temple while writing the book. This is not true. John Talmage explains that in spite of the relatively short time it took to produce the book, "the author not only left the Temple frequently, but managed to devote many hours a day to his regular duties as a member of the Council of the Twelve. He was spared most weekend stake conference assignments . . . He even slept at home most nights, but his hours at home were extremely limited and his family was keenly aware of the time-pressure problem."[88]

According to another rumor, when Talmage finished the book, Jesus himself appeared to him and told him he was pleased with the result. This story sounds similar to one church president Lorenzo Snow reportedly experienced in the temple,[89] and the two stories have probably become intertwined. Talmage was careful in recording spiritual experiences and did not leave an account of such a vision.

Both *The Articles of Faith* and *Jesus the Christ* are unique in Mormon literature in that they are the only two single-authored church-related books to have been commissioned by the First Presidency, reviewed by committees consisting of general authorities, and been published under the president of the church's official imprimatur. Both are seminal works, but even as Talmage acknowledged in his preface to *Jesus the Christ:* "It presents, however, the writer's personal belief and profoundest conviction as to the truth of what he has written." Neither book occupies the same status as scripture. Even so, they have a special place in our literature and, in the words of the apostle Paul, are "profitable for doctrine" (2 Tim. 3:16).

NOTES

1. John Talmage, *The Talmage Story* (Salt Lake City: Bookcraft, 1972), 226-28; hereafter cited as *Talmage Story*.

2. Bryant S. Hinckley, "James E. Talmage," *Improvement Era* 35 (July

1932): 524. Also see Albert Zobell, *The Parables of James E. Talmage* (Salt Lake City: Deseret Book Co., 1973), 65-66.

3. "III Term III Year, Examination Papers by J.E.Talmage, Normal Depart. April 4, 1879," cited in *The Papers of James E. Talmage, Register of the James E. Talmage Collection, Mss 229,* comp. Timothy Wood Slover (Harold B. Lee Library, Brigham Young University: Division of Archives and Manuscripts, n.d.); hereafter referred to as Talmage Papers. This register locates the Box and Folder of items in the Talmage Collection at the Lee Library. For this reference, see Box 9, Folder 7.

4. Dennis Rowley, "Inner Dialogue: James Talmage's Choice of Science as a Career," *Dialogue: A Journal of Mormon Thought* 17 (Summer 1984): 112-14. Also cited in *The Search for Harmony: Essays on Science and Mormonism,* ed. Gene A. Sessions and Craig J. Oberg (Salt Lake City: Signature Books, 1993), 43-45. *Talmage Story,* chap. 1.

5. James Talmage, "My Study of Astrology," *The Contributor* 14 (Nov. 1892): 33-36. A condensed version of this article is in the *New Era* 9 (Mar. 1979): 18.

6. *Talmage Story,* 18-19. In his journal, dated 3 March 1923, Talmage tells how he and some companions, en route from a church assignment, came upon an automobile accident "where I assumed the part of an amateur surgeon."

7. *Talmage Story,* 3-6; James E. Talmage, "An Unusual Accompaniment to a Baptism," *Improvement Era* 25 (June 1922): 675-76. Dennis Rowley, "Fishing on the Kennet: The Victorian Boyhood of James E. Talmage, 1862-1876," *Brigham Young University Studies* 33 (Summer 1993): 505-506, 519n87. This entire article is enlightening.

8. *Talmage Story,* 6-7. Also Rowley, "Fishing on the Kennet," 506-507. The accident occurred on 10 October 1873.

9. Reinhard Maeser, *Karl G. Maeser* (Provo, UT: Brigham Young University, 1928), 87.

10. As evidence of the discipline of the young student, at age fifteen James created a "Record Dated Aug. 20, 1878," in which he wrote the following:

> The notes, scraps, etc. presented here have been taken by the undersigned principally from lectures delivered by the professors, teachers, and students of the Brigham Young Academy, either during the regular school session of the institution, or in the societies connected with the same.
> Lectures, delivered by students have previously been endorsed by

the professors, hence they are considered equally authentic.

The notes have been taken, as presented and recorded for preservation with the intention of revising each subject at leisure, making improvements where admissible, and recopying each in a separate volume under a more thorough classification . . .

In the section titled "Index to Theological Questions and Answers," he outlined various doctrinal topics, for example, "Women, why no priesthood?" and the Negro and the priesthood. Talmage Papers, Box 9, Folder 5.

11. *Talmage Story*, 30.

12. Ibid., 38-39.

13. Rowley, "Inner Dialogue," 129; *Search for Harmony*, 61; Talmage Papers, Box 12, Folder 8.

14. Rowley, "Inner Dialogue," 127-28; *Search for Harmony*, 58-59.

15. *Talmage Story*, 81; Talmage Papers, Box 21, Folder 4.

16. For the duties of a "home missionary," see Glen Humphries, "Missionaries to the Saints," *Brigham Young University Studies* 17 (Autumn 1976): 76-79.

17. Talmage Papers, Box 14, Folder 10.

18. James E. Talmage, "The Need for Religion," delivered at the 103rd semi-annual conference of the LDS church, 3 October 1932. I have added titles to general conference addresses, since prior to 1942 they were not titled in the official conference reports.

19. For a brief discussion of one time when Talmage may have used the pulpit to put forth a political point, see Thomas G. Alexander, *Mormonism in Transition: A History of the Latter-day Saints 1890-1930* (Urbana: University of Illinois Press, 1986), 40.

20. Ibid., 52-53; also see James B. Allen, "Personal Faith and Public Policy: Some Timely Observations on the League of Nations Controversy in Utah," *Brigham Young University Studies* 14 (Autumn 1973): 77-98.

21. *Talmage Story*, 65-66.

22. Ibid., 70, and all of chap. 9.

23. Ibid., 135-37. In his journal, dated 27 April 1895, Talmage wrote:

This day will be remembered as the occasion of one of the hardest experiences and one of the heaviest burdens ever sent to us. Our sweet daughter left us this morning early: she died at 3:15 a.m. As she rallied under the influence of administrations and stimulants last evening we were flushed with trustful hope that she would be spared to us; at 1 a.m. today, when I called her mother from bed to nourish the child the baby seemed greatly improved; she gradually weakened however, and when next the mother was aroused, at 3 a.m., the child was evidently nearing the end. Fifteen minutes later the darling little one laid her pretty head upon my shoulder and was gone. The burden is hard to bear: our grief is acute, yet we try to see as indeed we feel the Hand of God in this sorrow as in our joys.

There are numerous journal entries in following years when the family would visit the grave of Zella, especially on Memorial Days.

24. Hinckley, "James E. Talmage," 567.

25. Ibid. Bryant S. Hinckley, president of the Liberty Stake (and father of Gordon B. Hinckley, later president of the Church of Jesus Christ of Latter-day Saints), was commissioned to write this series of articles on members of the Quorum of the Twelve. When he came to this letter from Talmage to Elsie, he wrote, "[James E. Talmage's] love and admiration for the woman whose wisdom and companionship have meant so much to him, his affection for his children and his solicitude for their welfare, is recorded in a correspondence which, we venture, will some day be found among the most precious and delightful things he has written."

26. *Talmage Story*, 189; Talmage Journal, 17 Oct. 1912.

27. See D&C 131:1-4; 132:19-20 (see the entire section).

28. Talmage Journal, 28 June 1890; 16 Jan. 1891; 10 Sept. 1894. An entry for 22 Nov. 1894 alludes to additional sealing activity.

29. Cited in Ernest L. Wilkinson and Cleon Skousen, *Brigham Young University: A School of Destiny* (Provo, UT: Brigham Young University Press, 1976), 89. For a treatment of this difficult period, see Edwin Brown Firmage and Richard Collin Mangrum, *Zion in the Courts: A Legal History of the Church of Jesus Christ of Latter-day Saints, 1830-1900* (Urbana: University of Illinois Press, 1988), chaps. 6-8.

30. *Talmage Story*, 90-91. The Thirteen Articles of Faith were re-adopted prior to sustaining the Manifesto to emphasize the fact that the church believes in "obeying, honoring, and sustaining the law."

31. James E. Talmage, *The Articles of Faith—A Series of Lectures on the Principle Doctrines of the Church of Jesus Christ of Latter-days Saints* (Salt Lake City: The Deseret News, Published by The Church of Jesus Christ of Latter-day Saints, 1899), 435-36, 440; 1924 ed., 424-25, 524-25.

32. "Items on Polygamy—Omitted from the Published Book," Talmage Papers, Box 23, Folder 8.

33. In Talmage's journal for 10 Jan. 1924 is his appointment letter from the Quorum of the Twelve Apostles. It indicates the inner workings of the council and is reproduced here:

ANNOUNCEMENT:

At a meeting of the Council of the Twelve Apostles held Thursday, January 10, 1924, in the Salt Lake Temple, the following action was taken:—

Elder Stephen L. Richards offered the following motion:—That it be the sense of the Council that Brother James E. Talmage be selected to act under the direction of President Rudger Clawson as the representative of the Council in giving aid to Stake Presidents and High Councils in the investigation and trial of alleged offenses and offenders against the marriage laws and the moral discipline of the Church and matters relating thereto, it being understood that it is the desire of the Council that the stakes and local jurisdictions shall assume responsibility for bringing offenders in such matters to trial and justice.

The motion was seconded by Brother Joseph Fielding Smith, and after a brief discussion was unanimously adopted.

[Signed Joseph Fielding Smith]
Sec'y.

Also see J. Max Anderson, *The Polygamy Story: Fiction and Fact* (Salt Lake City: Publishers Press, 1979), 146.

34. *Talmage Story*, 166. For other information regarding Talmage's impact on education in Utah, see Ralph V. Chamberlin, *The University of Utah, A History of Its First Hundred Years—1850-1950* (Salt Lake City: University of Utah Press, 1960), 177, 206-207. Also see Grant Larsen Wilson, "The Life and Educational Contributions of James Edward Talmage," M.A. thesis, University of Utah, June 1958.

35. *Talmage Story*, 138-40.

36. Talmage, *The Articles of Faith*, cover page.

37. Alexander, *Mormonism in Transition*, 281. Talmage Journal, 5 Jan. 1894; 13 Jan., 16 Jan. 1899.

38. In this interpretation of 1 Nephi 11:11, Talmage was preceded by Orson Pratt. See Orson Pratt, *Writings of an Apostle. Vol. II, Mormon Collectors Series* (Salt Lake City: Mormon Heritage Publishers, 1976), cited in "The Holy Spirit" from *A Series of Pamphlets by Orson Pratt*, 56.

39. Talmage, *The Articles of Faith,* 1st ed., 420-21; 1924 ed., 409. Talmage was not the first church writer to introduce the idea of progression among the kingdoms. See B. H. Roberts, *Outline of Ecclesiastical History* (Salt Lake City: Deseret Book Co., Classics in Mormon Literature, 1979); the book was originally printed in 1893. On pages 416-17 Roberts talks about "Progress Within and From Different Degrees of Glory." Talmage was a member of the reading committee that approved Roberts's original book. See Talmage Journal, 15 Aug. 1892. For an opposing view, see Joseph Fielding Smith, *The Doctrines of Salvation,* comp. Bruce R. McConkie (Salt Lake City: Bookcraft, 1955), 2:31-34.

40. James Talmage, "Our Bodies, Gifts from God," from the 84th semi-annual general conference, 6 Oct. 1913.

41. Lyndon W. Cook, "The Articles of Faith," *Brigham Young University Studies* 17 (Winter 1977): 254-56. See Talmage Journal, 29 Nov. 1893. For an excellent history of the Thirteen Articles of Faith, see David J. Whittaker, "The 'Articles of Faith' in Early Mormon Literature and Thought," in Davis Bitton and Maureen Ursenbach Beecher, eds., *New Views of Mormon History: Essays in Honor of Leonard J. Arrington* (Salt Lake City: University of Utah Press, 1987), 63-92; John W. Welch and David J. Whittaker "'We Believe . . .': The Development of the Articles of Faith," *Ensign* 9 (Sept. 1979): 51-55.

42. J. Reuben Clark, "Study Of Savior's Ministry Offers Wealth Of Faith, Virtue," *Church News,* 23 June 1956, 4, 9.

43. Frank W. Fox, *J. Reuben Clark: The Public Years* (Provo, UT: Brigham Young University Press, Deseret Book Co., 1980), 18; D. Michael Quinn, *J. Reuben Clark: The Church Years* (Provo, UT: Brigham Young University Press, 1983), 9, 286n21; Talmage Journal, 14 Sept. 1898.

44. Milton R. Merrill, *Reed Smoot: Apostle in Politics* (Logan: Utah State University Press and Department of Political Science, 1990), chaps. 1 and 2; Alexander, *Mormonism in Transition,* chap. 2; Joseph Fielding Smith, *Essentials in Church History* (Salt Lake City: Deseret Book Co., 1970), 509-11.

45. *Proceedings Before the Committee On Privileges and Elections of the United States Senate in the Matter of the Protests Against the Right of Hon. Reed Smoot, A Senator From the State of Utah, to Hold His Seat* (Washington, D.C.: Government Printing Office, 1905), 3:128; hereafter cited as *Smoot Hearings.*

Of interest in the Talmage Papers is the following document from B. H. Roberts to Joseph Fielding Smith, son of church president Joseph F. Smith, who worked in the church's historical department at the time. It outlines the strategy church leaders used during the Senate hearings. The items in brackets were written in by Roberts.

1. Obtain if possible when the four standard works, Bible, Book of Mormon, Doctrine and Covenants and Pearl of Great Price were accepted by the body of the Church as the Standard works of the Church. [(Oct. 6, 1902)]

2. Find the Temple Marriage Ceremony in the Seer published by Orson Pratt in Washington. [-Vol. 1 No 2 p 32 - H O Pamps Vol. 17 No 2]

3. Find the Journal of Discourses in which Amasa Lyman's discourse containing the Atonement is published. Mill. Star also contains said discourse. Find it in the Star [(Vol. 24 p 320)] as well as in the Journal for reason that there are some explanations, I think, in the Star which are not found in the journal. Also find the information about Lyman's excommunication, cause of, date, [(May 12-1870)] etc.

4. Obtain Journal of Discourses for July 8, 1855 containing President Young's sermon on the Kingdom of God. pp. 309-317. [-J of D vol. 2.]

5. Find President Young's discourse on Orson Pratt's work in which the President condemns much of the teaching of Orson Pratt, saying among other things "Orson Pratt's vain philosophy is no guide for the Latter-day Saints." We want this passage to offset the effect of Orson Pratt's statement concerning the nature of the Kingdom of God [D Weekly 14:372]

The above references are wanted to aid Brother Talmage in forming testimony to be given before the Senate Investigating Committee.

Also see "Scripture References and Information Suggested to James E. Talmage to Aid Him in His Testimony Before the Senate Investigating Committee Regarding Reed Smoot," undated, Talmage Papers, Box 23, Folder 12.

46. *Smoot Hearings,* 3:24-25.

47. Letter from Thomas G. Alexander, 19 Aug. 1993. Note Talmage Journal, 13 Jan. 1899: "In conversation Pres. Geo. Q. Cannon supported the view of the distinct personality of the Holy Ghost." Cannon may have been the "very much larger game" to which Talmage was referring. For the part Talmage and others played in the doctrinal development of the church, see Thomas Alexander, "The Reconstruction of Mormon Doctrine: From Joseph Smith to Progressive Theology," *Sunstone* 5 (July-Aug. 1980): 24-33.

48. Talmage Papers, Box 15, Folder 8; Talmage Papers at archives, Historical Department, Church of Jesus Christ of Latter-day Saints, Box 24, Folder 11; James E. Talmage, *Domestic Science* (Salt Lake City: The Juvenile Instructor Office, 1891), chap. 8 on "Ventilation."

49. Talmage Journal, 27 Sept., 30 Sept. 1909; James R. Clark, ed., *Messages of the First Presidency* (Salt Lake City: Bookcraft, 1970), 4:199-206.

50. *Talmage Story,* 174-75.

51. Talmage Journal, 7 Dec. 1911.

52. Ibid., 8 Dec. 1911.

53. *Talmage Story,* 172.

54. Clark, *Messages of the First Presidency,* 4:284-86; Talmage Journal, 16 July 1913, 1 Nov. 1931, 20 Jan. 1933.

55. Talmage Journal, 14 Sept. 1914. The so-called Talmage Room is on the fifth floor of the Salt Lake temple to the left of the Melchizedek Priesthood side of the Assembly Hall. The 1974 edition of Talmage's *The House of the Lord* (Salt Lake City: Deseret Book Co.) features a photograph of the Melchizedek Priesthood side of the Assembly Hall, but the door to the Talmage Room cannot be seen. In many entries in his journal, Talmage refers to "my room in the Temple." For a more modern example of the "Talmage Room" being used by a general authority, see Sheri L. Dew, *The Biography of Gordon B. Hinckley: Go Forward With Faith* (Salt Lake City: Deseret Book Co., 1996), 177.

56. Talmage Journal, 18 July 1905.

57. See the following supplementary materials that have been produced: *Study for the Melchizedek Priesthood and Priests, Church of Jesus Christ of Latter-day Saints, 1916, "JESUS THE CHRIST, by Elder James E. Talmage of the Quorum of the Twelve," Prepared and issued under the direction of the General Authorities of the Church, Salt Lake City, Utah, 1916.*

Lectures on JESUS THE CHRIST, Extension Publications, Adult Education and Extension Services (Provo, UT: Brigham Young University, Sept. 1963). This document covers lectures January-March 1963.

Of interest is the following editorial by Elder Mark E. Petersen of the Quorum of the Twelve, which appeared in the *Church News,* 17 Apr. 1983:

We Need to be Orthodox
IT SEEMS THAT there has always been a tendency on the part of some to speculate concerning our doctrines and to "enlarge upon them" with their own private notions, thus leading others astray.

Teachers have no right to mislead anyone by introducing unorthodox notions. And how do we define that which is unorthodox?

It is doctrine approved by the First Presidency of the Church. The prophet, seer and revelator determines what is true doctrine. Those who advocate teachings contrary to those approved by the First Presidency place themselves and others in an untenable position.

How shall we know what is truth? The scriptures are the foundation of our teachings and they do not change. President Joseph Fielding

Smith once said, "If I say anything that is contrary to the scriptures, the scriptures prevail."

That is the way it must be with all of us. The scriptures prevail!

To meet this situation in the days of President Joseph F. Smith, the First Presidency authorized Elder James E. Talmage of the Council of the Twelve to write two books: *Jesus the Christ* and *The Articles of Faith*.

THE BOOKS WERE COMMISSIONED by the First Presidency, edited by the First Presidency and distributed by them to the Church to help everyone understand the truth. These books still fulfill that purpose.

58. Malcolm R. Thorpe, "James E. Talmage and the Tradition of the Victorian Lives of Jesus," *Sunstone* 12 (Jan. 1988): 8-13. Also see Anthony A. Hutchinson, "LDS Approaches to the Bible," *Dialogue: A Journal of Mormon Thought* 15 (Spring 1982): 104-105.

59. Frederick W. Farrar, *The Life of Christ* (Portland, OR: Fountain Publications, 1972).

60. Thorpe, 11.

61. James E. Talmage, "Latter-day Saints and the Bible," delivered at the 84th annual conference, 5 Apr. 1914, and "The Book of Mormon and the Book of Isaiah," delivered at the 99th annual conference, 6 Apr. 1929. Talmage Journal, 27 Mar. 1904, mentions that he gave a talk on "The Higher Criticism" to the 27th Ward Mutual Improvement Association. There does not seem to be a written copy of this talk. Talmage was not the only church authority who wrote and spoke on Higher Criticism. See B. H. Roberts, "Higher Criticism and the Book of Mormon," *Improvement Era* 14 (June 1911): 665-77 and (July 1911): 774-86.

62. Farrar, 140n2.

63. The index to the 1902 edition of the Pearl of Great Price has six references to the "Son of Man," with each providing cross-references, all by Talmage.

The following entry from the "Record dated Aug. 20, 1878" by fifteen-year-old James Talmage (Talmage Papers, Box 9, Folder 5), comes from the section on "Theology," 96-97.

XXVII *"Son of Man"*—Why so called?

In several passages Christ is termed the son of man. Many of the prophets have been addressed by God as Son of Man; but Christ is the only one who calls himself so however. "The Man" is Adam, hence we may say son of Adam. Christ speaks of himself as such because he was preeminently the son of Adam:—"before Abraham was I." He refers by this that he is the firstborn of his Father. We are all children of God, but

Christ being the oldest, he is termed the son, just as the crown prince is termed the prince: whereas all the sons and daughters of the king, are princes and princesses.

64. Talmage Journal, 10 May 1915. The version contained herein is from the original proof sheets. For two other instances of post-conference editing, see Stan Larson, ed., *The Truth, The Way, The Life,* by B. H. Roberts (San Francisco: Smith Research Associates, 1994), lvii-lviii and references; and Peggy Fletcher, "Poelman Revises Conference Speech," *Sunstone* 10 (1985), 1:44-46.

65. *Talmage Story,* 180-81.

66. Ibid., 195. For context, see "Mormons Give Up Wheat," *New York Times,* 12 June 1918, 1; and James E. Talmage, "The Women's Relief Society," *Relief Society Magazine* 6 (Oct. 1919): 565-67.

67. "Sets Example for His Elders—Six Year Old Would Enlist," underneath, a smaller headline reading, "John Russell Talmage Offers Services to Country; Recruiting Goes On," *Salt Lake Tribune,* 31 Mar. 1917.

68. *Talmage Story,* 194; for a comprehensive listing of the circulation of the "Vitality of Mormonism" articles, see The Talmage Papers, Box 23, Folder 16; Box 24, Folders 1-4. James E. Talmage, *The Vitality of Mormonism* (Boston: The Gorham Press, 1919).

69. Talmage Journal, 6 Nov. 1916; *Talmage Story,* 193-94.

70. Talmage Journal, same date; *Improvement Era* 22 (Dec. 1918): 166-70; Joseph F. Smith, *Gospel Doctrine* (Salt Lake City: Deseret Book Co., 1919), 472-76. Also see D&C, explanatory introduction, and PGP, introductory note. For proceedings of the canonization process, see *One Hundred Forty-Sixth Annual Conference of the Church of Jesus Christ of Latter-day Saints,* 3, 4, 6 Apr. 1976, p. 29; and *Ensign* 6 (May 1976): 19.

71. Hollis Scott, "Oral History Interview with Helga Pederson Tingey, Secretary to James E, Talmage," Mar. 1976, 12, Talmage Papers, Box 24, Folder 8.

72. Talmage Papers, Box 23, Folder 13.

73. *Talmage Story,* 193.

74. Ibid., 208-209. In his journals Talmage makes numerous references to setting missionaries apart. The following incident is recorded in the family history of Crozier Kimball, who was set apart by Elder Talmage on 30 October 1928: "Elder James E. Talmage of the Council of the Twelve Apostles, set Crozier apart for this mission [to New Martinsville, West Virginia]. In the

middle of his prayer he hesitated for a few moments. Then he said, 'Brother Kimball, I see people gathering in crowds to hear the gospel from your lips this winter.' The promise was fulfilled; Crozier did speak to crowds and groups of people much more than to single individuals during this mission. He later said that groups of people would gather and stand in snow up to the tops of their shoes to hear him preach the gospel." See Marva Jeanne Kimball Pedersen, *Crozier Kimball: His Life and Work/Vaughn Robert Kimball* (Bountiful, UT: Crozier Kimball Family, Carr Printing, 1995), xx, 231.

75. *Latter-day Revelation—Selections from the Book of Doctrine and Covenants of the Church of Jesus Christ of Latter-day Saints* (Salt Lake City: Published by the Church, 1930); no author is indicated. In his journal dated 22 Nov. 1930, Talmage records the following, "I had the pleasure of presenting to the First Presidency advance copies of the little book '*Latter-day Revelation*' which is described on the title page as 'Selections from the book of Doctrine and Covenants.' The selections were decided upon by the First Presidency and the Twelve and the matter of arranging, editing, proof reading, etc., has been under my immediate direction, and I must be held personally responsible for the correctness of the type and matter." Talmage also reviewed the book in the *Improvement Era* 34 (May 1931): 427, and may have been responsible for the official announcement in the *Deseret News*, 24 Nov. 1931.

76. For a comprehensive analysis of the "Roberts/Smith/Talmage Affair," see Duane E. Jeffery, "Seers, Savants and Evolution: The Uncomfortable Interface," *Dialogue: A Journal of Mormon Thought* 8 (Autumn/Winter 1973): 41-75; Richard Sherlock, "'We Can See No Advantage to a Continuation of the Discussion': The Roberts/Smith/Talmage Affair," *Dialogue: A Journal of Mormon Thought* 13 (Fall 1980): 63-78; and Jeffrey Keller, "Discussion Continued: The Sequel to the Roberts/Smith/Talmage Affair," *Dialogue: A Journal of Mormon Thought* 15 (Spring 1982): 79-98. All three articles and others are reprinted in *Search for Harmony*. Also see Larson, *The Truth, The Way, The Life*. Larson's introduction is instructive as is the appendix which features "Correspondence Related to 'The Truth, The Way, The Life,'" 653-80.

A listing of letters by James E. Talmage, Sterling Talmage, John A. Widtsoe, Joseph Fielding Smith, and others pertaining to the evolution controversy can be found on the Internet under the title "The Sterling B. Talmage Papers (Accn724) Inventory at http://www.lib.utah.edu/spc/mss/accn724/accn724.html"; these documents are housed at the Marriott Library, University of Utah.

Also see James B. Allen, "The Story of *The Truth, The Way, The Life*," *Brigham Young University Studies* 33 (1993), 4:690-741.

77. There are three different printings of "The Earth and Man," the first

being the *Deseret News* version of 21 Nov. 1931; the second is the pamphlet of the same name; and the third is a reprint in *The Instructor* 100 (Dec. 1965): 474–77, and 101 (Jan. 1966): 9–11, 15. There are discrepancies among the versions, most notably changes in the order of paragraphs in the *Instructor* reprint.

78. Larson, *The Truth, The Way, The Life,* lvii, n77.

79. This document is located in archives, Vault M230 T147e 1931, Lee Library.

80. *Talmage Story,* 237.

81. Ibid., 112–14. Talmage Journal, 30 May and 31 May 1892.

82. To investigate this claim, I contacted Dennis Rowley, who said after a thorough review of the Talmage journals and other papers, he found no evidence for this claim. I also inquired at Princeton University (where Einstein taught). To date, no mention of Talmage has been found in the papers of Albert Einstein. Finally, John R. Talmage, the last living child of Elder Talmage, reported to me that the rumor was not true.

83. My purpose in mentioning this incident is to lay these rumors to rest, not to be controversial or to excuse such behavior. I have encountered several variations of the smoking story, and each differs from the original account.

84. Brian H. Stuy, ed., *Collected Discourses—Delivered by President Wilford Woodruff, His Two Counselors, The Twelve Apostles and Others* (Burbank, CA: B. H. S. Publishing, 1991), 4:281–86. Talmage Journal, 6 Apr. 1895.

85. James E. Talmage, "Hot Drinks are Not for the Body," *Improvement Era* 20 (Apr. 1917): 555–58.

86. Talmage, *The Articles of Faith,* 1st ed., 459–60; 1924 ed., 447–49. Also see Talmage, *Jesus the Christ* (1915), 29–31. Also Talmage, *The Vitality of Mormonism,* chap. 58, and *Sunday Night Talks by Radio* (Salt Lake City: Published by the Church, Deseret News, 1931), chap. 42, entitled "The Hygiene of the Soul."

87. Talmage Journal, 12 Mar. 1896; also cited in Richard S. Van Wagoner and Steven C. Walker, *A Book of Mormons* (Salt Lake City: Signature Books, 1982), 344–45.

88. *Talmage Story,* 182.

89. N. B. Lundwall, *Temples of the Most High* (Salt Lake City: Bookcraft, 1968), 139–42; *Deseret News,* 2 Apr. 1938, by Leroi C. Snow.

{1}

"An Unusual Accompaniment to a Baptism"

(from the *Improvement Era* 25 [June 1922]: 675-76)

During my eleventh year, in the Spring of 1873, I was stricken with a severe illness; and, as my parents afterward informed me, my life appeared to be near its close. My father associated this illness with the fact that my baptism into the Church had been deferred beyond the time at which it should have been attended to. At that time father was president of the Hungerford and Ramsbury branch of the Church.

As father afterward told me, he made solemn covenant with the Lord that if my life should be spared he would lose no time in having me baptized after my recovery. We were then living at Eddington, a suburb of Hungerford, Berkshire, England. Our house was within a stone's throw of one end of the great bridge that spans the Kennet River, an important tributary of the Thames. A mill race paralleled the river for a quarter of a mile or more, and between the two streams was a roadway for pedestrians. Because of possible interference by persecutors of the Latter-day Saints it was necessary that baptisms be attended to only in the night-time.

Ellen Gilbert, also in the eleventh year of her age, a faithful daughter of a devoted mother, was to be baptized at the same time. Ellen Gilbert's brother, Elijah, was then a deacon in the branch. Ellen Gilbert, now Mrs. Andrew L. Hyer, is living at Lewiston, Cache County, Utah, and her brother, Elder Elijah Gilbert, is at present a resident of Fairview, Idaho. I well remember the circumstances of the double baptism, and of the particular incident connected therewith.

On June 15, 1873, my father and Elijah Gilbert left our house shortly before midnight, traversed the Kennet bridge back and forth, looked around the neighborhood, and returned to the house telling us that all seemed clear, and that Ellen and I were to prepare to enter the water. In the interest of caution they went out once more, and returned with the same report. Ellen and I accompanied father and Brother Elijah to the place selected in the mill race for our immersion.

I was to be baptized first. As father stood in the water and took my hand, I being on the bank with Ellen and her brother, we were veritably horror-stricken by a combined shriek, yell, scream, howl—I know not how to describe the awful noise—such as none of us had ever heard. It seemed to be a combination of every fiendish ejaculation we could conceive of. I remember how I trembled at the awful manifestation, which had about it the sharpness and volume of a thunderclap followed by an angry roar, which died away as a hopeless groan.

The fearsome sound seemed to come from a point not more than fifty yards from us, near the end of the great bridge. The night was one of bright starlight, and we could have seen anyone on the bridge, which was built of white stone with low walls. Elijah Gilbert, with courage unusual for so young a man, started to investigate, but father called him back. Father, who was also trembling, as were the others, then asked me if I was too frightened to be baptized; I was too much terrified to speak, so I answered by stepping into the water. I was baptized, and Ellen Gilbert was baptized immediately afterward. As we started back to the house, not more than three hundred yards from the spot at which we had been immersed, father and Elijah went toward the bridge, surveyed the immediate vicinity, but failed to find any person abroad besides ourselves.

The affrighting noise had sounded to us as loud enough to be heard over a great area; but none except ourselves seemed to have heard it, as not even a window was opened by anybody in the neighborhood, and no mention or inquiry concerning the matter was later made by others. Neighborly gossip was quite the order of the time; and, surely, if that blood-curdling shriek had been heard by others than ourselves it would have been the subject of talk for many a day. But we heard it, as we shall never forget. Sister Ellen, Brother Elijah and I have spoken together on the matter as we have occasionally met. On January 20, 1912, I was a visitor at the home of Bishop and Sister Hyer, in Lewiston, Utah; and when mention was made of the unusual incident associated with our baptisms, I requested Sister Hyer to relate in detail the circumstance as she remembered it, for I had often wondered whether the distance of time had in any way distorted my view and rendered my remembrance inaccurate. I was struck by the strict agreement, even as to minute detail, between her recital and my recollection. On July 20, 1919, I was again in the home of Sister Hyer and made a similar request;

but Sister Hyer wisely suggested that as her brother Elijah was present he should be the one to tell the story. This he did, and his account agreed with our remembrance in all details.

{2}

Science and Religion

(Entries from the Journal of James E. Talmage, 1881-1926,
Archives and Manuscripts, Harold B. Lee Library, Brigham
Young University, Provo, Utah)

Feb. 7, 1881—Went to Salt Lake City to attend a series of two lectures to be delivered by Prof. R.A. Proctor. Attended his first lecture the same evening; etc.; "Birth and growth of Worlds." Have formed a decided opinion regarding Proctor's views, though that opinion of mine is certainly immature, and therefore I will refrain from expressing it, for I may change it. I will say, however, that, though Prof. Proctor's theory is logical and fascinating, I am able clearly to see how he lacks that firmness, which one who has just claim by his Priesthood on the spirit of god will possess. Proctor says that the theory of the winding up scene being at hand, is without foundation: that it is the "Cracked-brain project of the nineteenth century," as every century has been characterized by such alarm. Prof. Proctor with us, all will find out.

Feb. 8, 1881—Attended the second lecture of Professor Proctor in the evening. His theory is indeed beautiful but I modify his views to suit my own convictions. . . .

Dec. 12, 1881—I want to do good among the young—probably lecture amongst the Improvement Associations, and encourage the study of nature. I have thought to give a first lecture on the subject of harmony between Geology and the Bible—a subject upon which so many of our people have mistaken ideas. We sent off at once for a set of views costing thirty dollars for this lecture. . . .

June 17, 1882— . . . I have many times contemplated my probable destiny and mission in life without obtaining a satisfactory conclusion; but I have for some time past felt an intense desire to become familiar with the walks of Science for the Sciences have to be redeemed from their present position of infidelity & skepticism. The idea has been a favorite one for my meditations of late, and has formed the theme of my public speaking. I conclude that this great mission has to be performed by the Priesthood of God, and to lay a single stone in such work is perhaps my mission in life. . . .

Mar. 16, 1884—In the course of my studies I have naturally been brought face to face with the alleged atheistic tendency of scientific thought and the conflict usually said to exist between Science and Religion. Now, I have felt in a dilemma—and begin now to fancy I see a way out. I have been unable *to see* the point of conflict myself:— my belief in a loving God perfectly accords with my reverence for science, and I can see no reason why the evolution of animal *bodies* cannot be true—as indeed the facts of observation make it difficult to deny—and still the *soul* of *man* is of *divine* origin. The dilemma which has troubled me is this—being unable to perceive the great difficulty of which Scientists, and Theologians, and Scientific-theologians re- fer—I have feared that my investigation of the subject was highly superficial, for when such great men as most of the writers upon this subject are—find a puzzle, it would be high egotism for me to say *I* find no puzzle. And the fancied exit which I see has appeared from my reading some of John Stuart Mill's writings and I feel—that if I had none other idea of a Deity that those men have, viz., that of an unknown being, whose acts as Mill says *"contrary to the highest human morality"*—I too would hail atheism with delight. I could never believe in such a God as theirs, not though one should rise from the grave to declare Him to me. And just as certainly do I perceive that there can be no antagonism between the true science as revealed and made easy by the Priesthood, and the God whose attributes and passions of love and mercy are also declared by that same Priesthood. . . .

May 4, 1884—Have just returned tonight from service at the Westminster Presbyterian Church. The minister spoke against belief in Darwinism and like most ministers whose remarks I have heard or read upon this subject—showed his ignorance. He spoke much as an ordinary person would—*"Darwin.* Oh yes—says we come from mon- keys"—then condemns. I certainly think 'tis the ministers themselves who have bred the disgust with which most scientific people regard them—because they will dabble with matters from which their igno- rance should keep them at a safe distance. The speaker tonight brought out many noble principles, but in spite of his eminence as a preacher— self contradiction and inconsistency were apparent.

Really, I do not wonder that any scientific man refuses to belong to a church where he is told nothing but *"Only believe* & you'll be saved"—*"The blood* of *the Lamb* is *all powerful"*—"take up the cross of Christ" etc. The preachers always talk in metaphors—you can't bring them down to fact; and anything which will not bear scrutiny when stripped of fine language is to the scientific mind nonsense. Again, Darwin wrote for those who can understand him: some of whom will agree with & others oppose him: but he did not write for ministers who never read beyond other's opinions of the man, anymore than Plato or [?] wrote for babes and sucklings. . . .

June 8, 1885—Went to Salt Lake City by evening train to attend the lecture by *Monseignor Capel* on Science and Religion. I am glad to have heard the gentleman—but his arguments were in no respect stronger than I have heard brought out by students. I believe I could name three or four of my own students who could argue stronger than he did. He took a decidedly Catholic stance. . . .

June 27, 1888—In the evening according to previous appointment, I went to Springville to lecture there under the auspices of the Improvement Associations, on the subject of "Nature and Nature's God." I have been requested by the Springville people, since before the time of the accident to my eye, that I should speak in that place on "Evolution" as a partial offset to the tendency of certain atheistical doctrine [?] there through the teachings of a certain Dr. York. The subject was treated tonight according to my poor ability under the title first above named. I trust it did some good. . . .

Jan. 21, 1890—According to previous appointment, I tonight delivered a lecture on "The Theory of Evolution" at the University of Deseret under the auspices of the Delta Phi Society. The subject and the nature of the audience caused me to depart from my usual course in lectures,—I wrote and read the address; mainly that there may be no uncertainty to my expressions. While speaking extemporaneously, a person is liable by a slip to say the opposite of what he means. It is easy to omit a "not" or a "no" and cause a misunderstanding. . . .

Mar. 8, 1890—According to an appointment of long standing, I this day went to Provo and there delivered a lecture on the "Theory of Evolution" before the County Teacher's Convention. The convention, after listening to the lecture, asked permission to publish it. Because of the importance of the subject and the ease with which misunderstandings arise as to a speaker's intentions, I read the lecture from notes. . . .

Feb. 5, 1898—According to previous appointment I went by morning train to Logan. During the afternoon I delivered a lecture in the Temple, under the auspices of the Temple Association; subject

"Scientific methods and Motives." The address was well received, though I had expected some criticism of the choice of topic. It has become quite the fashion among some of our preachers,—the little-great men amongst us to denounce science and all its teachings, and this has been carried so far that many of our young people believe that science has no place in the religious soul, and that scientific teachings are contrary to the precepts of the doctrines of Christ. The leaders of our people are not so careless: they may as they do at times point out the dangers of man's philosophical systems, and such caution is good; but the lay speakers are apt to indulge in the common pastime of uninformed prejudice—denunciation.

May 2, 1899 [From the Manuscript History of the Church, the First Presidency's office.]—Presidents Snow and Smith were at the office. Dr. James E. Talmage called and had a long talk with President Snow on the subjects of philosophy, religion and science. Brother Talmage expects to go to Europe again, and President Snow offered to assist him in the sum of $300. Brother Talmage suggested the idea of his preparing the manuscript for a book on the subject of evolution, with the understanding that he was not to show the manuscript to any person until he had first submitted it to the Presidency. President Snow acquiesced in the suggestion. . . .

May 31, 1899—Closing lectures in my classes at the university for the year. Busy with preparations for my departure on another journey to England. Owing to my very busy condition in missionary labor last year I accomplished but little of the scientific work which I went to do, and I have been impressed with a desire to return. In recent conversations with the First Presidency, this desire was strengthened by the expressed wish that I would go. Indeed Prest. Snow first proposed that the Church propriate $300 for my expenses . . .

Sept. 27, 1909—Special committee meeting at the President's office, to consider a proposed article by the First Presidency on "The Origin of Man." . . .

Sept. 30, 1909—Committee meeting for further consideration of the article on "The Origin of Man." Meeting was held at my office. . . .

Sept. 13, 1899—Interview with the First Presidency for consultation regarding certain matters of scientific interest, and the views of the Church authorities concerning the same.

Dec. 19, 1911—Attended regular weekly meeting of the Deseret Sunday School Union. Then, in evening I delivered an address in the

Eleventh ward, under Improvement Assn. auspices on "The Origin of Man." This was virtually a repetition of the talk given in the 20th Ward a week ago and is in connection with current lessons in the Y.L.M.I.A. course of study.

Sept. 1, 1912— . . . Brief reports were made by the officers of the Y.M. and Y.L.M.I.A. and the rest of the evening was devoted to a lecture by myself on the subject of "Mormonism and Science." I returned home by interurban trains about midnight.

Mar. 12, 1922—While we were in Pittsburgh, President McCune informed me of an invitation extended by the "Free Thought Forum" of this city to address the body at 4:30 today. A meeting was held in the room we had occupied during the earlier part of the day. According to report there were over 300 present. I spoke on the "Origin and Destiny of Man," giving attention to the *distinction between the body only and the man,* and dealing with the subjects of ante-mortal existence, life beyond the grave, and the resurrection. I was listened to with every outward mark of close attention during the 50 minutes allotted to me. Then, according to the order, discussion was invited. The scene that followed is memorable and saddening. Sometimes several people were on their feet at once asking recognition of the chairman. None of them discussed the subject I had treated; but as I had quoted from the Bible, each directed his remarks to a denunciation of Holy Scriptures and some of them were blatant in proclaiming their atheism. There were three or four women who took part in the discussion, and these were even more extreme than the men. Such an exhibition of godlessness I have seldom seen; and the effect was not lost upon our missionaries and other members of the church who remained throughout the session. . . .

June 22, 1922—The American Association for the Advancement of Science, specifically the Pacific division, opened its annual session at the University of Utah today at 9 a.m. Elders John A. Widtsoe and Richard R. Lyman and I are fellows of the Association, and of course it is expected that we do our share of the work incident to carrying out the program. At the luncheon hour Dr. John A. Widtsoe gave an excellent address on "Research Problems of the Great Basin." In the afternoon I attended the meeting of the section known as The Western Society of Naturalists. The general topic for discussion was "Heredity and Evolution." Dr. David Starr Jordan spoke by way of reply to a recent statement by the President of the British Association for the

Advancement of Science, who said that we know little about the origin of species. Dr. Jordan holds that we know much about it.

I was profoundly impressed in listening to the several papers bearing upon this subject, that the evolutionists are much disturbed, their chief aim at the present time seems to be to counteract the general impression that evolutionists do not agree among themselves; nevertheless, that they do not agree is a well attested fact. . . .

May 19, 1923—At 6 p.m. I attended a social in open air at the home of President and Sister Maud Bentley, and I gave an informal talk in answer to questions relating to the subject of evolution. . . .

Apr. 20, 1925—[As mission president of the European Mission] This marks the beginning of a three days conference of the Royal Microscopical Society. I had received special and urgent invitation to be present: and in accordance with the expressed wishes of the First Presidency—that I attend as many of the scientific meetings as I can, I had accepted the invitation.

Nov. 19, 1926—["In Worthy Remembrance," From a Memorial Address delivered at the unveiling and dedication of the Karl G. Maeser tablet in Meissen, Germany. Printed in the Millenial Star, Dec. 2, 1926]

"To him [Karl G. Maeser] science and religion were the handmaidens of God, engaged in harmonious and reciprocal service, nurturing and leading the soul toward the state of perfection planned by the Divine Father. Who shall venture to challenge or deny such philosophy of life?" . . .

{3}

"The Effects of Narcotics upon the System"

(Entries from the Journal of James E. Talmage, while at Johns Hopkins University, 1884, Archives and Manuscripts, Harold B. Lee Library, Brigham Young University, Provo, Utah)

March 17—I have been engaged some time in the study of the effects of Narcotics upon the system, i.e. studying the same theoretically only. Today I found a gentleman who works in the same Laboratory as I, and who has for 2 years been addicted to the habit of eating Hashish or extract of Cannabis Indica. He was very willing to give me any data from his own experience; and gave me such.

March 18—My Hashish eating friend gave me further details at odd times today. Three of us in the University have entered upon the study of the Narcotics in use.

March 21—The result of our work in research upon Narcotics has been tolerably satisfactory. We utilize my friend referred to above, with his Hashish eating experience—and find four or five others whom he knows have also an experience upon the subject. But the effects experienced by the different ones are so widely different that we can scarcely draw a conclusion. The opium habit is well explained by books, and the bad after effects of the same are sufficiently appalling to keep down experimentation upon the subject. But, the ill effects are reported very low in the Hashish or Hemp administration; and we have concluded to try effect of small dose upon ourselves.

Of course, such a course is the proper one for the study of the effects of the drug, though I very much disliked the idea of doing such a thing, for as yet I have never known what it is to be narcotized either by tobacco, alcohol, or any drug. . .

March 22—This being Saturday, was the day I selected to study practically the effects of Hashish. This evening, after work and all was over, I took at 3 doses each an hour after the preceding, 5 grains solid extract Cannabis Indica. At this writing—midnight—5 hours since last dose, I have experienced no effect whatever. The effect is said to be widely different in different people.

March 23—Sunday. Spent quietly. Have had no result to be noted of my physiological experiment yesterday.

I do not feel inclined to try again till the end of next week—as the realization of the effects of the drug are not desirable on working days.

April 5—This evening—first opportunity which has presented itself—I attempted my experiment on the effects of Hashish as referred to March 22 (page 26). Took in all 15 grains. No effects.

April 6. Sunday . . . Continued my experiment by taking 20 grains Cannabis Indica and the effect was felt in a not very agreeable way. My fellow experimenters & I concluded I should take no larger dose—but perhaps vary the trial in the future. . . .

{4}

"The Birth and Growth of the Earth," An Address Given at Brigham Young Academy on 29 November 1884

(from *The Academic Review* 1 [December 1884]: 19)

THE BIRTH AND GROWTH OF THE EARTH was the subject of a public lecture delivered by the President of the Polysophical Society on Saturday evening, Nov. 29, and was illustrated by numerous and excellent lantern views. After dwelling upon the supposed origin of our earth, the speaker cited the most important arguments for and against the belief in a molten interior within a comparatively thin crust, and pointed out the evident conclusion that the crust must be undoubtedly thicker than has been traditionally believed for years. The formation of strata, and the dislocation and contortion of the same by volcanic and eruptive agencies next claimed attention; which was followed with remarks on the occurrence of living organisms in the later Eozoic and Paleozoic Rocks. The Trilobites, Crinzoids, Corals and Ammonites fossils were shown; followed by the flora and fauna of the Devonian Age. This was the age of fishes—all being of the Ganoid and Placoid orders; of which there were shown Pterichthys, Cephalaspis, Cocosteus and Dinichthys—fishes with skull shields large enough to protect the head of an elephant, strong enough to resist a musket ball, and hard enough to strike fire with flint. The Carboniferous Age was noted for its rank vegetation—monstrous tree-ferns and club-mosses—Calamites reaching to the height of twenty feet, while the only representation of the kind now extant—the "horse-tails"— scarcely even exceed two feet; Lepidodendra over sixty-feet high— with impressions on the stems resembling the scales of a Ganoid fish, and hence the name (meaning scale-stemmed); Sigillaria (seal marked)—supposed to have reached the height of ninety or more feet; while flattened stems have been brought to light in the Pennsylvania collieries, with a width of five feet.

The Mesozoic Age, or age of reptiles, was represented by the hideous Plesiosaraurus—twenty-five or more feet long, with whale-like paddles of seven feet in length; the Ichthyosaurus a fish lizard; the

Megalosaurus; the bat-like Pterodactyl with a spread of wings of twenty or twenty-five feet; the Iguanodon, the Hylaeosaurus and the Mosaaurus.

Among the mammals of the Cenozoic Age, there were represented the Paleotherium, Aneplotherium, Megatherium, glyptodon and Mammoth; and among birds, the Dodo.

Then Man is supposed to have appeared on the scene, and with his advent, the labors of the Geologist end; for "Geology, which is the story of the rocks, finds its climax in History which is the story of man."

{5}

"The Theory of Evolution,"
A Lecture Delivered before the Utah County Teacher's Association at Provo City on 8 March 1890

(from *The Theory of Evolution* [Provo, UT: Utah County Teacher's Association, 1890])

Mr. President, and Members of the Association:

It is with at least some realization of the honor attending the position that I stand before you now. This audience is composed largely of teachers, many of whom are of mature experience in the profession; being teachers, they must be more or less earnest thinkers; and to address a body of thinkers is an honor to any speaker. Relying upon this high standard of my hearers, I shall venture to treat the subject chosen by your President for the occasion, in a more technical and perhaps a less popular manner than would be advisable before a greatly mixed assembly. I shall believe that no one here has come for the purpose of being amused or entertained simply, but that the object of our gathering is to obtain instruction and to seek for truth.

I am especially desirous not to be misunderstood. The importance of the subject is such as to warrant no doubtful sentences or words with uncertain meaning. Yet any speaker may fail at times to convey his ideas in their fulness; he is liable to inadvertently omit a "not" or a "no" and thus express the opposite of what he intended to say. In consideration of these points, I shall ask your indulgence in a departure from my almost constant habit in public speaking, and shall read the greater portion of the address.

It is a subject of common interest. Today, scientists and laymen, and even ladies in their boudoirs talk of Evolution, and everyone must have an idea upon the subject, occasionally owned, but most frequently borrowed.

According to the generally accepted meaning, Evolution implies an unfolding, an unrolling, a developing; signifying therefore with respect to organisms, their growth to a perfect form. The Theory of Evolution then is that hypothesis by which man has sought to explain what he considers to be the probable origin of himself, and his surroundings. The establishment of the Theory of Evolution is to be explained by that innate tendency of man to search after the first or original of things. To the human mind there is something, aye, much, that is mystical in the idea of a beginning. The continuation of an action once begun is far more readily understood—is a natural process as we are apt to say: but the start, the origin—that is a far deeper subject; it partakes of the nature of a creation, and for that reason alone is suggestive of a power superior to that of man. It is at present a universal belief, that every living thing of earth has been developed from a particle of matter, in which there existed originally no discernible traces of the distinctive features which characterize the adult form. Such a particle is called a *Germ*.

The definition commonly applied to this much misunderstood term is "Matter potentially alive, and having within itself a tendency to assume a definite living form".

It is noticeable that the germs from which grow the most diverse of the orders of life, bear to each other, while still but germs, a marked resemblance. The highest powers of the microscope fail to reveal any differences sufficiently clear to be called distinctive, even between the germinal spots from which spring fishes, birds, or mammals; and in some cases human power is insufficient to detect the structural differences between the germ of a warm blooded quadruped, and that of certain plants. Yet shall we say there are no differences? The untrained eye may fail to recognize distinctive features between the seeds of radishes and turnips, but every thoughtful person will admit that such exist, and the subsequent growth will substantially establish the fact. It is absurd to hold that the germs of such divers forms are at all alike.

To illustrate the same more in detail, consider for a moment the case of the eggs of birds. The variations in outward appearance, size, etc., of the eggs of different species, are mainly dependent upon the quantity of food material stored within the shell, upon which the living germ subsists during the process of incubation. The embryonic points exhibit no recognizable differences; yet in the one case, the ovum produces a gaudy, shrill-voiced peacock, in another a plainly dressed, sweet toned lark, and in yet another, a savage eagle, or perhaps a timid wren.

Surely the possibility of the pea fowl's feather, the eagle's claw, or the lark's clear throat, lay hidden within the fragile shell. What an example of evolution there is here! What an unfolding! What a developing in the case of each creature to the full realization of the measure of its creation. Yet these differences are by many considered as mere distinctions between species; and that indeed bird and fish and mammal have all sprung from similar original germs.

To more properly consider the evidence on the subject thus broached, let us take a greater and more general view as to the full bearings of our theme. In its broader sense, the term *"Evolution"* is applicable to more than living organisms of earth. Man has sought to concoct a theory for the explanation of the development of every part of the great Creator's kingdom into which human thought has penetrated. The earth was not always as it is today. It has had a life history. There was a beginning to the globe; there will be an end to its present career. Hence the need, according to man's mode of thinking, of a hypothesis to explain the origin of this sphere, and the probable destiny toward which it is tending. The early history of the earth is hidden in the mists of the past, and many and diverse are the opinions of man regarding it. True it is, that the stony pages of our globe bear the record of numberless vicissitudes, strange metamorphoses; yet the earth did not record the story of its own beginning. It is written that "In the beginning"—when, how far in the ages of the past that beginning was no man can tell,—but "In the beginning, God created the heaven and the earth. And the earth was without form and void."

It is claimed by scientists, that the present condition of the earth indicates that this globe was once in a highly heated state, in a condition of igneous fusion in fact, and prior to that, as a nebulous gas. At that time, the particles of which the earth now consists were in a gaseous condition, forming a nebulous mass. Certain it is, that no tabernacle of life, plant, animal or human, such as the earth now supports, could have existed during those periods of extreme vulcanism. Then, it is said, these cosmic particles attracted each other, motion was thus established, nuclei were formed, condensation began, and continued till the earth took form, and was no longer void. Did our globe in that chaotic state, contain the germs of all subsequent being, or have such organisms since arrived upon the earth? Professor Tyndall writes: "Emotion, intellect, will, and all their phenomena, were once latent in a fiery cloud."—*Frag. of Science*. Again he says: "I discern in matter the promise and potency of every form and quality of life."

As a fair statement of the present meaning of the term, "Evolution," I quote the words of a professed disciple of the creed:—(See *Popular Science Monthly* March, 1888.)—"Plants and animals have all a

16

natural origin, from a single primitive living creature, which was itself the product of light and heat acting on the special chemical constituents of an ancient ocean. Starting from a single early form, they have gone on developing ever since, from the homogeneous to the heterogeneous, assuming ever more varied shapes, till at last they have reached their present enormous variety of trees and shrub, and herb and seaweed, of beast and bird, and fish and creeping insect. Evolution throughout has been one and continuous, from nebula to sun, from gas-cloud to planet, from early jelly-speck to man or elephant."

Having thus outlined the field of Evolution, it will be well to consider more in detail certain sections.

First, what is a species? As applied in the Life sciences, the term refers to any group of living things, which are closely allied in attributes, and which possess the power of indefinite multiplication of individuals through reproduction. It is a fact, known no less clearly to scientists than to breeders, that the results of union between different species are hybrids, which in themselves are incapable of reproduction. Here then, in the sterility of hybrids, is an easy method of identifying a species.

Now it is asked, is it not possible that the numberless orders of plants and animals now existing on earth, may be properly regarded as varieties or species of one common stock? Long ago this idea lay brooding in the minds of men. It is not a result of yesterday; the only thing modern about it is the form that it has now assumed as an alleged explanation for facts. In the eighteenth century, Lamar[c]k, and Erasmus Darwin—the grandfather of Charles Darwin, whose name is commonly coupled with any expression of evolutionary ideas—and many others, announced their belief that the diverse orders of animal and plants probably sprang from a common progenitor.

Buffon, the naturalist nobleman, was of the same opinion. He held, that since all animals, even those of the same species, vary within certain limits, such variations, infinitely accumulated, would suffice to account for almost any degree of ultimate difference. He scarcely more than hinted at a full expression of his belief, however; but this seeming hesitancy is fully explained by a consideration of his circumstances. In his day, the French monarchy was in a tottering condition, and it was the custom among his people to deal summarily with those whose ideas were at all offensive to the orthodoxy of the realm. This was true in every branch of human thought and activity.

Had our naturalist ventured an unmodified declaration of belief in a common general progenitor of living things, the powers of the times would doubtlessly have taken steps to effectually silence him. Still we must look upon Buffon as a pronounced evolutionist in thought.

Erasmus Darwin seemed to understand the full meaning of Buffon's hints. He became an ardent promulgator of the disconnected ideas which have since been woven into the fabric of the evolutionary hypothesis.

He said that "life began in very minute marine forms, which gradually acquired fresh powers and larger bodies so as to imperfectly transform themselves into different creatures." He pointed out that man possessed the power of changing the appearance, and even the habits of domesticated animals through selective breeding. He dealt especially with rabbits and pigeons; and in the words of a commentator he reasoned thus: "If man can make a pointer or a fan-tail out of the common sort, if he can produce a piebald lop-ear from the brown wild rabbit, if he can transform Dorkings into Black Spanish, why cannot Nature, with a longer time to work in, and endless lives to try with, produce all the varieties of vertebrate animals out of one single common ancestor?"

A few years later, Lamark openly avowed his belief that animals and plants were really descended from one, or, at most, a few common ancestors. He drew attention to the fact that the "species" of naturalists differed from "varieties" in being slightly more distinctly marked. "He thought organic evolution was wholly due to the direct action of surrounding circumstances, to the inter-crossing of existing forms, and above all to the actual efforts of the animals themselves. ★★★★ For him, the giraffe had acquired its long neck by constant reaching up to the boughs of trees; the monkey had acquired its oppossable thumb by constantly grasping at the neighboring branches; and the serpent had acquired its sinuous shape by constant wriggling through the grass of meadows."

All the opinions thus far quoted from, were extant before the time of Charles Darwin, who is so frequently regarded as the sole originator of evolutionary theories. There were many evolutionists before him. Even Herbert Spencer took cognizance of the growing belief in the *"development hypothesis,"* as evolution was then termed. Charles Darwin introduced a new element into the evolutionary idea—the element of *Natural Selection.*

Briefly expressed this means;—that among the almost numberless variations and differences which manifest themselves in the course of a few generations of living forms, many are positively disadvantageous to the organisms; and such bad variations tend to die out, because every disadvantage tells against its unfortunate possessor in the struggle for life.

If the variation be a good one, there is a strong tendency toward its perpetuation; for every such advantage makes its favorable influence felt in the race for life. The fittest therefore will tend to survive; while the weak and the unfit tend to speedy extinction. It is proper to suppose that individuals of any species would exercise choice in mating, so as to intensify pleasing variations. This principle of *Natural Selection* resulting in the survival of the fittest is in reality *Darwinism*. Evolutionism is not Darwinism. There were many evolutionists, and indeed some Darwinians before Darwin.

That Darwin's ideas may be clearly understood, his own words should be considered. In the "Origin of Species" he says: "I believe that animals are descended from at most only four or five progenitors, and plants from an equal or lesser number. Analogy would lead me one step further, viz.: to the belief that all animals and plants are descended from some one prototype."

Even at the risk of appearing tedious, I have sought to express, with some degree of fulness and fairness, the ideas of evolutionists upon Evolution. Great stress is laid today on natural selection: it is believed by some, that by natural selection species can be originated, and that by constant improvement through the operation of this principle, *man* himself has been evolved, and stands out today a monument of selective breeding.

In "Descent of Man", Mr. Darwin says:—"We thus learn that man has descended from a hairy, tailed quadruped, probably arboreal in its habits, and an inhabitant of the Old World. This creature, if its whole structure had been examined by a naturalist, would have been classed among the quadrumana, as sure as the still more ancient progenitor of the Old and New World monkeys. The quadrumana and all the higher mammals are probably derived from an ancient marsupial animal, and this through a long line of diversified forms, from some amphibian-like creature, and this again from some fish-like animal. In the dim obscurity of the past, we can see that the early progenitor of all vertebrata must have been an aquatic animal provided with branchiae, with the two sexes united within the same individual, and with the most important organs of the body (such as the brain and heart) imperfectly or not at all developed. This animal seems to have been more like the larvae of the existing marine ascidians than any other known form."

Such then is a fair statement of the Evolutionary Theory. What have we to say to it?

In the first place, supposing that undeniable proof had been furnished, that all existing forms of life had sprung from some primitive form, some primordial germ, the theory is very incomplete unless it offers an explanation of the origin of that germ. Can we find such life tissue?

Professor Huxley turned his attention to the gelatinous substance found in the ooze at the bottom of the deep seas: and announced his belief that it is a sheet of living matter, extending round the globe. It was composed he said, in large part of *Protoplasm,* the fabric from which living forms are woven. To it he gave the name of *Bathybius* from a pair of Greek words meaning *deep life,* and he assumed it to be the progenitor of all life on this planet.

This announcement was hailed with joy by those who awaited such that their theoretical conceptions as to the origin of life might be completed. Regarding it Strauss wrote in 1872 in "The Old Faith and New" as follows:

"Huxley has discovered the Bathybius, a shining heap of jelly on the sea bottom, Haekel, what he has called the Moneres, structureless clots of an albuminous carbon, which although inorganic in their constitution, yet are all capable of nutrition and accretion. By these the chasm may be said to be bridged, and the transition effected between the inorganic and the organic. As long as the contrast between the inorganic and organic, lifeless and living nature, was understood as an absolute one, as long as the conception of a special vital force was retained, there was no possibility of spanning the chasm without the aid of a miracle."

But it is known now that Bathybius is other than it was supposed by Huxley to be. The good ship *Challenger* dredged the bottoms of the deep over wide areas, and Bathybius was brought up from many parts of the globe, and in every case the substance has proved to be entirely inorganic, consisting mostly of calcium sulphate or gypsum. It is, therefore, incapable of nutrition and increase by multiplication, and the chasm between the organic and the inorganic is as wide as ever.

If Bathybius had been Protoplasm, it could not have existed as such in the fiery and nebulous stages of the earth's career. When the globe had cooled sufficiently to permit the condensation of water upon its surface, then Protoplasm could exist, but whence came it at that fortuitous time? Strictly orthodox evolutionists have been driven to the acceptance of some belief in *Abiogenesis,* or the doctrine of spontaneous generation of living things, from substances which were not living. This was taught by Aristotle in ancient Greece. He thought that the eels that swam in the Nile sprang into existence from the mud at the river bottom; that caterpillars were simply vivified portions of the leaves upon which they fed; that tadpoles, from which came toads and frogs, were generated from the life-giving action of the sun on the ooze of their marshy homes. Careful observations and experiments have been made, and today not a single case of spontaneous generation, even of microscopic bacteria, has been proved. All evidence points to the impossibility of such an occurrence. Without spontaneous generation, "miracle" in the words of Strauss, was and is still necessary to explain the advent, even of the hypothetical primordial germ.

Evolutionists see such; and concede this vital point of their theory.

Professor Huxley says:

"If the hypothesis of Evolution be true, living matter must have arisen from not-living matter: for by the hypothesis the condition of the globe was at one time such, that living matter could not have existed in it, life being entirely incompatible with the gaseous state."

And again he says:

"The properties of living matter distinguish it absolutely from all other kind of things; and the present state of knowledge furnishes us with no link between the living and the not-living."

In the same article:

"At the present moment there is not a shadow of trustworthy direct evidence that Abiogenesis does take place, or has taken place within the period which the existence of the globe is recorded."

The fertility of the human mind has suggested a remarkable avenue of escape from this labyrinth of incompetent theory. Sir William Thompson has come to the front with his poetical vision of "A moss grown fragment of a shattered world." He holds it probable, that by *chance* a flying meteor, from some exploded planet, having within or upon it the germ of life—plant, animal, or both—it matters not,—*accidentally* fell upon the earth, and the germ was sown; and after the lapse

21

of ages, the present inhabitants of the globe are the descendants. One could consistently think that such a theory argued on the part of its promulgators a belief in the hopelessness of their cause. It is a desperate catch at a straw in the hope of a partial rescue from drowning agony.

This beautiful world, this garden of life—planted by chance? A farmer preparing his soil, and trusting to the wind to bear seeds from preceding crops and sow the same. It is absurd. The mystery is no less dense than formerly.

But even Tyndall seems hardly satisfied that his theories account for facts, for he says: "Granting the nebula and its potential life, the question, whence came they? would still remain to baffle and bewilder us. The hypothesis does nothing more than transport the conception of life's origin to an indefinitely distant past."

Now for the argument's sake, granting that in some way the primordial germ, the primitive ancestor came to earth. What then? How have diverse species originated?

That variations do occur among animals and plants is beyond doubt. Equally certain is it that by human agency even, selective breeding may be so directed as to bring about great changes in development. From the wild and stunted ponies have come the Pereheron, the Norman, the Cleveland, and the Clydesdale. By man's care, the Alderney, the Devon, the Friesian, the Holstein, the Jersey, and the Durham cattle have been bred; each breed possessing distinctive qualities. From the hard, sour crab apple have come, under man's protection, many varieties of rich and mellow fruit, but they all are apples. From the wild dog rose have sprung hundreds of rich and rare varieties, but they all are roses. All of these are readily recognized as varieties of the same kinds. No florist has yet developed a rose from a tulip; human power is insufficient to cause a willow to bear acorns; the stock breeder cannot transform his cows into wool bearers, nor his dogs into horses. Even the amoebae, that structureless bit of jelly, produces only amoebae.

Taking the sterility of hybrids as a test, the first case of origination of a species through natural selection, has yet to be heard of. It is a fair proof of the evolutionary theory, to ask of its adherents to employ selective breeding, which may be called an artificial natural selection, and thereby produce two species, each of which shall be fertile in itself but the union of which shall produce sterile hybrids.

Says Prof. Kolliker, the eminent German authority on embryology:

"Great weight must be attached to the objection brought forward by Huxley, otherwise a warm supporter of Darwin's hypothesis, that we know of no varieties which are sterile with one another as is the rule among sharply distinguished animal forms. If Darwin is right, it must be demonstrated that forms may be produced by selection, which, like the present sharply distinguished animal forms, are infertile when coupled with one another, and this has not been done."

According to Darwinian natural selection, all organs with no well defined uses and functions will sooner or later become extinct; and the existence of any such is an argument against the truth of the theory. Darwin himself realized the weakness of his hypothesis, and wrote as follows, the sentences being in fact concessions.

Darwin in "Descent of Man," says:

"No doubt man, as well as every other animal, presents structures which, as far as we can judge with our little knowledge, are not now of any service to him, nor have been so during any former period of his existence, either in relation to his general condition of life or of one sex to the other. Such structures cannot be accounted for by any form of selection, or by the inherited effects of the use or disuse of parts."

And again:

"In the greater number of cases, we can only say that the cause of each slight variation and of each monstrosity lies much more in the nature or constitution of the organism than in the nature of the surrounding conditions, though new and changed conditions certainly play an important part in exciting organic changes of all kinds."

I take it to be a fair conclusion, that numerous and essential concessions on the part of any contending party are evidences of the weakness of the cause.

Here are more of such evidences.

Mr. Darwin in "Origin of Species," makes this expression:

"Natural selection can act only by taking advantage of slight successive variations; it can never take a leap, but must advance by short and slow stages. If it could be demonstrated that any complex organ existed which could not possibly have been formed by numerous successive slight or modifications, my theory would absolutely break down."

Note this from "Descent of Man:"

"I now admit, after reading the essay of Nageli on plants, and the remarks by various authors with respect to animals, that in the earlier editions of my 'Origin of Species,' I probably attributed too much to the action of natural selection or the survival of the fittest. I had not formerly sufficiently considered the existence of many structures which appear to be, as far as we can judge, neither beneficial or injurious; and this I believe to be one of the greatest oversights as yet detected in my works."

If natural selection cannot take leaps, as the author of that famous hypothesis has himself declared, then there must have existed a multitude of links between the highest apes and man, Why? What are the differences in structure between the body of an ape and that of man? Many osteologists have dilated on the similarity in bony parts of the two; and many others whose chief claim to notoriety rests upon the fact that they are opponents of evolutionary ideas, deny this. Facts however are sure to stand: they are independent of theory; they may be disproved; they cannot properly be denied simply.

It is a fact that certain of the bones of animals resemble corresponding bones in the human system. That we may speak of "corresponding bones" in this connection is a proof of close analogy between the two subjects. But it is not so much to the *bones* as to the *brain* which attention is most directed. And this is wise; for the brain appears to be the seat of the mind; and between the mind of man and that of the ape there is a colossal difference.

It is a fact that the cubic capacity of the highest ape's brain is 34 inches, and that of the lowest human brain is 68 inches. Evolutionists admit this. They admit further that no theory of natural selection can account for the brain of man, for that organ is much more highly developed than would have been needed for the successful struggle of man as an animal in the race for existence.

Here then we have a mighty chasm of difference—34 cubic inches cranial capacity as the highest animal attainment; 68 as the lowest human limit and no bridge between the two. That the *missing links* have not been found is not through lack of energy on the part of the searchers—years of agonizing effort have been devoted to the cause—but the great gulf still remains. There are the best of all possible reasons for the failure of evolutionists to point to the missing links.

Among fossil remains, there is never a doubt as to their animal or human origins. The first remains of man were undoubtedly those of beings who had the fullest claims to human position.

Prof. Dana says:

"No remains of fossil man bear evidence to less perfect erectness of structure than in civilized man, or to any nearer approach to the man-ape in essential characteristics. The existing man-apes belong to lines that reached up to them as their ultimatum; but of that line which is supposed to have reached upward to man, not the first link below the lowest level of existing man has yet been found. This is the more extraordinary, in view of the fact that, from the lowest limits in existing man, there are all possible gradations up to the highest; while below that limit there is an abrupt fall to the ape-level, in which the cubic capacity of the brain is one-half less. If the links ever existed, their annihilation without trace is so extremely improbable, that it may be pronounced impossible. Until some are found, science cannot assert that they ever existed."

Dana has given place to facts showing that the measurements of the bones of the man of Mentone, one of the earliest of human fossils thus far found, have the same proportions to one another as exist in human skeletons of today; the skull of this specimen is pronounced of excellent Caucasian type.

Evolutionists of the extravagant class are fast becoming fewer. The concessions they make year after year are so numerous and great, that the original aspect of the theory has been almost entirely lost.

Their hypothesis was a *deductive,* not an *inductive* growth, a result of speculation and not of observation. Even Haekel concedes this.

There are few rank Darwinians today. Indeed, the great naturalist's hesitancy and indecision have led one writer to declare that Darwin himself was not a thorough Darwinian.

Facts warrant me in asserting that the theory of evolution has been greatly injured through the vague, wild, aye, even insane enthusiasm of many of its professed adherents. Atheists have flocked to its standard, and with a pretense of defending its principles have hurled around their shafts of hatred toward their Godly parent. Aveling, in that dangerous little work *"The Students' Darwin,"* has gone mad in his endeavors to let readers know that he acknowledges no allegiance to the Christian God. To hold such conceptions he has a perfect right; but to inflict them on the public under the name of evolutionary tenets is unjust. It is as if some philanthropic physician, fearing an epidemic, and not willing to trust to the good judgment of the people, should mix physic with their flour in public supply stations. Such extravaganzas have drawn from the opponents of the theory much humor and irony.

The Evolutionists' *"Genesis, Chapter I.,"* is a fine sample of such satire. It is no every-day effusion, but one which, through a burlesque, has found place in the proceedings of learned assemblies. Perhaps I may be permitted to read it here:—

GENESIS - CHAPTER 1
ACCORDING TO THE EVOLUTIONISTS.

1. Primarily the unknowable moved upon Cosmos and evolved Protoplasm.

2. And Protoplasm was inorganic and undifferentiated; containing all things in potential energy; and a spirit of evolution moved upon the fluid mass.

3. And the unknowable said, "Let atoms attract," and they did so, and their contact begat light, heat, and electricity.

4. And the unconditioned differentiated the atoms each after its kind, and their combination begat rock, air, and water.

5. And there went out a spirit of evolution from the unconditioned: and working in Protoplasm, by accretion and absorption, produced the organic cell.

6. And cell by nutrition evolved primordial germ, and germ developed protogene, and protogene begat eozoon, and eozoon begat monad, and monad begat animalcule.

7. And animalcule begat ephemerae; then began creeping things to multiply on the face of the earth.

8. And earthy atoms in vegetable protoplasm begat the molecule, and thence came all grasses and herbs on the earth.

9. And animalcule in the water evolved fins, tails, claws, and scales; and in the air wings and beaks; and on the dry land they sprouted such organs as were necessary, being acted upon by the environment.

10. And by accretion and absorption came the radiata and mollusca, and mollusca begat articulata, and articulata begat vertebrata.

11. Now, these are the generations of the highest vertebrata in the cosmic period, when the unknowable evolved in the bipedal mammalia.

12. And every man on the earth while he was yet a monkey, and the horse while he was yet a hipparion, and the hipparion before he was an oredon.

13. Out of the ascidian came the amphibian and begat the pen-

tadactyle, and the pentadactyle by inheritance and selection produced the bilobate, from which are the simiadae in all their tribes.

14. And of the simiadae, the lemur prevailed above his fellows, and produced the platyrrhine monkey.

15. And the platyrrhine begat the catarrhine, and the catarrhine monkey begat the anthropoid ape, and the ape begat the longimanous ourang, and the ourang begat the chimpanzee, and the chimpanzee evoluted the what-is-it.

16. And the what-it-is went into the land of Nod, and took him a wife of the longimanous gibbons.

17. And in process of the cosmic, were born unto them and their children, the anthropomorphic primordial types.

18. The kornunculus, the prognathus, the traglodyte, the autochton, and the terragon; these are the generations of primeval man.

19. And primeval man was naked, and not ashamed, and lived in quadrumanous innocence, and struggled mightily to harmonize the environment.

20. And in the process of time, by inheritance and natural selection did he progress from the simple and homogeneous, to the complex and heterogeneous, and the weakest died, and the strongest grew and multiplied.

21. And man grew a thumb, for that he had need of it, and developed capacity for prey.

22. For, behold, the swiftest men caught the most animals, and the swiftest animals got away from the slowest men; wherefore it came pass that the slow animals were eaten and the slow men were starved to death.

23. And as types were differentiated, the weaker types continually disappeared.

24. And the earth was filled with violence, for man strove with man, and tribe with tribe, whereby they killed off the weak and foolish and secured the survival of the fittest.

The body of man bears some resemblance to the bodies of beasts. They share the common features of mortality. As with beasts, man needs food, else he starves; he may be poisoned; is subject to the same diseases; may receive or convey contagion through the medium of beasts; he dies; his body decays; it is flesh; it may be salted down; it could be pickled; it is of earth earthy.

19. For that which befalleth the sons of men befalleth beasts; even one thing befalleth them; as the one dieth, so dieth the other; yea, they

27

have all one breath; so that a man has no preeminence above a beast; for all is vanity.

20. All go into one place; all are of the dust, and all turn to dust again. —Ecclesiastes 3.

But the body is not the *man;* it were as wise to call the coat the *man.* Evidence is not lacking, though time forbids its introduction here, to show that man is dual.

The great Creator has not labored without a plan. When the mighty thought of a world flashed through His mind, He saw man as the crowning piece of the vast conception. It was no chance that man came when he did. His advent had been planned; the plan was executed in all its details.

No less eloquently than truly did the psalmist sing, "In thy book all my members were written, which in continuance were fashioned when as yet there was none of them." —Psalms 139: 16.

Man has been created in the image of Deity—the image of his Father. Though he may forget his royal lineage, and at times even disgrace his pedigree, yet he is of Godly descent. He bears within his mind half forgotten memories of his former royal abode. Those are the sentiments which at times invade his soul—thoughts that are unutterable. Those were the songs that Hugo heard, but could not sing, for in their expression the capacities even of his musical tongue were exhausted—the language failed.

"Like harp strings that are broken asunder
 By the music they throb to express."

To him who will but listen, silence is vocal with the whispers of man's noble condition.

Do but follow Job's advice:

7. But ask now the beasts, and they shall teach thee; and the fowls of the air, and they shall tell thee;

8. Or speak to the earth, and it shall teach thee; and the fishes of the sea shall declare unto thee.

9. Who knoweth not in all these that the hand of the Lord hath wrought this?

10. In whose hand is the soul of every living thing, and the breath of all mankind. —Job 12.

Is evolution true? Aye! true evolution is true. The evolution that means advancement, progress, growth, to a full realization of the intended measure of the creation of all things, that is true. The power by which

"Every clod feels a stir of might.
   An instinct within it that reaches and towers,
And, groping blindly above it for light.
   Climbs to a soul in grass and flowers,"
That is the evolution of the heavens.

The influences that developed from the cave hut to the mansion, from the fire-hollowed canoe to the iron clad and the Great Eastern, from the pack mule to the locomotive and the electric car, from the foot messenger through all the gradations of flags and signal-fires to the telegraph and telephone, from the pine torch to the electric lamp—that is evolution. It shows in every step of the *evolver*. There is a design; there must needs have been a designer.

But the evolution that looks upon the work and denies the need and proof of an artisan; that gazes upon the inspiriting canvas, and says there was no artist; that dwells in the protection and comfort of an edifice of beauty and claims there never was an architect; that scans the face of the time piece of the universe and says, "this all is chance"—that is false evolution, illogical, unscientific, untrue. It bears no marks of growth, but of shrinking; not of development, but of diminution; not of advancement, but of retrocession. Man has the right of Jehovah's commission as the ruler of all other earthly creatures. He is endowed with all necessary attributes for his kingly position.

The insect is fitted for its abode on the leaf; the fish for the water; the bird for the air; each beast for its allotted life; and so man for his. No one form can be transmuted into another. The thought that it could be otherwise is far more wild than the alchemist's dream of transmuting base lead into royal gold. In the fable of old, the frog burst when it tried to appear as an ox. Each after its kind—each to its sphere—this is the song of nature; and its praise to Nature's God, and

"God is law, say the wise, O, soul and let us rejoice;
For if He thunder by law, the thunder is yet his voice.
Speak to Him thou, for He hears, and spirit with spirit may meet;
Closer is He than breathing, and nearer than hands and feet."

{6}

"My Study of Astrology"

(from the *Contributor* 14 [November 1892]: 33-36)

Many readers of The Contributor have doubtless heard or read of the science of astrology. The name has descended to us from a pair of Greek words—*astron* meaning star, and *logos,* a discourse or treatise. According to the derivation of the term, therefore, astrology is the science that deals with the stars. As popularly understood, however, astrology has to do not alone with the laws that control the movements and varied appearances of the heavenly bodies, for these subjects belong to the more exact science of astronomy, (from *astron* star and *nomos* law), but also with the real and the many fancied influences which these heavenly bodies are said to exert upon the earth and its surroundings.

As an excuse for my seeming presumption in speaking upon this dark subject, let me assure the reader that I have had some personal experience in the pursuit of the study, a few items of which I am not likely to wholly forget. Years ago, while a romping, careless school boy in far-off England, I was fortunate or unfortunate as you may choose to take it, to make acquaintance with an aged sage who placed implicit trust in the indications of the stars. He deplored in strong terms the neglect by the many and scorn by the few with which his pet science was treated, and then, finding my boyish fancies aroused by his marvelous stories of stellar influences, and the possibility of penetrating futurity and of stealing the secrets of destiny, he supposed that he had found in me a promising student of astrological lore; so he devoted himself with great energy to instruct me in the mysteries of this species of the black art. I drank at this fountain of error with increasing thirst, and trusted in his words with all the power of a child's simple faith. But first a word as to astrology itself.

It is the belief of many that the sun, the moon, and the planets of our solar system, as also the constellations of fixed stars, produce well defined effects upon the earth. It was once generally supposed, and indeed it is still believed by a few, that the sun and the planets, take turns in ruling the earth and its inhabitants, each of the orbs holding sway for an hour at a time, and then giving way to the successor. Beside this hourly order, the heavenly bodies were said to assume varied powers over our planet in monthly periods, the particular influence exerted by any body depending upon its own nature, and upon the constellation in which it appeared to be at any particular time. The planets, it must be remembered, revolve around the sun as does the earth, consequently they are continually changing their relative locations with respect to the other stars, which do not belong to our system and which, being so distant from us as to undergo no apparent changes of position with regard to one another, are called fixed stars. The order in which the bodies of the solar system assumed control over the earth was Sun, Mercury, Venus, Moon, Mars, Jupiter, and Saturn; the other planets Uranus and Neptune not being then known.

To each of these bodies were attributed individual characteristics, and corresponding influences. To the Sun belonged the attributes of brilliancy, progress and growth; and a person born during any hour of the Sun's ascendency would be endowed with physical strength and mental acumen. Mercury was supposed to impress his children, and during his hour of ascendency to influence the whole earth with the characteristics of quick action, and spasmodic effort, and with but feeble powers of persistency or continued perseverance. Venus was regarded as the source of love and beauty, and during her hour of power the lover was thought to be more ardent in his suit, and the maiden more coy and subtle in her charms. A person born under the rule of Venus was supposed to be of an exceptionally affectionate disposition. The Moon was said to exert an influence of dullness as typified by her faint light, and absence of warmth, and persons born under her influence were thought to be of necessity quiet in nature, feeble in intellect, and subject to moods and changing spells in accordance with her own phases, indeed our words *lunacy* and *lunatic* (from Latin—*luna,* the moon) as applied to the condition and the victim of insanity, bear testimony to this astrological belief. Mars was the god of battle, and the ruddy planet bearing that name was said to give rise to war-like tendencies; and today even we speak of a person possessing such characteristics as being of a *martial* nature. Jupiter is the giant planet, moving through his extended orbit with majestic tread; and his subjects were thought to be as dignified in character and demeanor as himself; and furthermore to be of sanguine temperament and cheerful disposition and to be fond of good things. From such conception sprang our word *jovial* like unto Jove or Jupiter. Saturn was fickle and crafty, he cast an influence of distrust everywhere, he engendered jealousy; and we trace this superstition to-day to the adjective *saturnine* as applied to a heavy and unreliable nature.

These beliefs are rejected now by all but the eccentric few, yet the old superstitions have had in their day a powerful effect on the minds of mankind. We see evidence of such in the form and use of many of the words of our language, some of which, as lunacy, martial, jovial, and saturnine have been already referred to. We speak of any calamity as a *disaster;* this word is composed of *dis* a prefix implying bad or ill, and *aster*, from the Latin *astrum* a star, and therefore the word signifies a bad star and evidently refers to the astrological belief that the heavenly bodies are responsible for the evils that befall mankind. So the word *contemplation* is from *con* against, and *templum,* a space which was marked out by the astrologer through the aid of his divining staff, and the word to day signifies an attentive mental examination. So we may detect an astrological air about many other terms such as *aspect, consider, moonstruck, ascendency, mercurial,* etc. By a literal construction we imply a belief in astrological theories whenever we use such words.

But to return to my personal escapades in the field of astrology. I was duly instructed in the rules of the "science" by the star-gazing sage who had taken such a fancy to me. Before I was ten years old, I had learned to cast the horoscope, and to compute the benign and the malignant spirits of any person, the exact time of whose birth I could learn. My faith in these indications was so strong that I never could trust a schoolfriend, boy or girl, who had been born under the ascendency of Mercury or Saturn, and I think I would not have doubted a child of Mars, Jupiter, or the Sun though such a one had sought my life. A class-mate whom I found to have been born under the Sun's rule was always wise in my eyes, though now I am sure he made many miserable blunders, and the sayings of a certain child of the Moon were ever foolish to me, though in the schoolmaster's judgment that same one had been placed near the head of the class. But the master deserves excuse for his mistake, he probably had never studied astrology. On rare occasions, when paternal permission was obtained to go a 'fishing, I was scrupulously careful to compute the position of the planets, and learn the hour at which the power of the Moon was weak; for the fishes being under the dominion of the queen of night would be protected during her reign.

But my faith in astrology was soon to undergo a change. Among my schoolmates was a big, blustering fellow, who ruled as the autocrat of the playground, maintaining his sway by force of animal might. We all acknowledged his supremacy and paid him tribute of our property, a five-fold tithe of our sweetmeats, marbles, and pins. And further, he compelled us to work his sums for him, to draw his maps, and write his essays, and if any such effort received less than high commendations at the class, the author of the work was sure to feel the might of offended majesty at the next recess. If any boy appeared to doubt his authority, or failed to pay him servile homage, the tyrant was apt to apply the effectual remedy of a severe drubbing which rarely failed to bring the rebel to a sense of his duty. But worse than this, our oppressor happened to be the scion of a family somewhat distinguished by wealth—a rare accomplishment in those days and parts—he was the subject of the teacher's marked favor in consequence; and this was even more galling than the yoke of actual bondage which the fellow fastened upon us.

But there came a day when I felt within me those swelling impulses that are known only to a would-be savior or deliverer of his kind. I consulted the stars; and determined to break the fetters that bound us and to set myself and my school-fellows free. My faith in the success of the undertaking was so unbounded, that I had no thought of dividing the honors of conquest with anyone; I would fight the battle alone. Being on speaking terms with the autocrat's sister, I managed to find from her the date of Ben's birthday; but this was not enough, "I must know also the *hour* at which this remarkable piece of humanity had made a first appearance on the earth.["] The girl, in entire ignorance of the purpose for which I intended to use the information, questioned her mother, and brought me word that it was within half an hour of midnight on a Friday. With this information I hurried home, and at once proceeded to compute his nativities, with as much care as if he had been a prince of the realm. Ah! I might have known it: the horoscope gave his character in detail: he was a son of Saturn, born when the planet was in ill-conjunction: what wonder then that he was untrustworthy, mean, and cruel? Then I cast the horoscope of the future, and found that at a convenient hour, five o'clock in the afternoon on Wednesday, the next day but one, his star would be declining, and mine would be in the ascendency; this augured ill luck to him at that time and good fortune to me, in any undertaking. Surely the day of our de iverance [sic] was near at hand: the stars had promised to help me in my dangerous enterprise, and victory was assured. Brute force should be subdued by the power of superior knowledge.

So on the morning of the appointed day I confronted his saturnine majesty on the play-ground, and challenged him to meet me that evening at five o'clock, boldly expressing my determination to show him who would be master from that time forth. His surprise made him dumb for an instant, then he indulged in a loud laugh and cuffed my ears; but this I bore with no attempt at retaliation, for the time of revenge had not yet come; besides, I consoled myself with the reflection that it is the lot of all heroes in the cause of liberty to suffer insult at the hands of tyranny. During the day I received many a hearty wish for success; but feeble faith in my cause was plainly portrayed in every face.

At five o'clock we were at the appointed place; a score of boys were there to see fair play done. My antagonist was nearly a foot taller, and fully a stone heavier than I, but these were trifles below notice; had I not the happy assurances of the stars that I should win? I made a speech to the burly fellow, setting forth a few of his many acts of oppression and cruelty, and closed with a studied flourish, declaring that henceforth we would be free. This was received with a laugh of derision by my opponent; and the hostilities began. They did not last long. The conflict though fierce was decidedly brief. I discovered myself by degrees, lying on the ground, cheek cut, eyes bruised, nose smashed, a couple of teeth loosened and a quantity of hair gone. The bully retired without a scratch.

As I slowly made my way homeward, I was in an unusually thoughtful state. I began for the first time in my life to have serious doubts as to the infallibility of astrological indications, after all. Amongst the family my appearance created considerable consternation; then my worthy sire reminded me of his oft repeated injunctions against fighting; and to impress the lesson firmly upon my mind he proceeded to illustrate his lecture by sundry strokes with the buckle end of a stout strap. This was convincing; my doubts vanished, and with them all my confidence in the horoscope. I know that astrology was a fraud. From that day to the present I have been unable to revive any interest in the fallen science. A few months ago, after twenty years absence, I visited again the home of my childhood, and on a Wednesday afternoon, precisely at five o'clock, I went to the scene of my

34

bloody defeat in sweet liberty's cause; but the remembrances thus awakened were sorrowful, and I soon left the spot.

However, the little astrological knowledge which I gained was of inestimable benefit to me; it taught me the absurdity of its own professions. There is no astrology in the world of science today, though I doubt not that there has been a true science of the stars in days now past. When divine inspiration was regarded as an indispensable element of scientific investigation, then the stars declared their hidden secrets to the mind of the seer. To this the scriptures bear abundant testimony. The two great lights which the Creator placed in the firmament of heaven were to be "for signs and for seasons;" and the greater light was "to rule the day, and the lesser light to rule the night[.]"

In a terrible interview between divine majesty and human weakness, the Almighty demanded of his prophet Job (Job xxxviii, 31, 32), "Canst thou bind the sweet influence of Pleiades, or loose the bands of Orion? Canst thou bring forth Mazzaroth in his season? or canst thou guide Arcturus with his sons?"

Deborah the prophetess, singing with Barak a song of praise, that Israel had been delivered from the yoke of Jabin and Sisera, declares (Judges v, 20) "They fought from heaven the stars in their courses fought against Sisera."

At the time of Christ's birth a new star appeared in the firmament, and the oriental magi, recognizing its import sought the place of the heaven-born child that they might do him honor, "saying, where is he that is born king of the Jews? for we have seen his star in the east and are come to worship him." (Matt. ii, 2.)

And that Savior, afterward declared among the signs of his second coming (Luke xxi, 11 and 25) "fearful sights and great signs shall there be from heaven," "and there shall be signs in the sun, and in the moon and in the stars, and upon the earth distress of nations with perplexity, the sea and the waves roaring." And further we are told (Matt. xxiv, 30) among these terrible events, "And then shall appear the sign of the Son of man in heaven. The Revelator, with vision quickened by celestial light saw in the last days" (Rev. vi, 12-14); "the sun became black as sackcloth of hair, and the moon became as blood; and the stars of heaven fell unto the earth even as a fig tree casteth her untimely figs when she is shaken of a mighty wind. And the heavens departed as a scroll when it is rolled together."

With this portentious declaration, modern revelation is in perfect accord; (Doctrine and Covenants lxxxviii, 87) "for not many days hence and the earth shall tremble and reel to and fro as a drunken man, and the sun shall hide his face, and shall refuse to give light, and the moon shall be bathed in blood, and the stars shall become exceedingly angry, and shall cast themselves down as a fig that falleth from off a fig tree."

But the Latter-day Saints can rejoice in the consoling promise of their Father that the day shall come when all knowledge that ever has been upon the earth shall be restored, and moreover when a fullness of knowledge shall be given, (Doctrine and Covenants cxxi, 28 and 30-32) "a time to come in the which nothing shall be withheld. ★★★ And also if there be bounds set to the heavens or to the seas, or to the dry lands, or to the sun, moon or stars. All the times of their revolutions, all the appointed days, months and years, and all the days of their days, months and years, and all their glories, laws and set times shall be revealed, in the days of the dispensation of the fullness of times, according to that which was ordained in the midst of the council of the Eternal God of all other Gods, before this world was, that should be reserved unto the finishing and the end thereof."

Let us then refrain from unfounded conjecture concerning the mysteries of the heavens; and await the divine bestowal of that knowledge when such will be to us of the greatest good; lest the powers of evil take advantage of our impatience, and instil error into our souls. On themes of such mighty import no power below that of God-given inspiration should presume to instruct.

{7}

Four Blessings Given to James E. Talmage

I.

A Blessing Given to James E. Talmage,
16 December 1892, by Elder Lorenzo Snow,
President of the Quorum of the Twelve Apostles

(from the Journal of James E. Talmage, 16 December 1892,
Archives and Manuscripts, Harold B. Lee Library,
Brigham Young University, Provo, Utah)

By request I went this evening to Ogden, and there delivered a lecture to the Student's Society of the Weber Stake Academy; subject—"A peep through the Microscope", with optical lantern illustrations. Stayed at night at Bro. Dalton's house,—the lodging place of Bro. Isgreen, the Principle of the Academy.

On the train en route to Ogden, I had a long and interesting conversation with Apostle Lorenzo Snow, President of the Quorum of the Twelve. He spoke to me at length concerning the Church School Cause, and encouraged me in my labors in the same. Then taking me by the hand, he pronounced over me words of counsel and blessing, and that too by the spirit of prophecy; for so he declared to me: and so the testimony in my own heart bore record. As soon as possible,—within a quarter of an hour after the interview closed, I wrote down, as fully as I could remember, the sentiments he expressed.

Said he[,] "I do not know exactly why, but I feel, and have always felt a deep interest in you. I want you to feel encouraged in your labors, and to cultivate a love for life and a desire to live, for I tell you, you shall live till you are satisfied with life; and if you so desire till you are a very old man. You shall attain to the very highest pinnacle of fame, that your heart may aspire toward; and you shall reach a position which very few men in the church will attain. The Lord has wondrously blessed you; you are endowed with talents many and great,—endowments for which many men would give a fortune of millions of dollars; and if you will continue to cultivate a spirit of humility, and fail not to give to God the glory for your successes, achieved through His favor, you shall be blessed of god, more and more, and your heart shall be filled with blessings indescribable. You are called to fulfill a mission of rare and great importance in the Church, and the Lord will assist you".

I was deeply affected at his words; and I asked of him as a favor to offer criticism and instruction whenever he saw me wandering from the track of the Gospel, for I have seen so many men, highly favored of God fall away through pride and arrogance. To this President Snow replied,—"Brother Talmage, I will do so, but I prophecy to you, as Joseph Smith prophesied to me once,—though your weaknesses may be many, and your failings not a few, yet the Lord will not permit you to live to wander entirely from the path of right. God bless you, and you shall be blessed".

Oh, how can my heart contain the blessings of my Father! God grant me power to live for them and to resist the tempations that come my way.

★ ★ ★

II.
A Blessing Given to James E. Talmage, 26 October 1893, by Patriarch William J. Smith

(from the Journal of James E. Talmage, 26 October 1893, Archives and Manuscripts, Harold B. Lee Library, Brigham Young University, Provo, Utah)

Today, Elder Wm J. Smith, one of the Patriarchs of the Stake, called at my office on business, and while there told me that he had for me a blessing. Placing his hands upon my head he blessed me as follows; his words being taken in writing, as he spoke, and afterwards written out:—

Salt Lake City, Utah, October 26, 1893. Blessing, given under the hand of Patriarch William J. Smith, upon the head of James Edward Talmage, son of James J. Talmage and Susannah Praeter; born at Hungerford, Berkshire, England, Sept. 21, 1862.

Brother James Edward Talmage, greatly beloved of the Lord: I place my hands upon thy head, even the crown of thy head, in the name of Jesus Christ, the son of the Living God, to bestow upon thee a Patriarchal and a father's blessing as it may be given by the spirit of truth unto me, and by virtue of the Eternal Priesthood, I seal and confirm upon thy head all of thy former blessings, baptisms and confirmations, ordinations, and every blessing that has been bestowed upon thee by the spirit of revelation, that all may be fulfilled in the due time of the Lord unto thee; and not a word fail thee, or promise that the Lord has made unto thee. I bless you in your high and holy calling that the spirit of God may be your constant companion, that you may be wise and skillful in all your undertakings, and profession that you may not be excelled [?] by man's, because thou art taught of God; and He will be with thee wherever thou goest, and bless all that thou puttest thy hand to do; and thy heart shall be perfectly satisfied. Seek unto Him for wisdom and knowledge, skill and ability to peform thy duty and it shall be given thee. And the Lord shall be with thee in dreams and visions in different languages and the interpretation of the same. Thou shalt have the spirit of revelation, and prophecy and discernment; your eye shall be like the eye of the eagle to see near by and afar off, with power to discern every false spirit under the whole heavens, that thou may'st not be deceived thereby: that thou may'st have power over devils and demons and that cruel and wicked monster that fell before the throne of God, that thou may'st escape his grasp. Thy tongue shall be loosed, and thou shalt proclaim the gospel of Jesus Christ in power to the convincing of the honest in heart; and they shall know that the Lord is with thee and that the spirit of revelation is upon thee to a great extent; and thy faith shall be like unto Moses, and the brother of Jared; and thou shalt have power to perform any miracle that was ever wrought by man upon the earth, for the salvation and deliverance of Israel. I bless you to be faithful in all time to come, that your feet may never stray from the path of Christ. Thou shalt live to see Israel gathered from the four quarters of the earth, to assist in the redemption of Zion, and be gathered to the center Stake, and be a minister in that Holy Temple or Temples of thy Father's house, for thy ancestors and also the house of Israel. Thou shalt have the ministering of angels to stand by thee, and protect thee from all evil: not a hair of thy head shall fall by the hand of an enemy, and thy joy shall be full in the Lord, and in the power of his might. I bless you that you may thrive and prosper in the Land, amongst the people of the Lord, that thousands may rise up and call thee blessed of the Lord. I bless you with the blessings of Abraham, Israel and Jacob, with all that appertains to the new and everlasting covenant; that your posterity may be numerous as Jacob's of old; and that no good thing shall be withheld from thee until thy heart is perfectly satisfied. Thou art of the chosen seed of Israel, of the house of Joseph through the lineage of Ephraim, lawful heir to the blessings of the Gospel; and the Eternal Priesthod shall be bestowed upon thee till thou hast received a fullness; and the blessings that were sealed upon thy tribal lineage shall be upon thee, and upon thy posterity after thee while time shall last. I seal thee up unto Eternal Life to come forth in the morning of the First Resurrection with all thy Father's house with their inheritance in the New Heavens and upon the New Earth, when it is sanctified and made the eternal abode of the righteous. According to the Holy Order and sealing power that bonds on earth and looses, and binds in heaven and looses, I seal these blessings upon thy head in the name of the Father, Son and Holy Ghost. Amen.

* * *

III.
A Blessing Given to James E. Talmage,
21 August 1899, by Patriarch Jesse B. Martin

(from the Journal of James E. Talmage, 21 August 1899, Archives and Manuscripts, Harold B. Lee Library, Brigham Young University, Provo, Utah)

In the evening Patriarch Jesse Martin who was visiting the folks, gave me a patriarchal blessing. It reads as follows:—

A PATRIARCHAL BLESSING, given by Jesse B. Martin, upon the head of James Edward Talmage, son of James J. and Susannah Talmage, born Sept. 21st, 1862, at Hungerford, Berks, England.

JAMES EDWARD, in the name of Jesus Christ, I lay my hands upon thy head, and give thee a Patriarchal Blessing; for thou art a literal descendant of Ephraim, and entitled to all blessings pertaining to that tribe. And thou shall have all things given unto thee through thy holy anointings, that shall prepare thee for a fulness of glory in the Celestial Kingdom of God. For thou art one of the chosen of the Lord, to do a great work among the Saints of the Most High, as well as amongst the world. And the Lord shall bless thee with the discernment of spirits, and thou shalt not be deceived by wicked and designing persons. And the time is not far distant when thou shalt be called and set apart and ordained as one of the Apostles of Jesus Christ in this dispensation. And thou shalt do much good among the people in preparing them to go to the Center Stake of Zion; for the Holy Ghost shall rest down upon thee in all thy labors, and thou shalt speak forth words of truth with power and much assurance, and thousands will flock around thee to hear thy words; and thy influence among the people shall cause many to turn from their wayward ways and serve the Lord more perfectly. And thou shalt have the privilege of going with the Saints of God even to the Center Stake of Zion, and do much good in helping to build that beautiful Temple; for the Saints will listen to thy words and thy counsel as they would to an angel from the presence of God. Thou shalt enter into that Temple when it shall be prepared for the reception of Jesus Christ; and thou shalt see the Redeemer and know that He is the Son of God. And thou shalt travel from place to place with the Apostles of God and organize stakes in the land of Zion; for thou ha[s]t been chosen to do this great work, and thou shalt never be forsaken by thy Father in Heaven; for thou art of royal seed, and shalt accomplish a great and glorious work for the redemption of the human family. Thou shalt be a savior upon Mount Zion, because of the work thou shalt do for thy friends that have passed away behind the vail. And thou shalt be ready and prepared to meet the Savior when He shall come upon the earth. And thou shalt enter into the great feast as one of the wise, and shall feast and drink wine with the Apostles of old, and with Jesus Christ here upon this earth. Let thy heart be comforted, and fear not the powers of darkness, for thou shalt have power over all evil spirits that come in thy way, and they shall have no power to tempt thee more than thou canst bear.

And I seal thee up against the power of the Devil, and he shall not lead thee from the Church of Jesus Christ. And I seal thee up unto Eternal Life, to come forth in the morning of the First Resurrection.

All these blessings I seal upon thy head in the name of Jesus Christ; Amen.

★ ★ ★

IV.
A Blessing Given to James E. Talmage, 14 October 1900, by Patriarch John Smith

(from the Journal of James E. Talmage, 14 October 1900,

In the evening I called upon Patriarch John Smith by invitation, and accompanied him to the sacrament meeting in the 14th Ward; where President David Cannon of St. George and I occupied the stand during the meeting, addressing the people in the order named. After meeting, Patriarch Smith, Bishop George H. Taylor and I administered to the 13 year old son of the Bishop. The boy is suffereing from an attack of typhoid fever. At the house of Bishop Taylor, Patriarch Smith conferred upon me a patriarchal blessing which I copy here.

A BLESSING given by JOHN SMITH, Patriarch, upon the head of James Edward Talmage, son of James Joyce Talmage and Susannah Praeter Talmage, born in Hungerford, Berks, England, September 21st, 1862.

Brother James Edward Talmage, According to thy desire I place my hands upon thy head to pronounce and seal a blessing upon thee. And I ask God the Eternal Father for His Spirit to indite thy blessing, and to fill thee with the influence thereof, to give thee strength of memory that you may comprehend not only thy duty but the blessings promised unto the faithful. for thou art numbered among the sons of Zion who were chosen at their birth to labor in the ministry, to labor in the interest of the youth of Zion, and to assist in gathering Israel.

From early youth thou wert taught of thy parents the principles of truth and virtue, for which the Lord was well pleased, and gave thine Angel charge concerning thee, who has watched over thee thus far, preserved thee from the evils of the world, the power of the destroyer and those who fain would have led thee into by and forbidden paths.

From thy youth thou hast been true to thy trust, honest in thy belief, and firm in thine integrity, and for this the blessing of the Lord has attended thy labors, opened the eyes of thine understanding that thou hast seen things as they are; and as thy duty has been known to them thou hast cheerfully rendered obedience, for which thou shalt verily receive thy reward. And as thou hast been called to go or come by the Priesthood, thou hast been faithful; and in thy journeyings amongst strangers thou hast found friends; and thou hast without fear or favor proclaimed the words of life and salvation unto all who would listen; and thy word has on many occasions fell with power, and the influence thereof will remain and bring forth fruit in time to come.

Therefore I say unto thee be of good cheer for the Lord is pleased with thy integrity, and His favor shall go with thee. It is thy duty to preside in Council among the brethren; to guide and to guard the minds of the youth; to be one of the watchmen upon the towers of Zion. It is thy privilege when necessary to have the gift of discernment that you may detect error and also evil. It is thy province to defend the oppressed, to chide the guilty, and to pass sentence upon the wicked. Therefore remember to be cheerful in thy deportment.

Thou art of Ephraim which is the lineage of thy progenitors, many of whom look to thee for salvation, as thou art the legal heir to this privilege, holding the Priesthood. It is thy privilege to live to a good old age, and the will of the Lord that you should be an instrument in His hands in doing much good and become a mighty man in Israel. And I say unto thee, in thy reflections go back to early youth and thou shalt realize that the hand of the Lord has been over thee for good, that thy life has been preserved by an unseen power for a purpose. Thou shalt also realize that a decree of the Father has gone forth and that thy mission is barely begun.

Hold sacred thy covenants and no power shall stay thy progress; and thou shalt have joy in thy labors spiritual and temporal. Thou shalt have great faith in the ordinances of the Lord's House. Thou shalt lay hands upon the sick and they shall recover, for this is one of thy gifts which thou shalt receive through prayer and faith.

Thy children shall grow up around thee, bless thee in thy old age, and hold thy name in honorable remembrance. Therefore be comforted for all shall be well with thee here and hereafter. Thou shalt also secure unto thyself an inheritance among those who shall stand upon Mount Zion, saviors of men.

Therefore look forth to the future with pleasure.

This Blessing I seal upon thee in the name of Jesus Christ; and I seal thee up to eternal life to come forth in the morning of the First Resurrection, a savior in thy father's house.

Even so. AMEN.

{8}

"The Articles of Faith"

(Entries from the Journal of
James E. Talmage, 1891-1901, 1922-24,
Archives and Manuscripts, Harold B. Lee Library,
Brigham Young University, Provo, Utah)

Sept. 11, 1891—Today I had an interview with the First Presidency of the Church, relative to the Religion Class system. Being the Superintendent of such classes for this Stake, and having found from the labors of the past, that the Bishops of many of the wards feel that they have now all they possibly can carry in the way of special organizations. I asked instructions from the authorities as to the proper procedure. Plans for some change in the system are pending, and another appointment for an interview was set for Monday next. . . .

Sept. 14, 1891—Met by appointment with the First Presidency relative to the Religion Class system (See Sept. 11). It is the intention of the brethren to cause to be published a class-work on Theology, for use in Church Schools, and in Religion Classes generally. The need for such a work has long been felt among the teachers of the Latter-day Saints. The plan of the work is not fully matured as yet, the probability of issuing a series of two or three books is strong. Several preliminaries have to be arranged before the work is begun; but the First Presidency have expressed to me their intention of appointing me to do the labor. I find myself very busy already, but I have never yet found it necessary to decline any labor appointed to me by the Holy Priesthood; and in the performance of duties so entailed as my day, so my strength has ever been. . . .

Jan 31, 1893—This day in an interview with Presidents Woodruff and Smith of the First Presidency, I was appointed to now proceed with a work before given and subsequently withdrawn. (See record of Sept. 14, 1891, Journal Vol. V p. 74) I am requested to prepare a work on Theology, suitable as a text-book for our church schools and other organizations. In making the appointment Pres. Woodruff gave me his blessing. Told the brethren that I would accept the appointment as a mission; with no expectation of any pecuniary reward should the work ever be published, hoping that the book would be sold more cheaply if I waived all claim to royalty in the sale. Without the blessing of the Almighty, and the support of the brethren I should shrink from even attempting such a work. . . .

Feb. 22, 1893—Being at the President's office early this morning I had a conversation with President Woodruff concerning the Seer Stones spoken of yesterday, and particularly of the stone owned by Bro. Rushton, which latter I showed to the President. He attributes no importance at all to the stone; and he sustains me in my opinion concerning Mrs. Russel and her divinations. Later in the day Bro. Rushton called upon me and gave me a history of the stone. He found it in Nauvoo, associated with a valuable record, and with a store of gold; but neither the record nor the gold could he obtain. He claims that the location of the stone was revealed to him in a day vision thrice repeated; and at first it was under a seal, the nature of which he declined to explain. He says the stone possesses a celestial and a terrestrial side, and is capable of revealing matters connected with this world and the spirit land. One surface of the stone is devoted to the Ten Tribes, and in that the Seer can perceive the place and circumstances of that people beyond the ice. Bro. Rushton says the stone served him to locate the burial places of several of Joseph Smith's kindred, the prophet having placed several of the brethren under covenant to bury his dead together. Since that work was accomplished, Rushton has lost his gift, but lives in hope that it will be restored to him. The stone he believes will be of service in the vicarious work of the Temples by revealing the condition and desires of those behind the vail. Bro. Rushton and I met Pres. Woodruff, but Rushton declined to explain to the President the nature of the seal under which the stone was laid. Pres. Woodruff says he has but little encouragement to offer for the use of Seer Stones.

At night I attended the monthly meeting of the Home Missionary Quorum. A matter was there discussed, which I have already spoken upon in public a few times of late, and which I have asked counsel upon from the authorities:—the unseemly anxiety approaching curiosity on the part of some people for miraculous manifestations at the approaching dedication of the Salt Lake Temple. I believe that we should exercise faith in God for His blessings: leaving Him to decide what particular manifestations would be for our good. For my part, the

Lord does not favor me with visual or oviricular manifestations, yet I have an abiding faith in His supporting care.

This day I received from the First Presidency a letter of appointment for the work mentioned under the date of Jan. 31, last: (see page 170, this book.) The letter reads: -

Office of the First Presidency,
Salt Lake City, Utah
Feb. 20th/93

Dr. James E. Talmage,
    Salt Lake City,

Dear Brother: -

From conversations we have had with you in the past, we know that you in common with many others who are connected with the educational interests of our Church have seen the great need of properly arranged text and reference books in theological and religious subjects, for use in our Church Schools, Sunday Schools, etc.

It is our desire that a book suitable for the purposes named should be placed in the hands of our people as soon as possible. Knowing your experience in this direction we should be pleased to have you prepare such a work. We understand it is your intention not to make any charge for the preparation of this work so that it may be placed on the market at so low a price that it will be within the reach of all; with this suggestion we hastily concur.

Wishing you the fulfillment of every righteous desire in your calling as a teacher of the youth of Israel, we are

> Your Brethren:
> W. Woodruff
> Jos. F. Smith

(Pres. Geo. Q. Cannon, the second member of the First Presidency was not in the city at this time.) . . .

Oct. 20, 1893—Today it was decided by the Presidency of the Church, with several of the Apostles sitting with them in council to establish in connection with the Church University a Theological Class, to meet for the present on Sundays at 12:15 p.m. I am appointed to take charge of it; indeed I must take the blame for the subject having been brought up for consideration, as I myself suggested it having been impressed for a long time with the opinion that some theological work should be done in the Church Univ. from the beginning of its career of actual work. . . .

Oct. 25, 1893—Attended regular monthly meeting of the Home Missionary Quorum. One of the most important items discussed at the meeting was the duties of the Saints regarding Fast Day observance; another topic which seemed to be of interest was that of the Theological Class about to be established in connection with the Church University (See Oct. 20, p. 94). . . .

Oct. 29, 1893—This is the appointed day for the organization of the Theological Class in connection with the Church University. At 12:15 p.m. the time set: the large lecture room in the University building was filled to overflowing: every seat being occupied. Chairs were brought from the College adjoining and every corner taken possession of while the aisles were filled, and the stand crowded, many sitting on the edge of the platform. I had not even dreamed of such a class. As it was first suggested to my mind I saw a small body of University and College students with perhaps a few outsiders; but the Presidency of the Church (See Oct. 20, p. 94) directed that the scope of the class be enlarged. Had not the counsel which had made so large a class possible originated with the authorities of the priesthood, I should mistrust the outlook. Things great, substantial, and lasting have usually small beginnings. Our class has a very large inception. The Presidency of the Stake, High council, etc., were represented; prominent elders, patriarchs and others of the Stake authorities together with Elder George Reynolds of the Council of Seventies were present. I thank the Lord for so encouraging an outlook. So many applicants had to be denied admission that it was decided on the recommendation of Prest. Angus M. Cannon to adjourn the class at its close to meet next Sunday in the Stake Assembly Hall.

The work outlined for the class is the consideration of the "Articles of Faith" of our Church: the Presidency having directed that I present to the class in the form of lectures the matter which I am preparing with a view to eventual publication as a text book for the theological organizations of our church schools, and such classes. May divine blessings rest upon the effort.— . . .

Nov. 5, 1893—Second session of the University Theology Class

47

held today in the Stake Assembly Hall. Between 500 and 600 persons attended, and the interest manifested was of the most encouraging order. To assist in the work of the class printed outlines of the study are prepared: today a double sheet was distributed, giving the lessons of last Sabbath and today. We appreciate the generosity of the Stake officers in their placing the Assembly Hall at our disposal, though the house is hardly adapted for a class. I confidentially expect the numbers to fall off as soon as the gloss of novelty has worn away; then we may return to our own building.

Nov. 6, 1893—Today the Presidency of the Church gave instructions that the lectures delivered before the University Theology Class be published in full in serial form, and that the arrangements for republication in book form be left for subsequent consideration. The "Juvenile Instructor" was selected as the organ of publication. . . .

Nov. 16, 1893—Inasmuch as the Theology Class lectures are to be serially published (See Nov. 6, p. 102), I requested of the First Presidency, the appointment of a Committee on Criticism to whom I could refer the matter before publication. I am very desirous that proper criticism should be made, to avoid serious error. The following Committee was appointed in stated order: - (1) Apostle Francis M. Lyman (Chairman) (2) Apostle A. H. Cannon: (3) Pres. Geo. Reynolds (4) Elder John Nicholson: (5) Dr. Karl G. Maeser. The Committee (last two absent) held a session today in the Temple. . . .

Nov. 26, 1893—No diminution in size of the Theology Class. Pres. Geo. Q. Cannon was present today though as he sat amongst the audience his presence was not known to many until after the close of the session. He expressed himself as very highly pleased with the class. The question of abandoning all review work in the class owing to the difficulty of getting the students to speak sufficiently loud in so large a house has been with me a serious one: but Pres. Cannon recommends the continuation of the exercise even though there be difficulties in the way. The President of the Stake, one of the Presiding Bishopric, one of the First Presidents of Seventies, two of the General Sunday School authorities were present today. . . .

Nov. 29, 1893—Wife and I went to the Temple with the intention of attending to ordinance work for the dead. Immediately after the opening exercises, however, I was called out to attend a consultation between the Committee appointed to assist me in the Theological Class work, and the First Presidency of the Church. Wife carried

48

through her part of the Temple labor; but my work was put off. The consultation referred to lasted between two and three hours. There were present all of the First Presidency and three of the Quorum of Twelve Apostles. I brought before the Presidency, asking for rulings, the following subjects:—

1. The changing of Article 4 of the Articles of Faith from the old form:

4. We believe that these ordinances are: First, Faith in the Lord Jesus Christ; second, Repentance; third, Baptism by immersion for the remission of sins; fourth, Laying on of Hands for the Gift of the Holy Ghost.

so as to designate faith and repentance in some other way than as ordinances which they are not. The following form was adopted

4. We believe that the first principles and ordinances of the Gospel are: (1) Faith in the Lord Jesus Christ; (2) Repentance; (3) Baptism by immersion for the remission of sins; (4) Laying on of hands for the Gift of the Holy Ghost.

2. The proper form and ceremony of baptism whether in case of rebaptism or in any other occasion, additions to the revealed formula, such as, "for the remission of your sins" or "for the renewal of your covenants." The decision was that any additions to the revealed form, or any other departure therefrom is unauthorized, and to be deprecated. The authorized form is that given in the Doctrine and Covenants.

3. The authority for rebaptisms:—The authorities were unanimous in declaring that rebaptism is not recognized as a regularly constituted principle of the Church; and that the current practice of requiring rebaptism as a prerequisite for admission to the temples, etc. is unauthorized. Nothing should be put in the way of anyone receiving his covenants by rebaptism if he feels the necessity of so doing: and of course, in cases of disfellowship, or excommunication, a repetition of the baptism is required, but the making of rebaptism a uniform procedure is not proper. It was declared to be at variance with the order of true government in the Church to require baptism of those who come from foreign branches to Zion, bringing with them certificates of membership and of full standing. Pres. Geo. Q. Cannon expressed the opinion that the practice of repeating baptism came from the example and teaching of Pres. Brigham Young in the days of first

migration to these parts: when the journey meant a long separation from organized branches and wards of the Church: and consequently an interruption in the observance of regular Church duties. The conditions are changed now: and the counsel given for special circumstances should not be made applicable to general procedure under all circumstances. Danger was seen in the practice of repeated baptisms:—such may be made like the confessional of the Catholics: a premium on sinning [?].

Several minor points were ruled upon, comprising—unpardonable sin: murder and shedding of innocent blood.

In the afternoon a meeting of the Presidency and the Twelve was held at the Temple, at which all the points named above were ratified as set forth. I was told by one of the Apostles on our Committee that I was authorized to proclaim this as doctrine in the Theological Class. . . .

Dec. 3, 1893—*Sunday*. Usual meetings. The Theological Class was attended by about 1100 persons. . . .

Dec. 10, 1893—*Sunday*. Usual meetings. Very large attendance at the Theological Class. In the evening Elder John Harrison and I officiated as Home Missionaries in the 17th Ward. . . .

Dec. 17, 1893—*Sunday*. Large attendance (between a thousand and eleven hundred students) at the Church University Theological Class today. . . .

Dec. 24, 1893—*Sunday*. Usual meetings. Large attendance at the Church Theological class. . . .

Dec. 31, 1893—*Sunday*. Meetings as usual. About 1100 present at the Theological Class. In the evening by call I addressed the saints in our own Ward meeting. And so the year ends. It has been a year of great things in general and in my life particularly. It has witnessed the dedication of the House of the Lord; and the accomplishments of much labor therein. The world boasted and rejoiced over the great Fair [Chicago]: and great events have rolled like a tide over the shores of history. I am thankful. . . .

Jan. 2, 1894—Lengthy meetings with the Theology Class Committee, and the First Presidency reading lectures already delivered before the class. I am grateful for the supervision thus exercised, and the assistance so afforded. . . .

Jan. 5, 1894—Met with Theological Class Committee and Presidency in lecture work. The subject of "*The Holy Ghost*" formed the topic. Pres. Cannon in commenting on the ambiguity existing in our printed works concerning the nature or character of the Holy Ghost expressed his opinion that the Holy Ghost was in reality a person, in the image of the other members of the Godhead,—a man in form and figure: and that what we often speak of as the Holy Ghost is in reality but the power or influence of the Spirit. However the Presidency deemed it wise to say as little as possible on this or other disputed subjects. . . .

Jan. 7, 1894—*Sunday*. Large attendance at the theological Class. In the evening Elder F. M. Lyman and I officiated as Home Missionaries in the 18th Ward. . . .

Jan. 12, 1894—A meeting of the Theological Class Committee, and the Presidency, to consider the subject of the sacrament. After the acceptance of a paragraph written by me on the duties of the priesthood in seeing that the Sacrament is not administered to any but Church members, and to none who are unworthy, I asked concerning the custom of administering the sacrament in our Tabernacle, where all classes assemble, where indeed it is known that many outsiders partake and others show by strong demonstration their scorn for the ordinance, where in short no supervision that is effective can be exercised. In answer I found that the First Presidency and the Twelve were united in desiring the administration of the sacrament removed from the Tabernacle to the Ward houses, where the local authorities could properly guard the sacredness of the ordinance. I understand instructions to this effect will soon be issued. . . .

Jan. 14, 1894—*Sunday*. Nearly 1100 at the Theological Class. To my pleasure Father, Mother and Albert attended. . . .

Jan. 21, 1894—*Sunday*. Usual meetings: large attendance at the Theological class. . . .

Jan. 28, 1894—*Sunday*. Today the fourteenth session of the Church University Theological Class was: and the attendance was the largest yet seen: between 1000 and 1200. To my surprise I was called upon in the afternoon to address the Tabernacle congregation. . . .

Feb. 4, 1894—*Sunday*. By special appointment I attended today a meeting of the Committee by the Presidency of the Church to listen to and report on the matter of a pamphlet now in course of preparation by Elder B. H. Roberts, subject:—"Succession in the Presidency of the Church." We have held many meetings on this matter during the past week; today we heard the last of the reading before the work goes to press. It is an excellent preparation, and will doubtless do much good.

Its chief purpose is to settle certain false claims of the "Josephite" Church, to the succession of the priesthood.

At the meeting of the Theology Class today, the attendance was very large;—nearly or quite 1200 present. Prest. Joseph F. Smith honored us with a visit, and spoke a short time. . . .

Feb. 11, 1894—*Sunday.* Usual meetings. In the morning I attended the Sabbath School for the Deaf and Dumb. Very large attendance at the Church University Theology Class. Today witnessed a slight change in the matter of conducting the class. It being deemed wise by the Presidency of the Church that I should hasten through with the lectures lest anything of the contemplated change in the University matters should occur; and thereby change the Theology Class, it has been decided to drop the review part of the work, devoting nearly all of the time of the class to lectures. . . .

Feb. 18, 1894—*Sunday.* Theological Class and Usual Meetings. At Prayer Circle, by appointment I officiated in the dedicatory prayer. . . .

Feb. 25, 1894—*Sunday.* Over 1200 were present at the Theological Class session today. At the Prayer Circle I officiated at the altar by appointment. . . .

Mar. 4, 1894—*Sunday.* Attended meetings of the Stake conference; this is the third day of the session. The Theological Class was omitted today in consequence. . . .

Mar. 11, 1894—*Sunday.* Usual meetings, except the afternoon prayer circle: that organization being now appointed to meet in weekly session at the Temple: and for the present the time is set— Saturday 5 p.m. At the theological class today a very large congregation was present. In the evening, by previous appointment I delivered a lecture in Sugar House Ward under the auspices of the combined Mutual Improvement Associations of the Ward: Subject— "Blasphemy." . . .

Mar. 18, 1894—*Sunday.* Twentieth session of the Theology Class today: and the attendance was the largest yet witnessed. In the evening Elder George Blair and I officiated as Home Missionaries in the Seventh Ward. An excellent influence prevailed during the meeting. . . .

Mar. 25, 1894—*Sunday.* Unusually large attendance at the Theology Class. . . .

Apr. 1, 1894—*Sunday.* At this the twenty second session of the Theology Class the attendance was as large as if not indeed larger than that of any previous session. Today marked the last meeting of the class, its discontinuance having been determined upon yesterday or the day before by the First Presidency. the reasons for this action are briefly these:—(1) It is plain that in the event of my accepting any prominent position in the State University it would be manifestly inconsistent for me to occupy so distinguished a place among the Theology Class of our people, the University being a strictly non-sectarian institution. There will be I think opposition enough to the change in the University administration without complicating matters by offering other excuses for attack. (2) The Presidency are loath to appoint a successor in the instructorship of the Theology Class, as the projected work is still unfinished; and if such an appointment were made, the work would have to be carried in one of two ways,—as the independent treatment of the subject by the new instructor;—and this course they deem objectionable, as it is the design to publish the lectures in book form, and the volume would then be the joint work of two; or the lectures would have to be presented as mine being simply delivered by another; this latter course would remove little if any of the objection now offered to my continuing with the work as in the past. (3) The Presidency have warned me repeatedly of my having too much work on my hands: and they seem determined to relieve me of some.

At the session today, I disposed of as many of the incidental questions as possible, then finished the lecture on the *Gathering*, as per leaflet No. 17: then announced the discontinuance of the class. This announcement caused considerable consternation: and I feel that there has been a true appreciation of the work of the class. A letter from the First Presidency, addressed to myself, advising the discontinuance and citing the reasons therefore, was read by Apostle Abraham H. Cannon one of the Committee on Theology Class appointed by the First Presidency. He and Elder George Reynolds, another of the Committee made remarks eulogizing the labors of the class. A vote of thanks was heartily rendered the instructor. I feel much regret in seeing the class come to a close,—regret that circumstances render such a course advisable for I believe the class has taken a hold on the minds of the members. I would at least have wished to see the completion of the lectures on the Articles of Faith; but the lectures not yet delivered, will be published with those already given. For the need of success that has come to the class I reverentially acknowledge the hand of God. May the seed so planted, yet produce a healthful growth and pleasing fruit.

In the evening, Elder Parry and I officiated as Home Missionaries in the 19th Ward. . . .

Dec. 27, 1898—Began the reading of manuscript for a proposed theological publication; the reading was before a committee created at my request by action of the First Presidency of the Church. The history of the affair is briefly as follows:—Years ago, while I was officially connected with the Church School work, the First Presidency expressed to me their desire to have prepared a book or a series of books, suitable for use as textbooks in theological classes of the Church: (see Journal entry, Sept. 14, 1891; vol., page 74-). This developed into a request that I write such a book (Jan. 31, 1893, Journal vol. 6, p. 170) and a letter of appointment to the work dated Feb. 20, 1893 was received Feb. 22, 1893: (see last date, Journal vol. 6, p. 183). When the theology class in connection with the Church University was established I was appointed instructor, and the work decided upon was a series of lectures on the "Articles of Faith," the plan being that I present in lecture form the matter which would have been published as the substance of the proposed book (See Oct. 20, and 29, 1893: Journal vol. 7, pages 94 and 101). At my request a committee was appointed to pass upon the matter of the lectures (see Nov. 6, and 16, 1893: Journal vol. 7, pages 102 and 103). Twenty-two lectures were given before the class: then on April 1, 1894 (Journal vol. 7, p. 134) the class was discontinued owing to my call to the presidency of the University of Utah. I was counseled to drop the work of preparing the unfinished part of the lectures for the time being, in view of my busy condition. Part of the matter presented to the class was published in serial form in the "Juvenile Instructor" commencing Nov. 15, 1893, and running to Aug. 15, 1894. Many requests, personal and official have been made for the continuation of the work. The subjects of the "articles" not presented before the Church University class were subsequently treated before other classes and theological organizations. Not until this autumn have I been able to resume the work of writing the lectures. For three months past I have been suffering from my baneful affliction of sleeplessness, and my nights, often extending until daybreak have been devoted to writing the matter, which is now practically completed. The printed parts have been completely re-written, and the unpublished part has been added. As stated, at my recent request, the First Presidency appointed a committee to hear and pass upon the matter in its present form. This is really the old committee reconstituted, the only change in the personnel being the appointment of Apostle Anthon H. Lund in place of Apostle Abram H. Cannon deceased. Apostle F. M. Lyman continues as chairman: the other members are Elders George Reynolds, John Nicholson, and Karl Maeser. Two sittings, each two hours, were held today, and such are to continue daily with as few interruptions as possible until the reading is finished. . . .

Jan. 5, 1899—Finished the reading of the manuscript on "Articles of Faith" to the Committee. Committee passed a unanimous vote of hearty approval: and referred the question of publication to the First Presidency. . . .

Jan. 13, 1899—Meeting with the First Presidency and the Committee on the lecture book; at which the latter referred certain points of doctrine and instructions as to the manner of publishing. As the book has been written by appointment previously made I knew not whether to consider my mission completed now that the Mss. has been approved, or to regard myself as under appointment until the book appears in print. I was surprised at a suggestion made by the committee a few days ago, and still more so at the approval of the suggestion by the First Presidency that the book be published by the Church. I was not aware that such an honor had ever been paid to one of our writers; and I hardly felt to urge the matter for I don't think the Church is rightly [?] to be made responsible for the slips and errors which will inevitably appear in the book. The details of publication were not settled today. One of the questions referred to the First Presidency by the Committee was as to the advisability of reprinting the lecture entitled "*The Holy Ghost*" which appeared in the "Juvenile Instructor" soon after its delivery in the theology class of the Church University. I remember that considerable discussion attended the reading of the lecture before the former committee prior to its delivery. (See January 5, 1894: Journal VII, p. 116) The question hung upon the expediency and wisdom of expressing views as definite as those presented in the lecture regarding the personality of the Holy Ghost when marked ambiguity and differences of opinion appeared in the published writings of our Church authorities on the subject. The lecture was approved as it appeared in the "Instructor." I have incorporated it in the prospective book in practically an unaltered form. President Snow took the article under advisement today. In conversation Pres. Geo. Q. Cannon supported the view of the distinct personality of the Holy Ghost and stated that he had [the word "actually" is crossed out] heard the voice of the third member of the Godhead, actually talking to him. . . .

January 16, 1899—Meeting with the First Presidency on the lecture book matter. President Snow announced his unqualified approval of the lecture on the "Holy Ghost"; and directed its insertion. The preliminaries relating to publication were furthered.

Jan. 17, 1899—Final word from the First Presidency regarding the publication of the lectures. It has been decided that the Church publish the work. This action will give the book greater prestige, and will doubtless add to its usefulness among the people. I am sensitive of the confidence in the work thus shown by the authorities, and of the honor thus given to myself. The printing will be done at the "Deseret News" office—the Church publishing establishment. I am notified that new type is to be purchased for the work, and I am asked to make the selection. An edition of 10,000 copies is ordered. As to the financial phase of the undertaking I note this:—In my first acceptance of the appointment to prepare a text-book for use in the theological organizations, I expressed a willingness to undertake the work, without hope of royalty or other pecuniary advantage from the sales, provided the book could be sold at cost. In a reply to this the First Presidency wrote me under date of February 20, 1893, as follows: *We understand it is your intention not to make any charge for the preparation of this work so that it may be placed on the market at so low a price that it will be within the reach of all; with this suggestion we hastily concur.*

In presenting recently the question of publication before the Committee, and the First Presidency, this offer of mine was commended as liberal and praiseworthy; although some opposition was referred to, the thought of some of the brethren being, that the waving of the royalty would either make so little difference in the price of the book as to be inappreciable, or, should the cost of publication permit a markedly low price to be charged, there would be a danger of some-what demoralizing effect on home publications in general. Pres. Geo. Q. Cannon was outspoken in the belief that no unusually low price should be set on the book. Nevertheless my offer was treated from the first as fully accepted. In an itemized estimate of the cost of publication, H. G. Whitney, Business Manager of the "News" establishment, writes me under yesterday's date that the new type needed will cost about $200.00 and that "the work with typesetting and paper will cost . . . $1500 to $1600 on an edition of 10,000," to which is to be added 25 cents per copy for cloth and binding. It is proposed to charge not less that $1.00 per copy of the cloth-bound book. Evidently this allows considerable profit, which I am told will accrue to the Church. While the purpose of my offer to do the work without charge was to secure a selling price of the book at cost, I do not demur to this plan of a moderate profit being made for the Church. I have tried to do the work in the true spirit of making an offering to the Church, and I leave the matter to the authorities. If I can feel that the Lord has accepted my humble and imperfect offering I shall count myself as richly recompensed. But the work is not yet finished; the Mss. is to be prepared for the press, and the labor of carrying the book through will be considerable. . . .

Feb. 25, 1899—At last typographical work has begun on the "Articles of Faith" book. (See entry for Jan. 17th last) New type was ordered from the East, and the kind selected had to be made to order, then a delay was caused by the recent snow blockades on the railways: and the last lot of type arrived yesterday. The first form of the book was placed in my hands for proof reading tonight. The plan is to keep up the printing operation night and day if necessary so as to bring out the book by or before the time of April conference. . . .

Mar. 10, 1899—In this evenings issue of the "Deseret News" appeared the first public announcement of the prospective book on the "Articles of Faith." This first mention is made by the President of the Church, in the manner following:—

EDITOR'S TABLE.
OFFICIAL ANNOUNCEMENT.
THE ARTICLES OF FAITH, BY DR. JAMES E. TALMAGE.

During the early part of April there will be issued by the Deseret News a new Church work entitled "The Articles of Faith," the same being a series of lectures on the principal doctrines of the Church of Jesus Christ of Latter-day Saints, by Dr. James E. Talmage. The lectures were prepared by appointment of the First Presidency, and the book will be published by the Church. It is intended for use as a text book in the Church Schools, Sunday Schools, Improvement Associations, quorums of the Priesthood, and other Church organizations in which the study of Theology is pursued, and also for individual use among the members of the Church. The work has been approved by the First Presidency, and I heartily commend it to members of the Church.

LORENZO SNOW.

The work of printing is progressing at the rate of a form (16 pages) every day; and the assurance is still held that the work will be completed by the approaching April conference. . . .

April 1, 1899—Read proof of last form on the "Articles of Faith" book. The preface will be put to press under date of Monday next (The 3rd) and my work on the book is finished for the present. I read proof of the first form (16 pp.) Feb. 25: one form per day was promised: 32 forms have been completed in the 30 intervening days (Sundays excepted). . . .

April 4, 1899—First copies of the book left the bindery. The earliest issues were taken to the office of the First Presidency. The matter of the lectures with appendix and index occupy 490: the book in its entirety 498 pages. The title page is as above [copy of title page glued in journal]: for that I am not responsible as it was prescribed by the First Presidency. President Snow disapproved of my preference of "Elder" as the title of the author, saying that the name as given above [Dr. James E. Talmage] would be more assuming to non-members of the Church into whose hands the book may come. I have copyrighted the book in my own name, and will assign the right for the first edition to the Church In defense to my wish to have the work sold at the lowest possible price, the cloth-bound copy is offered at $1.00; prices of other bindings $1.50 to $2.50. Actual cost of the cloth-bound copy as per statement of the "Deseret News" Manager is 45 cents. . . .

Feb. 10, 1900—The "Deseret News" announced this (Saturday) evening that since April 1st last, six thousand (6000) copies of the book "The Articles of Faith" have been sold; and asserts that this is the largest sale of any home publication in the same length of time.

March 17, 1900—Attended meetings in Second Ward at 8 p.m. incident to the Relief Society work, and by previous appointment delivered an address. This evenings issue of the Deseret News announced that 7200 copies of the "Articles of Faith" have been sold. (Compare Feb. 10 last.) . . .

March 29, 1901—Meeting with the First Presidency and the Publication Committee relative to the issue of a second edition of "The Articles of Faith". The first edition has been practically exhausted for some time—only a few copies in expensive bindings remaining.

This evening I presided at the meeting of the Microscopical Society of Utah, and delivered an address. . . .

May 5, 1901, Sunday—Usual meetings. At the Temple Fast Meeting in the morning I was one of a number of speakers. Afternoon session of the Committee with whom I confer on the revision of "The Articles of Faith" soon to be put to press for a second edition. . . .

May 31, 1901—When I submitted manuscript for the "Articles of Faith", the book that I had prepared in response to the appointment of the First Presidency, I asked no royalty on the sales or other pecuniary return; indeed I felt honored in being able to do that little for the good of the Church. There was some hesitation on the part of the First Presidency in accepting the gift, partly owing to a request of mine that the book be sold strictly at cost, and partly because of Pres. Snow's statement that a proper payment ought to be made. The first edition of 10,500 copies has been sold, and copy for a second issue is now in the hands of the electrotypers. (See entry for 10th inst.) Several times I have been called into conference with the publication committee and with the Presidency relative to the transfer of my copyright to the Church; this the authorities desire, and for the same the Presidency declare a payment ought to be made. The brethren have urged the matter with such kindness that I could not well do otherwise than express acquiescence. I was asked to name a sum that would be satisfactory; this I declined to do, saying that I had offered the work as a gift. Pres. Snow replied that it had been accepted as a gift, but they desired to make a present in return. Today Pres. Snow informed me of the decision reached, and I was handed a check for Fifteen Hundred Dollars. I made the legal transfer of copyright to the work, and assigned all claims incident to the first edition. . . .

Jan. 27, 1922—Fri. In addition to ordinary duties I had an important consultation with the First Presidency today and they reached the decision that in view of the great demand for "The Articles of Faith", which has not been revised through many editions, that I devote my time to a revision of the book named, with the view to bringing it out in improved form, and with such changes in the text as may be deemed advisable—and that this work take precedence over my writing the book on "Priesthood". . . .

Sept. 6, 1922—Wed. The rest of the day I spent in my room in the Temple. . . .

Nov. 2, 1922—Thurs. I devoted a good part of the afternoon to writing. . . .

Jan. 27, 1923—Sat. Was engaged in office work and theological research. . . .

July 6, 1923— Fri. I spent the greater part of the day in the Temple, engaged on revision work on the "Articles of Faith". . . .

Aug. 21, 1923- Tues. Spent a good part of the day in the Temple engaged in the revision of "The Articles of Faith". . . .

Sept. 11, 1923—Tues. Spent the greater part of the day at Hammond, Indiana, in business with the W.B. Conkey company. Made adjustments of several printing matters relating to the publication of our standard works, and considered the preliminary points requiring attention connected with the possible bringing out of the new edition of the "Articles of Faith". Returned to Chicago in the evening, and was gratified in receiving a letter from Maia, written immediately after her arrival home. All were reported well. . . .

Nov. 27, 1923—Tues. Attended meeting of the Deseret Book Company with the manager and secretary, and afterward an executive meeting of the committee itself. The rest of the day was devoted to work on the "Articles of Faith". . . .

Dec. 4, 1923—Tues. After my trunk arrived [he was in Chicago] I spent a good part of the remaining time going over some parts of the copy to be presented to the printers for the bringing out of the new issue of the "Articles of Faith". . . .

Dec. 11, 1923—Tues. Spent the day at Hammond, Indiana, reading proofs of different parts of the book as set up in the varied styles of type. Went into details as to arrangement. Returned to Chicago at night. On reaching the hotel I was surprised to find my trunk missing from my room. Inquiries revealed the fact that the porter had mistaken the number of the room from which a trunk was to be taken, and that my trunk had already been sent to Detroit as personal baggage.

Dec. 12, 1923—Wed. Spent some time at the Chicago headquarters of the W.B. Conkey Company, and had personal conversation with Mr. Henry Conkey, who since the death of his respected father is the head of the company. My trunk was recovered and returned to my room. . . .

Dec. 17, 1923—Mon. Reached home between 8 and 9 a.m. Found that wife Maia had been ill and still suffering from a severe cold, with threatened pneumonia. I learned with sorrow of the death of my niece, Susa Harding, daughter of my sister Alice, in Provo. She has long been a sufferer from heart and lung trouble and passed away suddenly. Today my secretary and I began reading by copy the first installment of proofs of the forthcoming book. . . .

Dec. 19, 1923—Wed. Maia is still ill, but we trust the pneumonia will be averted. I spent the greater part of the day in proof reading. . . .

Jan. 1, 1924—Tues. Today was begun with the encouraging word over long distance phone that my brother George in Springville is greatly improved. I devoted the greater part of the day to work in the office, owing to pressure in proofreading the forthcoming book, the revised edition of the "Articles of Faith". However, I spent a delightful two hours at home with the family at New Year's dinner, and after this I returned to the office and worked until a late hour. . . .

Jan. 18, 1924—Fri. Attended meeting of the Deseret Book Company Committee during the forenoon, was in consultation with the First Presidency and others, and put in a particularly busy day in correspondence. It has been deemed advisable that I go to Chicago and Hammond, Indiana, to expedite the work on the new issue of the "Articles of Faith"; and I am to leave tonight by the Continental Limited, accordingly. . . .

Jan. 21, 1924—Mon. Visited the missionary company and rendered them some assistance. They left by early afternoon train. Was in early communication with the W.B. Conkey Company and attended some revised proof sheets. . . .

Jan. 26, 1924—Sat. Each day since last entry has been devoted to work on the book proofs. Spent this day at Mission headquarters, the occasion being a conference of the Chicago branches, or as we say, through a regrettable double use of the term, a conference of the Chicago Conference. Meeting with the missionaries covered in all four hours, at which the twenty-two present made their individual reports after which President Taylor and I addressed them at some length. From 3:30 until 8 p.m. the missionaries and I were engaged in checking up on the references following the chapters in the "Articles of Faith". It was a pleasing experience to them and one of assistance to me. Only one error was found, and this made the effort worth while, affording opportunity for its correction. . . .

Feb. 7, 1924—Thurs. Spent day in Hammond, Indiana, and made arrangements as to details in the matter of binding the book. Returned to Chicago at night. . . .

Feb. 9, 1924—Sat. The proofreading is finished. In the course of the work I have been impressed by the thought of bringing out a cheaper edition of the "Articles of Faith", so as to place it within the reach of more people. Several letters from Mission Presidents have come to hand, answering my inquiry as to their wishes in the matter; and without exception they urge strongly that such an edition be published. On Thursday last I went into details as to cost of production, etc., with the W.B. Conkey Company, and telegraphed the First Presidency, asking their approval of the plan to bring out an edition of ten thousand copies, to be known as the *Missionary Edition*. In general style similar to the *Missionary Edition* of the Book of Mormon.

As no reply had arrived by this morning I sent a fast day message, requesting answer today. In a little over two hours I had the response, in the form of a message authorizing the publication as requested by me. I immediately closed the contract with the W.B. Conkey Company. . . .

March 3, 1924—Mon. Had a very busy day in office work and consultations. The first copies of the new issue of the ARTICLES OF FAITH arrived today, and appear to be very satisfactory. . . .

April 14, 1924—Mon. Office work and consultations occupied the day. The first copies of the *Missionary Edition* of the "Articles of Faith" arrived today. The books come up to the standard of expectation, and the First Presidency and others express full satisfaction. . . .

{9}

The Articles of Faith, First Edition

(Selections from *The Articles of Faith—*
A Series of Lectures on the Principle Doctrines of
the Church of Jesus Christ of Latter-days Saints
[Salt Lake City: The Deseret News, Published by
The Church of Jesus Christ of Latter-day Saints, 1899])

[Note: The following selections are taken from the first edition of James Talmage's The Articles of Faith, printed in 1899 and endorsed by church president Lorenzo Snow. From the 1899 edition to the 1924 revision, the author incorporated changes ranging from correcting punctuation to reconsidering church doctrines. The format of the first edition resembled a catechism, with notes at the end of each chapter and a series of questions in the back of the book. In the 1924 edition the questions were removed and the notes were placed in the back of the book. The contents of the first edition were presented as a series of lectures. In the 1924 edition these were changed to chapters. The selections that follow represent changes most often referred to when comparing differences between the first and second editions.]

★ ★ ★

Existence is Eternal
(from Lecture II, "God and the Godhead," pp. 32-34)

9. Man's inborn consciousness tells him of his own existence; his ordinary powers of observation prove the existence of others of his kind, and of uncounted orders of organized beings; from this he concludes that something must have existed always, for had there been a time of no existence, a period of nothingness, existence could never have begun, for from nothing, nothing can be derived. The eternal existence of something then, is a fact beyond dispute; and the only question requiring answer is, what is that eternal something; that existence which is without beginning and without end? The skeptics may answer, "Nature; matter has always existed, and the universe is but a manifestation of matter organized by forces operating upon it; however, Nature is not God." But matter is neither vital nor active,

nor is force intelligent; yet vitality and ceaseless activity are characteristic of created things, and the effects of intelligence are universally present. True, nature is not God; and to mistake the one for the other is to call the edifice the architect, the fabric the designer, the marble the sculptor, and the thing the power that made it. The system of nature is the manifestation of that order which argues a directing intelligence; and that intelligence is of an eternal character, coeval with existence itself. Nature herself is a declaration of a superior Being, whose will and purpose she portrays in all her varied aspects. Beyond and above nature, stands nature's God.

10. While existence is eternal, and therefore to being there never was a beginning, never will be an end, in a relative sense each stage of organization must have had a beginning, and to every phase of existence as manifested in each of the countless orders and classes of created things, there was a first, as there will be a last; though every ending or consummation in nature is but the beginning of another stage of advancement. Thus, man's ingenuity has invented theories to illustrate, if not to explain, a possible sequence of events by which the earth has been brought from a state of chaos to its present habitable condition; but by those hypotheses, this globe was once a heated ball, on which none of the innumerable forms of life which now tenant it could have existed. The theorist therefore must admit a beginning to earthly life, and such a beginning is explicable only on the assumption of some creative act, or a contribution from outside the earth. If he admit the introduction of life upon the earth from some other and older sphere, he does but extend the limits of his inquiry as to the beginning of vital existence; for to explain the origin of a rose-bush in our own garden by saying that it was transplanted as an offshoot from a rose-tree growing elsewhere, is no answer to the question concerning the origin of roses. Science of necessity assumes a beginning to vital phenomena on this planet, and admits a finite duration of the earth in its current course of progressive change; and in this respect, the earth is a representative of the heavenly bodies in general. The eternity of existence then is no more potent as an indication of an eternal Ruler, than is the endless sequence of change, each stage of which has both beginning and end. The origination of created things, the beginning of an organized universe, is utterly inexplicable on any assumption of spontaneous change in matter, or of a fortuitous and accidental operation of its properties.

11. Human reason, so liable to err in dealing with subjects of lesser import even, may not of itself lead its possessor to a full knowledge of God; yet its exercise will aid him in his search, strengthening and confirming his inherited instinct toward his Maker. "The fool hath said in his heart there is no God." (Ps. 14:1) In the scriptures, the word fool (Prov. 1:7; 10:21; 14:9) is used to designate a wicked man, one who has forfeited his wisdom by a long course of wrong doing, bringing darkness over his mind in place of light, and ignorance instead of knowledge. By such a course, the mind becomes depraved and incapable of appreciating the finer arguments in nature. A wilful sinner grows deaf to the voice of reason in holy things, and loses the privilege of communing with his Creator, thus forfeiting the strongest means of attaining a knowledge of God.

★ ★ ★

The Holy Ghost
(from Lecture VIII, "The Holy Ghost," pp. 166–67)

9. In the execution of these great purposes, the Holy Ghost directs and controls the numerous forces of Nature, of which indeed a few, and these perhaps of the minor order, wonderful as even the least of them seems to man, have thus far been made known to the human mind. Gravitation, sound, heat, light, and the still more mysterious, seemingly supernatural power of electricity, are but the common servants of the Holy Spirit in His operations. No earnest thinker, no sincere investigator supposes that he has yet learned of all the forces existing in and operating upon matter; indeed the observed phenomena of nature, yet wholly inexplicable to him, far outnumber those for which he has devised even a partial explanation. There are powers and forces at the command of God, compared with which, electricity, the most occult of all the physical agencies controlled in any degree by man, is as the pack-horse to the locomotive, the foot messenger to the telegraph, the raft of logs to the ocean steamer. Man has scarcely glanced at the enginery of creation; and yet the few forces known to him have brought about miracles and wonders, which but for their actual realization would be beyond belief. These mighty agencies, and the mightier ones still to man unknown, and many perhaps, to the present condition of the human mind unknowable, do not constitute

the Holy Ghost, but the mere means ordained to serve Divine purposes.

10. Subtler, mightier, and more far-reaching still than any or all of the physical forces in nature, are the powers that operate upon conscious organisms, the means by which the mind, the heart, the soul of man may be affected. In our ignorance of the true nature of electric energy, we speak of it as a fluid; and so by analogy the forces through which the mind is governed have been called spiritual fluids. The true nature of these higher powers is unknown to us, for the conditions of comparison and analogy, so necessary to our frail human reasoning, are wanting; still the effects are experienced by all. As the conducting medium in an electric current is capable of conveying but a limited current, the maximum strength depending upon the resistance offered by the conductor; and, as separate circuits of different degrees of conductivity may carry currents of widely varying intensity; so human souls are of varied capacity with respect to the diviner powers. But, as the medium is purified, as the obstructions are removed, so the resistance to the energy decreases, and the forces manifest themselves with greater perfection. By analogous processes of purification, may our spirits be made more susceptible to the power of life, which is an emanation from the Spirit of God. Therefore are we taught to pray by word and action for a constantly increasing portion of the Spirit, that is, the power of the Spirit, which is a measure of the favor of God unto us.

★ ★ ★

The Kingdom of God
(from Lecture XX, "Christ's Reign on Earth," pp. 376-78)

21. Kingdom and Church—In the Gospel according to Matthew, the phrase "kingdom of heaven" is of frequent occurrence; while in the books of the other evangelists, and throughout the epistles, the expression is "kingdom of God," "kingdom of Christ," or simply "kingdom." It is evident that these words may be used interchangeably without violence to the true meaning. However, the term kingdom is used in more senses than one, and a careful study of the context in each instance may be necessary to a proper comprehension of the writer's intent. The most common usage's are two:—1. An expression synonymous with "the Church," having reference to the followers of Christ without distinction as to their temporal or spiritual

66

organizations. 2. The designation of the literal kingdom over which Christ is to reign on the earth in the last days.

22. When we contemplate the Kingdom in the latter and more general sense, the Church must be regarded as a part thereof; an essential indeed, for it is the germ from which the Kingdom is to be developed, and the very heart of the perfected organization. The Church has existed and now continues in an organized form, without the Kingdom as a visibly established power with temporal authority in the world; but the Kingdom cannot be maintained without the Church.

23. In modern revelation, the expressions "kingdom of God" and "kingdom of heaven" are sometimes used with distinctive meanings,—the former phrase signifying the Church, and the latter the literal kingdom which is to overshadow and comprise all existing national divisions. In this sense, the Kingdom of God has been set up already in these the last days; its beginning, in and for the present dispensation, was the establishment of the Church on its latter-day and permanent foundation. This is consistent with our conception of the Church as the vital organ of the Kingdom in general. The powers and authority committed to the Church, are then the keys of the Kingdom. Such meaning is made clear in the following revelation to the Church: "The keys of the kingdom of God are committed unto man on the earth, and from thence shall the gospel roll forth unto the ends of the earth, as the stone which is cut out of the mountain without hands shall roll forth, until it has filled the whole earth * * * Call upon the Lord, that his kingdom may go forth upon the earth, that the inhabitants thereof may receive it, and be prepared for the days to come, in the which the Son of Man shall come down in heaven, clothed in the brightness of his glory, to meet the kingdom of God which is set up on the earth. Wherefore, may the kingdom of God go forth, that the kingdom of heaven may come, that thou, O God, mayest be glorified in heaven so on earth, that thine enemies may be subdued; for thine is the honor, power and glory, forever and ever." (D&C 65: 2, 5-6)

24. At the time of His glorious advent, Christ will be accompanied by the hosts of righteous ones who have already passed from earth; and the Saints who are still alive on earth are to be quickened and caught up to meet Him, then to descend with Him as partakers of His glory. With Him too will come Enoch and his band of the pure in heart; and a union will be effected with the Kingdom of

God, or that part of the Kingdom of Heaven previously established as the Church of Christ on earth; and the Kingdom on earth will be one with that in heaven. Then will be realized a fulfilment of the Lord's own prayer, given as a pattern to all who pray: "Thy kingdom come. Thy will be done in earth, as it is in heaven." (Matt. 6:10; Luke 11:2)

25. The disputed question "Is the kingdom already set up on earth or are we to wait for its establishment until the time of the future advent of Christ, the King?" may properly receive answer either affirmative or negative, according to the sense in which the term kingdom is understood. The Kingdom of God as identical with the Church of Christ has assuredly been established; its history is that of the Church in these the last days; its officers are divinely commissioned, their power is that of the holy priesthood. They claim an authority which is spiritual, but also temporal in dealing with the members of the organization—Church or Kingdom as you may choose to call it—but they make no attempt, nor do they assert the right, to modify, assail, or in any way interfere with, existing governments; far less to subdue nations or to set up rival systems of control. The Kingdom of Heaven including the Church, and comprising all nations, will be set up with power and great glory when the triumphant King comes with His heavenly retinue to personally rule and reign on the earth, which He has redeemed at the sacrifice of His own life.

26. As seen, the Kingdom of Heaven will comprise more than the Church. The honorable and honest among men will be accorded protection and the privileges of citizenship under the perfect system of government which Christ will administer; and this will be their happy lot whether they are actually members of the Church or not. Law-breakers and men of impure heart will meet the judgment of destruction according to their sin; but those who live according to the truth as they have been able to receive and comprehend it, will enjoy the fullest liberty under the benign influences of a perfect administration. The special privileges and blessings associated with the Church, the right to hold and exercise the priesthood with its boundless possibilities and eternal powers, will be, as now they are, for those only who enter into the covenant and become part of the Church of the Redeemer.

★ ★ ★

Progression Between the Kingdoms
(from Lecture XII, "Religious Liberty and Toleration," pp. 420-21)

24. The Kingdoms with Respect to One Another—The three kingdoms of widely differing glories are themselves organized on an orderly plan of gradation. We have seen that the telestial kingdom comprises a multitude of subdivisions; this also is the case, we are told, with the celestial; and, by analogy, we conclude that a similar condition prevails in the terrestrial. Thus the innumerable degrees of merit amongst mankind are provided for in an infinity of graded glories. The Celestial kingdom is supremely honored by the personal ministrations of the Father and the Son. The Terrestrial kingdom will be administered through the higher, without a fulness of glory. The Telestial is governed through the ministrations of the Terrestrial, by "angels who are appointed to minister for them." (D&C 76:86, 88)

25. It is reasonable to believe, in the absence of direct revelation by which alone absolute knowledge of the matter could be acquired, that, in accordance with God's plan of eternal progression, advancement from grade to grade within any kingdom, and from kingdom to kingdom, will be provided for. But if the recipients of a lower glory be enabled to advance, surely the intelligences of higher rank will not be stopped in their progress; and thus we may conclude, that degrees and grades will ever characterize the Kingdoms of our God. Eternity is progressive; perfection is relative; the essential feature of God's living purpose is its associated power of eternal increase.

★ ★ ★

Social Order of the Saints
(from Lecture XXIV, "Practical Religion," pp. 454-55)

16. Social Order of the Saints—In view of the prevailing conditions of social unrest, of the loud protest against existing systems, whereby the distribution of wealth is becoming more and more unequal—the rich growing richer from the increasing poverty of the poor, the hand of oppression resting more and more heavily upon the masses, the consequent dissatisfaction with governments, and the half-smothered fires of anarchy discernible in almost every nation—

69

may we not take comfort in the God-given promise of a better plan, a plan that seeks without force or violence to establish a natural equality, to take the weapons of despotism from the rich, to aid the lowly and the poor, and to give every man an opportunity to live and labor in the sphere to which he is adapted? From the tyranny of wealth, as from every other form of oppression, the truth will make men free. To be partakers of such freedom mankind must subdue selfishness, which is one of the most potent enemies of godliness.

{10}

"Items on Polygamy—Omitted from the Published Book," Undated, Written for Inclusion but Not Published in *The Articles of Faith,* First Edition

(from James E. Talmage Papers, Archives and Manuscripts, Harold B. Lee Library, Brigham Young University, Provo, Utah)

Polygamy—An Ancient Practice—As made known in the revelation (Doc. & Cov. 132) concerning the eternity of the marriage covenant, the order of celestial marriage may include a plurality of wives. While the practice of polygamous (Note) marriage has been condemned by christian sects in general, it was doubtless the system under which (by most of) the patriarchs of old: and in view of this fact, it is known in the Church today as the system of patriarchal marriage. The custom has survived the lapse of time, and is still a traditional and common practice amongst a large proportion of the human family.

The Jewish scriptures conclusively prove that polygamy was not merely tolerated *by the Lord,* but positively approved by the Lord in olden times. Abraham was a polygamist, yet the Lord treated him with spiritual favor, established with him a covenant for all time (Gen. 17:1-4), and moreover bestowed upon his polygamous child a special blessing (Gen. 17:20). Jacob, whose God-given name-title Israel is still the honored designation of the chosen people, was the husband of four living wives; yet unto him the Lord confirmed the covenant made with his grandfather Abraham (Gen. 28:13), and granted special blessings to his polygamous wife Rachel (Gen. 30:22-23), and also to Leah the first wife for having given another woman to her husband (Gen. 30:17-18). Moses also possessed a plurality of wives (Exo. 2:21; Numb. 12:1; Judges 4:11), yet he was made the mouthpiece of God unto Israel, and through him the laws of the people were established, but in no instance do we find the polygamous relationship denounced; on the contrary special provision was made for the treatment of polygamous children (Deut. 21:15-17).

Through another enactment, polygamy was made compulsory

among the Israelites under certain conditions, and the penalty of lasting disgrace was decreed against him who refused to meet the requirement. The law was to the effect, that if a married man died without children, it should be the duty of the brother of the deceased to take the widow to wife, in order that he might have a posterity in his dead brother's name; no distinction was made as to the single or married state of the surviving brother; and compliance with the law might necessitate a polygamous relationship (Deut. 25:5-10). Samuel, a favored prophet of God (I Sam. 3:19-21) was the offspring of plural marriage (I Sam. 1:1-2, 19-20). David, Israel's mighty king, specially chosen of God, had many wives and concubines (I Sam. 25:42-43; II Sam. 5:13; 12:7-8); yet of him we read that he "did that which was right in the eyes of the Lord, and turned not aside from anything that he commanded him all the days of his life, save only in the matter of Uriah the Hittite" (I Kings 15:5). The exception here noted in David's righteous life was a grievous sin; for he had committed adultery with Bathsheba, the wife of another; and moreover planned the death of her husband. The child resulting from this sinful association was smitten with death in spite of David's earnest supplications (II Sam. 12:15-23): yet another child, Solomon, which Bathsheba, as David's polygamous wife bore to him, was loved of the Lord (II Sam. 12:24), became the recipient of unprecedented blessings (I Kings 3:5-15; 4:29-34) and succeeded his father on the throne of undivided Israel (I Kings 1:13). Moreover, he was honored in being permitted to build a temple to the Lord (I Kings 5:5) a privilege denied to his father David (I Chron. 22; 28:3), and on the completion of the sacred structure, the Lord made known his acceptance of this work of a polygamous son, by miraculous manifestations (I Kings 8:10-11; 9:1-3; II Chron. 7:1-3, 12). Solomon also was a polygamist (I Kings 11:1-3); for this he was not accounted a sinner, but for having married women of idolatrous nations, and in sanctioning their god-less practices (Verses 4-13).

The instances cited may suffice to show that the seal of divine approval as set upon the polygamous system, which characterized the history of ancient Israel, and while illegitimate children were stigmatized as objects of shame (Deut. 23:2), the issue of polygamous marriage were in many instances the recipients of special honors as has been shown. As a crowning example, let it be remembered that according to New Testament authority, Christ himself was born in

72

polygamous lineage, among his earthly progenitors there were many polygamists, and children of such, including even Solomon, the son of Bathsheba (Matt. 1).

Plurality of wives in this dispensation. The Latter-day Saints do not base their defense of the doctrine of polygamy as it was taught and practiced for a time within the Church upon the scriptural justification of the system which existed of old; nor upon arguments as to the propriety and expediency of the practice, some of which have been urged by those who would make it appear that plural marriage best subserves the interests of society. The sole and sufficient reason which led the church to promulgate the doctrine was that the Lord had by revelation taught it and had commanded its acceptance in the present dispensation. The revelation here referred to was given to Joseph Smith in 1831; but for several years after that time it was made known to a few of the leading officials of the Church only; and not until 1841 did the prophet allow its practice or introduce it by his own example. The written revelation was published to the Church under date of July 12, 1843 (Doc. & Cov. 132). In this declaration of the divine will, the Lord justified Abraham, Isaac, Jacob, Moses, and other holy men of old in their marriage relations, declaring that they had all received their wives, by command of God, and under the conditions of the celestial covenant, and that in this thing they sinned not, except as some of them, David and Solomon for example, took wives not given of God. The command to re-establish the sacred ordinance of celestial marriage, including plurality of wives was definite and binding on the Church. The people received it as a divine requirement, and entered upon its practice with the sentiment of the Christian world and their own traditional conceptions of propriety in full opposition.

The story of their fidelity to this principle in the face of sectarian persecution of the bitterest kind, under the harrasments of hostile, and as the people truly believed, unconstitutional legislation, is more a matter of history. The first anti-polygamy enactment by the Congress of the United States became a law July 1, 1862; for twenty years however the statute was practically a dead letter; it was held by eminent legal authority to be unconstitutional and therefore void, and little effort was made to enforce its provisions. In 1882, and again in 1887, additional laws were framed against the practice of plural marriage, and when the Supreme Court finally decided that the laws were valid, the people could but submit (See page — [no reference indicated]). The discontinuance of plural marriages was decreed by the Church, through a manifesto issued by the presiding authority and adopted by the people October 6th 1890. *Note* [no reference indicated].

{11}

"The Methods and Motives of Science," An Address Delivered in the Logan Temple on 5 February 1898

(from the *Improvement Era* 3 [February 1900]: 250-59)

It is possible that a question may arise in the minds of some as to the propriety of this choice of subject for treatment within these sacred precincts. The thought, if it occur at all, is probably dependent upon the very prevalent idea that science is a man-made system, of earth earthy; and that its study is attended with possible if not certain dangers to the faith which man should foster within his soul toward the source of superior knowledge and true wisdom. Indeed, there are many who openly declare that a man cannot be both scientific and religious in his views and practices. Yet there is probably little justification for this conception of supposed antagonism between the healthful operation of man's reason in his effort to comprehend the language of God as declared in the divine works, and the yearnings of the human heart for the beauties of the truth that is revealed by more direct communication between the heavens and the earth. It is not my purpose on this occasion to deal with the trite topic of religion versus science, but rather to speak of the motives that impel the scientific man in his labor, and the fundamental principles of his method. Such an inquiry, if prosecuted in the spirit of scientific research, cannot be out of place even here; and if the effort be strengthened by our instinct of reverence for truth and its divine source, it will be found to be friendly to faith and akin to worship.

The word "science" with its many derivatives, and such combinations as "scientific habits" and "scientific spirit" are of common usage today. In spite of the vague and indefinite way in which these and other expressions are used by those who are habitually inaccurate in their sayings and doings, the terms have come to have a meaning specific and definite. Science is not merely knowledge; a simple accumulation of facts, of however valuable a kind, would not constitute a science, any more than a collection of brick and stone, wood, iron and glass, sand, lime, and all other necessary materials of construc-

75

tion, would constitute a house. The parts must be placed in proper relative position, and only as this true relationship is established and maintained, will the structure approach completeness, or even the condition of convenient service. Science is collated knowledge; its material are arranged in orderly manner, its facts are so classified and placed as to afford for one another the advantage of mutual support, as the walls bear the roof, and the foundations the walls.

Our rational conclusions regarding the propriety of any occurrence or cause of action are based on two distinct mental processes:— (1) observations and apprehensions of facts, and (2) the shaping of opinions and judgments in accordance with those facts. Concerning such Winchell has said, "Aptness, readiness, and spontaneity in the execution of those processes constitute what we mean by the scientific habit. Eagerness to act on determinations reached by such processes is the scientific spirit. The scientific habit of mind is therefore the precise habit required for most just judgments within the sphere of all activities possessing an ethical character ★★★ This spirit, first of all, loves the truth supremely. It feels that the passive acceptance of error is an affront to truth and intelligence. It therefore seeks earnestly to arrive at truth and to avoid error either in conception or conclusion. It therefore maintains a habit of watchfulness and scrutiny. It seeks to be accurate in its observation of facts, in its collocation of them, and in the inferences drawn from them. It is cautious; it pauses and reflects; it repeats its observations; it accumulates many facts to enlarge the basis of its generalizations. It enounces inferences tentatively and verifies them at every opportunity. It refuses to swerve from the teachings of the evidence. Interest, prejudice, friendships, advantage, all must be pushed aside. An attitude of absolute indifference toward collateral ends must be maintained. It knows no motive but one, that is the exact truth. This is true judicial attitude. It is an ideal attainment. Probably under human conditions it is never reached; but the scientific spirit approaches it as the asymptote approaches the curve."

This spirit is that of the just judge who is above all human temptation toward bias or prejudice, and in this degree well may we call it an ideal attainment. Man is a creature of bias, a bundle of prejudices, some of them good, many of them assuredly bad. The world teems with dread examples of this prejudice; we scarcely know where to look for an unbiased decision. This spirit sits in judgment, but not as the dumb jury in the box, sworn to decide upon such evidence and that only, as sharp-witted lawyers are able to bring forward, or such as a biased judge may see fit to allow; compelled to ignore every fact, the admission of which has been ruled out through some technical victory of the interested pleader; not sworn to render a verdict according to the law as construed by the court, who may or may not be true and worthy; but sworn to try every issue by the most crucial tests, to search for evidence in every nook and corner of the world; to count no costs of court in securing testimony, to search not for evidence on one side alone, but for evidence though it prove or disprove, to construe the law in the spirit of the law-maker and according to equity, to strive not for triumph but for truth, to know no victory but the discomfiture of error and the vindication of right. This spirit will impel him upon whom it rests to a condition at least approaching absolute unselfishness; he must sink himself with all his desires and preconceived opinions, into oblivion. As he works, he is a machine finely constructed, nicely adjusted; responding to every mani-festation of force, recording every movement, calm, deliberate, un-emotional. Not as the magnetic needle, which is held by the attractive force of that greater magnet, the earth, so that it cannot move in response to another force, unless this latter be strong enough to overcome the earth's directive power; but like the *astatic* needle, the pronounced tendency of which to swing North and South is over-come, so that it is rendered free to recognize and obey the outer force.

With such purpose and motive the scientific man strives to de-velop his power of accurate observation, and to train his reason in the forming of judgments on the facts supplied through observation. Every teacher knows how deficient is the ordinary student in the perform-ance of these processes. Observations incomplete, and in other ways unreliable as a basis for opinion and judgment, are in the usual order. It is difficult to bring the mind into a condition of neutrality; we persist in thinking that we see things as we believe they ought to be, or perhaps as we would like to have them, rather than as they are. Lack of skill in observation, aided by active and untrained fancy, is capable of working miracles on a scale otherwise unknown. It is said that the veteran microscopist, Dr. Carpenter, once had his attention directed to the work of a young student, who offered for inspection a marvelous collection of drawings representing alleged revelations of the micro-scope; there were animals never seen before or since by others; and all of these he had discovered, so Dr. Carpenter was told by an enthusi-

77

astic acquaintance, in spite of his inexperience and the imperfections of his instrument. The master's reply was: "Say not in spite of but because of those disadvantages".

May I offer another illustration? A tyro in the use of the microscope found a dead cat lying in a pool of water; the water was stagnant and filthy; he placed a drop under his glass, and saw to his amazement numerous living creatures darting through that liquid drop, which to them was a world, chasing, tearing, rending, devouring one another. Those creatures he declared, though infinitesimally small, had all of them the general appearance of cats; the departed spirits of all the cat tribe were there congregated. Confident of the result of a further observation, he put the carcass of a dog in another pool, and when decay had reached a convenient stage he examined that water and demonstrated to his own satisfaction that the liquid was swarming with canine ghosts. 'Tis a pity did not mix a drop of water from each of the pools; he might have heard the savage barks and have seen the fur fly. He confidently communicated to a friend that he had found the land, or rather the water, of departed spirits. The friend proceeded to test his conclusions, and fully demonstrated their falsity. Wherein lay the error? Was it in the glass? No, the second observer used the same instrument; it rested with the man. One was in a fit condition to consider evidence and to give judgment, the other was prejudiced; one was sober, the other was drunken with the wine of his own bias; one was sane, the other mad. Even in the seemingly simple operation of sketching, but few are able to show a thing as it is; some features are sure to be exaggerated, others suppressed; characteristics not appearing in the original are introduced, and essentials are entirely omitted. I speak not of the ideal representations in the work of the artist, his purpose is not so much to copy nature as to portray the beauties, which, while appealing to his trained eye, may be beyond the perception of others.

But even the highest development of skill in observation does not insure correctness of judgment. We may err in interpreting the simplest facts, and the same fact may impress different people in many ways. A well-trained ear might be able to analyze the ticks of a telegraphic receiver, but a knowledge of the code is essential to a proper interpretation of the sounds. We blame the barometer as an untrustworthy instrument, if a rise be not followed by fine weather, or a fall by rain; forgetting that it revealed a change of atmospheric pressure only, and that the definite prophecy of fair or other conditions was not made by the barometer but by ourselves, as a judgment which was perhaps poorly supported.

The cultivation of the scientific spirit has been objected to for many reasons. We are told that it is opposed to the poetic impulse and tends to quench the emotional fire which is essential to the growth of man's perfect nature; and that it is therefore bad. Such a conclusion is hastily drawn; it is contrary to fact. There is no truer poet than the man of science, he must needs indulge his imagination as much as does the singer who deals with sweet sounds, the one who pours out his soul in verse, or he who finds expression for his ideal in beauteous forms in stone, or in colors in canvas. But the scientific man knows that when he sings, the demands of melody and the requirements of harmony may lead him to exaggeration; he remembers that when he makes verses his ardor to secure rhythm and rhyme may intoxicate him; that in the use of chisel and brush he aims rather to please than to teach.

As already stated, the purpose of art is not simply to imitate nature; else photography would be in higher esteem than painting; for it is an evident fact that the good photograph is a likeness representing the subject as it is, while the painted portrait is often an attempt to show the artist's ideal. Art strives to recognize and portray this ideal in nature. The mission of poetry, which is but one manifestation of the spirit of art, is to please, incidentally it may teach, but its prime purpose is not didactic. The poet's effort is to find and show forth beauty. And yet the scientist is poetically inclined; he is a lover of beauty in its highest, purest phases. He stands side by side with his brother the poet, in the presence of the simplest manifestations of beauty, admiring the colors of the flower, entranced with the sweet song of the bird and the murmuring of the wind. But he goes farther than his brother, analyzes the color and the sound, and strives to trace these effects back to their causes.

There are other and higher manifestations of beauty than those which appeal only eye to eye, harmony of color and sound. There is the beauty of adaptation, the fitting of purpose to end, the existence and operation of law. To this, the highest type of beauty, the scientist is passionately devoted. He is a lover of beauty for its own sake; not because it pleases his eye or ear, but because it appeals to his reason and judgment; he loves it for its intrinsic worth. Novelty sways him but lightly; truths to others old and gray, are yet youthful and rosy to him; his affection knows no cooling as the charms of fresh acquaintance disappear; he cares less for the face and the figure than for the heart and its prompting. Tell me, which is the true lover and which is the admirer only, he who is charmed by complexion and bust, or he who is attracted by the spirit, though it be encased in a body that is feeble and scarred? Let the poetic feeling be indulged; its indulgence oft-times marks the higher moments of our existence; but in these exalted states we do not work methodically and systematically; as Winchell has said, were the Creator to unveil his face to us, our power of work would be gone, we could do naught but worship.

Again, I hear some say that this scientific tendency is of doubtful propriety, for being cold, calculating, discerning, judging, its devotee being cautious and at times even skeptical, he has no place in his soul for trusting, all-abiding faith; in other words, that the scientific spirit being in contrast with the poetic, is opposed to faith. The conclusion upon which such a statement rests is plain, that he who makes it classes faith as a poetic impulse, an emanation of the art spirit. As if faith were a mere emotion, its purpose solely to please; as if it had its foundation in the sweet but yet light bubbling poesy. It has a deeper seat, a firmer anchorage. Liken it to a tree, then its roots penetrate to the profoundest recesses of the soil. The scientific spirit is the fruit of that tree. None sees more clearly than does the scientist the necessity of all-abiding trust, none recognizes more readily than he the existence of laws which he has scarcely begun to comprehend, the results of which are nevertheless exalting. Faith is not blind submission, passive obedience with no effort at thought or reason. Faith, if worthy of its name, rests upon truth; and truth is the foundation of science.

The scientific worker pursues his investigation step by step, inviting inspection and criticism at every stage. He makes as plain a trail as he can, blazes the trees of his path through the forest, cuts his footprints in the rocks that others may more readily follow to test his results. He welcomes every new worker in the field, for the work of others will diminish the chances of error going undetected in his own. The scientific man welcomes the stimulant of competition, but has no room within his soul for feelings of rivalry.

In this day competition is severe, even fierce indeed; but the scientific spirit would make it friendly and ennobling. Its possessor acknowledges freely and gladly the aid he has gained from others. I see about me men who are ungrateful in the extreme, knowing only their own achievements, and having but a blind eye for all that was done before, and which made their work possible. They seek to blot out from the canvas on which they are permitted to work, the whole background of the picture, failing to see how they spoil their own foreground by so doing. I have little sympathy for the man who boasts that nothing was done in the field til he came in at the gate. And so of the bricklayer who thinks that he and he alone has reared the house, while but for the stonemason he would have no foundation on which to build. The man who comes into position and immediately sets about demolishing the work of his predecessor, or, if he cannot dispense with it, who hides it, or disguises it, that it might appear as his own, has none of the scientific spirit, which is the spirit of manhood and of honor. Shame upon him who speaks slightingly of those who pioneered the way and made the path along which he travels with comparative ease! Double shame on the boy who sneers at the old-fashioned ways of father and mother; perhaps they were more typical representatives of the spirit of true propriety in their early days than is he in his.

As with individuals so with institutions. There are some that seek to grow upon the ruins of others. The promoters of such see no good outside their own plans. They detest competition, and feel that they have a patent to the field. They advertise by denouncing others. Modesty has not a seat within their walls, manhood resides far from them. Look at the business advertisements of the day: every manufacturer, merchant, or huckster warns you against all others of his trade. He is a paragon of perfection, and the only one of his kind.

The scientific spirit acknowledges without reserve the laws of God, but discriminates between such and the rules made by man. It abhors bigotry, denounces the extravagances of the blind zealot, religious or otherwise, and seeks to perfect the faith of its possessor as a purified, sanctified power, pleasing alike mind and heart, reason and soul. In the charges that have been preferred by the theologians against science, and the counter accusations by the scientists against theology, it is evident that in each case the accuser is not fully informed as to what he is attacking. Irrational zeal is not to be commended; and the substitution of theory for fact, though often declared to be the prevailing weakness of the scientist, is wholly unscientific.

But it is easy to denounce; so to do is a favorite pastime of ignorance. That scientific theories have been and are being discarded as unworthy because untrue is well known; but no one is more ready to so renounce than the scientist himself. To him a theory is but a scaffolding whereon he stands while placing the facts which are his building blocks; and from these he rears the tower from which a wider horizon of truth is opened to his eye. When the structure is made, the scaffold, unsightly, shaky, and unsafe, as it is likely to be, is removed. 'Tis not always possible to judge of the building from the rough poles and planks which serve the temporary purpose of him who builds. Yet how often may we hear from our pulpits, usually however when they are occupied by the little-great men, scathing denunciations of science, which is represented as a bundle of vagaries, and of scientific men, who are but Will-o-the-wisps enticing the traveler into quagmires of spiritual ruin. Would it not be better for those who so inveigh to acquaint themselves with at least the first principles of the doctrines of science? So general has this practice become amongst us, that the most inexperienced speaker feels justified in thus indulging himself, and in the minds of many the conclusion is reached, none the less pernicious in its present effects because unfounded, that the higher development of the intellect is not a part of the Gospel of Christ. I speak not against the true inspiration which as a manifestation of the spirit of prophecy has in many instances clearly indicated the errors of human beliefs. Were I to deny the existence of such a power and the potency of revelation I would be false to my love of science and its work, a betrayer of the testimony within my own soul.

I place the prophet before the philosopher; of the two I have seen the former go less frequently astray; he is guided by a "more sure word," he is a privileged pupil of the greatest Master. Yet revelation is not given to save man from self effort; if he want knowledge let him ask of God, and prove himself worthy of the desired gift by his own faithful search. Such are the teachings of our Church. The leaders amongst us, those who are acknowledged as prophets and revelators to the people, are not heard in authoritative denunciations of the teachings of science. Yet under the freedom allowed by our liberal Church organization the lay speaker is prone to indulge in unguarded criticism, and the undiscriminating hearer is apt to regard such as the teachings of the Church. The scientist in his self-denying earnest labors is a true child of God; as he is strengthened spiritually will his work be the better. The scientific spirit is divine.

{12}

"An Inspiring Thought,"
An Address Delivered on 27 April 1902

(from "Services at the Tabernacle.
Interesting Discourse by Dr. James E. Talmage.
A Progressive Religion.
The Church is Abreast of the Times
And Its Advancement is Due to Revelations from God,"
Deseret Evening News, 28 April 1902, p. 8)

Dr. James E. Talmage was the speaker of the afternoon. He prefaced his interesting discourse by saying it was an inspiring thought to know that thousands of the people were gathering together from Sabbath to Sabbath to find out God and His ways. He had learned that there is an inspiration in an earnest, devout desire, and that it calls forth those words and thoughts that are best fitted to the needs of the people. It is no light thing to gather and pray or to do aught in the name of Christ, when it is done unworthily. All Christians know that mighty things have been wrought in the name of Christ, and happy is he who does all things in His name.

In undertaking to worship God, it is requisite that one should know something of God. A man cannot be saved in ignorance. That does not necessarily mean illiteracy. A man may be weighted down by some kinds of knowledge and yet be ignorant in the eyes of God. The man who is able to say in his heart, "God is love," has learned something of the power and sanctity of love.

In this day much is heard of the rapid advancement in the arts and sciences; that man has learned the secrets of nature which will revolutionize society. It is a good indication that the human race is advancing, and the Latter-day Saints desire to be up with the times. This, the speaker thought, was a commendable ambition, if it did not lead to an appetite for mere novelty, whether the new thing were better or worse than the older one. The question was then asked, should not people also make advancement in their worship. The speaker thought they should do so. He then pointed out how the religious teachings of the Saints were an advancement, in relation to the revelations of God and other vital principles. What would students think of their professor in chemistry, geology or any of the other sciences, if he should say there was nothing for them to do but read the books of the past; that no more light or knowledge on those subjects was to come forth? That teacher would be denounced as a fossil and not entitled to respect. It is beginning to be recognized that the religion that is not progressive is as devoid of life as much as is the science that is not progressive.

The great difference; between the works of man and the works of God is that man's works end with themselves, while the works of God are eternal. Dr. Talmage stated that men who had put aside their prejudices had acknowledged to him that the Church of Jesus Christ of Latter-day Saints was abreast of the times. And that which appealed most to the speaker, was the spirit of freedom in the Church. Its song was the song of liberty; liberty of heart and mind as well as the body.

In no feature is the progress of the Church more emphasized than in its teachings regarding the status and mission of women. Those teachings are that woman is man's equal and she is not made to suffer for the sins of man. In those early days when the legislature of Utah was composed almost entirely of members of this Church, woman was given her political franchise the same as man. It was subsequently taken away by act of Congress, but was restored when Utah became a state of the Union. The Church is bold enough to go so far as to declare that ["]man has an Eternal Mother in the Heavens as well as an Eternal Father, and in the same sense We look upon woman as a being, essential in every particular to the carrying out of God's purposes in respect to mankind." The marriage relations between man and woman is not looked upon merely as a convenience, but as a Divine order to exist for time and through all eternity. This matrimonial agreement must be sealed by one bearing Divine authority.

The speaker then discussed the subject of pre-existence and declared that nothing came by mere chance. God knew us all before we came here, and the command to "multiply and replenish the earth," was not a new one. It was merely a statement of law that had always been in operation. Teach a man that he evolved from a brute: that he will die like a brute, and he will live like a brute. Teach him that he is a son of God and he will strive to be worthy of the title.

Dr. Talmage expressed the sentiment that man should have more pride; real pride; that pride, that would not permit him to sink to the level of sin. "Teach him that he is not only a prince of earth but a born son of the King of Kings, and has a place in His palace on high, if he does not forfeit his title to it.

The speaker dilated earnestly upon the principle of modern revelation, and pointed out many Divine and rational truths that had been brought to light through that means. He described the belief of the Latter-day Saints in relation to the salvation of all men. This life is but a prelude to the life that is to come, and therefore every act or word here is significant. Man is here to demonstrate the metal he is made of, and his fitness to occupy the position he is seeking in the world to come.

The speaker concluded with an eloquent appeal to the people to repent of sin and turn unto God.["]

{13}

"Lord of All"

(from the *Improvement Era* 11 [August 1908]: 769-72;
written for publication in Japan)

It is one of the weaknesses of man to question the omnipotence of God. Human ignorance challenges Divine wisdom. The infinitesimally small arrays itself against the infinitely great. The atom believes itself the universe.

It is my privilege to retire at intervals to a place of seclusion and rest, in the upper part of a large building, far above the rattle and roar of the city street. My room is lighted by large windows; and these, whenever I leave them ajar, afford egress to a variety of winged visitors of the insect tribe, such as flies, gnats, beetles, bees and butterflies; and, if I leave the casements open when I work at night, moths that fly in the darkness come to me. When I retire to this room after an absence of several days, I find a number of insects on desk, table and floor. Their deaths are evidently due to the dry atmosphere of the closed room.

Three days ago, while I was writing in the room, a wild bee from the neighboring hills came to visit me, entering through the crevice of the slightly opened window. When I was ready to leave, I threw the casement wide, and tried to drive the bee to liberty and safety. I pursued the flying creature, vigorously striking and swishing with a towel, knowing well that if it remained in the room it would die. The more I tried to drive it out, the more fiercely did it resist. Its erstwhile peaceful hum became an angry roar; its flight became hostile and threatening. At last it caught me off my guard, and stung my hand—the hand that had tried to drive it to safety. Then it alighted on a carved projection of the ceiling, beyond my reach of aid or injury.

Today, I returned to the room, and found the shriveled corpse of the captive bee on my desk where it had fallen from the ceiling-point of fancied safety.

To the bee's short-sighted mind I was a foe, a persistent pursuer, a mortal enemy seeking its destruction. Yet, in truth I was its friend, offering a ransom of the life it had forfeited through its own error,

86

striving to drive it in spite of itself from the prison of death to the open air of liberty.

Notwithstanding the sharp wound of its sting, I had no unkind thought, but rather pity and commiseration for the foolish creature. The bee paid for its stubbornness with its life.

As to ourselves and the bee, are we so exalted that the analogy fails?

Since the beginning of human history, man has sought to measure Omnipotence by human standards. Fleeting pleasure has been preferred to enduring happiness; the gilded bauble of the present is chosen rather than the true gold of eternal worth.

To gauge Omnipotence by the yard-stick of mortal weakness, to arraign Omnipotence at the bar of human wisdom—this is no achievement worthy of modern praise, no mark of civilization or advancement. Yet such has been the usual course of man from the earliest time.

It is written in Arabic lore of the long ago that a holy man once questioned the deeds of an angel of God. Thus runs the story:

An angel came to earth on special errand bent. Moses, the lawgiver of Israel, met him and said: "Let me go with thee that I may learn how God doth deal with man." The angel replied: "Thou couldst not understand my acts; yet, if thou wilt, thou mayest go with me; but question not what I shall do, whate'er it be."

Moses and the angel journeyed together. They came to the shore of a lake whereon were many fishing boats. From one of these the angel struck away the boards, and the boat sank near to the shore. Moses was angered and demanded, "What means this? Dost thou destroy without cause?" The angel answered, "I told thee thou couldst not understand."

Anon they met an Arab boy wending his way joyously along the road. Upon him the angel breathed the breath of death; the boy fell and expired. Then Moses spake, "what ill deed is this? Dost thou slay the innocent?" Again the angel said, "I knew thou couldst not understand. Question me not; or leave me."

Onward they journeyed. They entered a village on the outskirts of which they stopped at a cottage. The garden wall was old and crumbling. The angel pushed upon it and it fell, crushing and spoiling the garden growth of vegetables and herbs. Then Moses broke forth, "Why doth thou destroy and spoil?" The angel answered, "I told thee thou couldst not understand. Now here we part, thou and I. Go thou the ways of earth, while I follow the appointed ways of heaven. Yet,

87

before thou leavest I would thus make plain, that the name of my Lord be exalted and extolled:

"The boat I broke belonged to poor fisher folk. Without the boat their livelihood is gone. But there cometh now a king's company along that coast, seizing all goodly boats. When the king's company had passed, the fisher folk, who are faithful before the Lord, will raise their boat while all the rest have gone.

"Touching the Arab boy—he was a goodly youth, but so great a power hath Satan over him that had he lived two moons more he would have slain his brother. Now his brother lives to bless his people, and the boy dies without guilt of blood.

"As to the cottage and the garden wall–two worthy men live there. Their father loved his Lord. The father for safe keeping hid a treasure beneath the wall; this the sons will find, building up the ruins, and they will be enriched." (Paraphrase of No. 77 of Pearls of the Faith, as translated by Sir Edwin Arnold; "Praise him, Al Mutahali; whose decree is wiser than the wit of man can see." Compare Koran chap. xviii.)

Thus it is shown that mortal afflictions ofttimes mean Divine blessings.

Yet, let it not be thought that dread calamities and dire distresses occur as a direct result of the will and purpose of a loving God. He rejoices not in the anguish and suffering of his children. Having endowed them with the rights of agency and individual freedom, he permits the exercise of this agency even to the bringing about of suffering and vicissitude. Even the Omnipotent may not shield man from the ill effects of voluntary actions without infringing upon the rights of free agency. There is no caprice in the dealings of God with man. If the Creator arbitrarily exempted some of his children from the ills naturally resulting from their acts, he could as well honor and aggrandize others beyond their merits.

It is no result of Divine will that people sin, that men follow debauchery and vice. Neither is it God's will that nations proclaim war, and send forth armies and navies to destroy or be destroyed. It is the will of God that in such dire contingencies the ordinary course of events, the natural sequence of cause and effect, be not interfered with. The Almighty is able to turn and overturn the results of human acts so as to conduce to eventual good.

Such a consummation, however, is neither justification nor excuse for wrong-doing. The ill-inspired sinners who crucified the Christ are answerable for their motives and their acts, though the sacrifice on Calvary has proved the world's redemption.

We proclaim the atonement wrought by Jesus Christ, the means of salvation provided by the Son of God, the voice of the Lord as heard in this age—the dispensation of the fulness of times. This proclamation is to all people; it is the message of deliverance from sin and its sorrow, the decree of liberty, the charter of freedom.

In olden times the Lord of heaven spoke by word of mouth to his chosen oracles. We proclaim that he speaks today. Why should the dead past be law to the active present? Is the voice of God silenced? Is his arm shortened that he cannot reach his children? Can he no longer speak to be heard, or move to be felt?

We proclaim the present God, the speaking, moving, active God, the God who recognizes the free agency of his children and who holds them accountable for their acts.

{14}

Calling and Ordination to the Apostleship

(Entries from the Journal of James E. Talmage,
7-8 December 1911,
Archives and Manuscripts, Harold B. Lee Library,
Brigham Young University, Provo, Utah)

Dec. 7, 1911—Shortly after 4 o'clock this afternoon, I learned of a call for me which must mark a great change in my work. This is no less than a call to the Holy Apostleship. Action was taken at this day's council meeting of the First Presidency and Twelve, whereby Apostle Chas. W. Penrose was sustained as Second Counselor in the First Presidency to succeed the late President John Henry Smith. I believe that all Israel will feel as I do—that this call is from the Lord. The Presidency, thus completed, will have my fervent support and prayerful service. The selection creates a present vacancy in the Council or Quorum of the Twelve and to this exalted and special office I am called. The announcement of my having been chosen came as a wholly un-heralded action. I was with President Joseph F. Smith until a late hour yesterday, but by no word, act or intimation was such action suggested to my mind. I know not that the President had then considered it, were such an office offered me as a position in secular life I might be tendered, I feel that I would shrink from the responsibility and hesitate even if I did not actually decline, but I hold myself ready to respond to any call made upon me by and in the Priesthood.

Apostle Anthony W. Ivins, called upon me about 4 p.m. on a matter of business and there told me with evidences of affection and emotion of the action taken by the Council. He testified to me that the call was from the Lord. Even at this time the announcement had been printed in the Deseret News, and within a few minutes I had many calls by phone from brethren who assured me of their support. May the Lord grant me His, and enable me to be a true witness of Him.

Within half an hour after the news had reached me, Maia, my wife, came to my office and assured me of her loving support. She had learned of the call while she was attending a meeting of the General Board of the Young Ladies Mutual Improvement Association. I feel that I need the help of my wife and family. I have looked upon myself as a lay member in the Church though I know that a patriarch Jesse Martin of Provo gave me to understand that, and I would be called and ordained one of the Twelve Apostles.

Dec. 8, 1911—At 11:30 this forenoon I was ordained an Apostle of the Lord Jesus Christ, and was set apart as one of the Twelve Apostles of the Church of Jesus Christ of Latter-day Saints. The ordinance was performed in the President's office, by President Joseph F. Smith, assisted by his counselors, Presidents Anthon H. Lund and Chas. W. Penrose, and by President Francis M. Lyman, and Elders Hyrum M. Smith, Geo. F. Richards and Jos. F. Smith Jr., of the Council of the Twelve.

I pray for strength to honor this divine calling. The brethren testify to me that the call is from the Lord. To it I respond with prayerful trust. The official report furnished me is as follows.

Ordination and setting apart of James E. Talmage as an Apostle of the Lord Jesus Christ, and a member of the Council of the Twelve, under the hands of Presidents Joseph F. Smith, Anthon H. Lund, Charles W. Penrose, Francis M. Lyman, George F. Richards and Jos. F. Smith Jr., being all the members of the Council that could be reached, at the president's office, Friday morning, Dec. 8, 1911, President Smith officiating.

★ ★ ★

"Before proceeding with the ordination, President Smith asked President Lyman if he had anything to say to Bro. Talmage. In answer President Lyman said that he had already had a long talk with Bro. Talmage instructing him with respect to the duties that would devolve upon him as an Apostle of the Lord, Jesus Christ, together with the great responsibilities attaching to that calling. He also said that he had instructed Bro. Talmage with respect to the necessity of his being in perfect accord with the brethren of the Twelve, informing him also that in all their private councils it would be his privilege to freely express his own individual views but that after doing so it would become his duty to be united with this brethren on the conclusions and decisions arrived at, even should the conclusions and decisions be contrary to his own views and judgment, also that everything talked about and done in a Council capacity should be held in strict confidence as matters sacred to the Council, not to be made known to anybody, his own wife and members of his family included. That he had also instructed Bro. Talmage it would become his duty to hold himself in readiness to go and come at call, and that his duties as Apostle should take precedence over all others whether of a public, private, or domestic nature; to all of which he asserted. And Prest. Lyman added that he was perfectly satisfied with Bro. Talmage and was prepared to welcome him into the Quorum of the Twelve.

★ ★ ★

"Bro. Talmage now received his ordination which was as follows:

Dear Brother James E. Talmage, as your fellow servants and as Apostles of the Lord Jesus Christ, in authority of the holy priesthood, which is after the order of the Son of God, we lay our hands upon your head, and ordain you an Apostle in the Church of Jesus Christ of Latter-day Saints, and also set you apart to be one of the Quorum of the Twelve Apostles, and confer upon you all the keys, rights, privileges, blessings, ministries and authority, pertaining to this high and holy calling, to the end that you may be, as you have been heretofore, but more abundantly, a living witness to the divinity of the lord Jesus Christ—a special witness of Him unto all the world, knowing and understanding as though you had seen by the sight of your eyes, and heard by the hearing of your ear, that the Lord God Almighty, our Heavenly Father, sent forth His Son unto the world, to become the Savior and redeemer of mankind; and that He did come, that he did live and die and rise again, and ascend on high, and that He does now sit enthroned with power and dominion on the right hand of the Father, and He has chosen His own brethren from time to time to be his fellow-laborers in the world, to administer to the children of men for their own salvation & exaltation, and they and all mankind through them might be brought to a knowledge of the Father and the Son.

"Now our dear brother in the Lord, we bless you and ordain you, conferring upon you the holy Apostleship, with all that pertains to this high and holy calling; and we pray God to bestow upon you the spirit of this calling abundantly and continue unto you the spirit of humility and meekness even more abundantly than you have ever experienced it heretofore, that you may be most exemplary and most efficient in the performance of your duties, and be an honor to the cause of God.

"Father, bless this thy servant and accept of him and fill him with the light of truth, the gift of the Holy ghost, and the testimony of

Christ, that he may labor diligently for the salvation of souls, and that his labors may be acceptable in thy sight.

"We seal upon you Brother Talmage, all these things, by authority of the Holy Priesthood vested in us; and this we do in the name of our Lord and Master Jesus Christ, even so, Amen."

★ ★ ★

This being done President Smith and all the brethren present congratulated Brother Talmage, and extended to him the right hand of fellowship.

(Signed) Geo. F. Gibbs

[Secretary to the First Presidency]

★ ★ ★

The occasion is to me one of irrepressible reverence and sanctity. To me the calling of an Apostle of the Lord Jesus Christ has always been one of special sanctity requiring the unreserved devotion of the man so honored. It is a calling above any office, station or title that man can confer.

{15}

"The Significance of Easter,"
An Address Delivered on 7 April 1912

(from *Eighty-second Annual Conference
of the Church of Jesus Christ of Latter-day Saints*
[Salt Lake City: Published by the Deseret News, 1912],
pp. 124-29)

It is with feelings of genuine gratitude that I stand before you to add
my testimony to those to which you have listened. A more inspiring
sight than that before me could scarcely be imagined, and certainly
could not be desired. It is doubtful if anywhere else in this great land
a larger gathering graces this Easter day. I feel that the Latter-day Saints
have manifested most praiseworthy interest in their religion, most
commendable sincerity, and genuine devotion to the cause of truth in
the attention they have given in this Conference.

This is indeed a day of days to all Christians. While it is true that
the Easter celebration has its counterpart in many pagan customs,
nevertheless Easter stands today for Christian belief, profession, and
hope. It is the gladsome day of the year; and we believe that in this
present year the anniversary comes at very nearly the actual and correct
date. It is the anniversary of the greatest event in all history, the most
effective miracle known to man—a miracle surpassing all that the mind
of man could of itself conceive. It was upon the day we now com-
memorate that victory over the tomb was proclaimed and the glad
tidings of eternal life were made known.

The Latter-day Saints believe in the literal resurrection of the
body. They accept the biblical doctrine in all its beauty and simplicity.
They do not invest it with foreign mysteries, nor do they read into the
sacred record interpretation and meaning not inherent therein. The
Latter-day Saints believe that this life is a necessary part of the education of the soul, that it is a stage marking advancement and progression;
that only those of the sons and daughters of God who were worthy
were permitted to take upon themselves mortal tabernacles upon the
earth. They believe that death is just as much a part of the divine plan
as is birth; and that death is but a passing from one necessary stage to

another yet more advanced. They believe, without question or doubt, that the body and the spirit shall again be united in a literal resurrection; and be it remembered, the resurrection of the body is the controlling thought and the central idea of Easter service. The man who believes in the resurrection of the body must base his belief upon revelation; and the man who so believes is inconsistent if he questions the truth declared in absolute and literal revelation from God.

It is a fact that we look around in nature vainly for any analogy of the resurrection. I have never been in harmony with the attempts of some to find analogies in nature where they do not exist relating to this great event of such surpassing importance. The egg, which is exhibited as the Easter symbol, has been pointed to as an instance of life after death. It has been said that the coming forth of the bird from the tomb-like recess of the egg is an instance of the return of life from death. The analogy is faulty; the example is not good; for be it understood that the egg that can hatch or may hatch is not dead; and if it be truly dead, it does not again come to life. The bursting forth of the buds in the spring time, the putting on of their foliage again by the trees, has been strained by some and pressed into service as another instance of a resurrection from the dead; but I believe that this is equally faulty, for the tree that is dead does not put forth leaves in the spring, and the plant that is dead does not again bear blossoms. The sleep of the insect by which it passes from the crawling larva into the death-like, corpse-like chrysalis, from which, after a time, the winged imago comes forth in all the glory of maturity, has been used by others as an instance of the resurrection. But, again, this is faulty and untrue, for the chrysalis is not dead, and if it were it would not burst forth into the winged beauty that crowns the sequence of insect life. When we accept these natural occurrences as analogies of the bodily resurrection from death, we are lead to regard favorably also that analogy which some attempt to affirm, that the crucified Christ was not dead, but that He was in a state of coma, or trance, and came out from that condition by a simple process of revivification, and was seen again of men, not as an immortal Being but as a man who had revived from a faint. Jesus died upon the cross. His spirit was literally and actually separated from His body; that body was not in a state of suspended animation, while still alive, that body was dead in the sense of being an untenanted tabernacle of clay, and it was only by the power of God that it could be again brought to life. Let us not deny the literalness of the resurrection as made known through the revelations of God. We believe that we shall in very truth die, and that the spirit—that immortal part of man, which existed before the body was framed, and which shall exist and continue to live after that body has gone to decay, that spirit shall take upon itself again this tabernacle of earthly element, immortalized, however, and destined to serve it as a fit garment through all eternity.

The Latter-day Saints have been charged with great literalness, with astounding simplicity, and as one critic put it to me, with a brutal materiality, in their doctrine. We acknowledge the charge in the sense in which it was meant, although we may object to some of the adjectives. The Latter-day Saints are just so simple-minded that they are willing to believe the Lord when He speaks, and take Him at His word. We rejoice in the hope and the assurance of a glorious resurrection. We rejoice in the work that was inaugurated at that first Easter period, for and in behalf of the dead. For while the body of the Christ lay in the tomb, as we learn beyond question, His spirit went to the spirits in prison, to those who were held in bonds because of their disobedience, to those who had not been privileged to learn of the redeeming efficacy of the Gospel; and He introduced and inaugurated there a missionary labor that has been going on ever since—a missionary work compared with which that which we attempt to do here upon earth, with our two thousand missionaries out in field, is not even as a drop compared to the ocean. Men are needed for missionary service among the dead. Who are the dead but those who once have lived? God is Lord of both the living and the dead; and all live unto Him. If it be true that the man who is now living cannot hope to enter into the Kingdom of God unless he complies with the simple law and requirement laid down by the author of our salvation, namely, that we must be born of water and of the spirit, that applies equally to each and every one of the uncounted myriads who have lived and passed beyond.

The doctrine of salvation for the dead came as a revelation to the earth. It had to be made known anew; for while it had been known of old, it, like many other of the saving doctrines of the Gospel, had been lost sight of and forgotten. The labor in behalf of the dead was cited by Paul, an apostle of old, as an argument and evidence of the resurrection; said he: "Else what shall they do which are baptized for the dead, if the dead rise not at all? Why are they then baptized for the dead?" [1 Cor. 15:29] Throughout the centuries of the deep night of the apostasy, not a single ordinance was performed in behalf of the dead. Yet, the ranks of the dead at that time were increasing by uncounted thousands. We are greatly behind in the work, but the Lord has provided a means by which it shall be done, and by which it is the privilege of those who come in at the door themselves to hold that door open to admit others, others who were once among the living and are now among the dead.

To me there is special significance in our assembling upon this block, by the great temple that is consecrated mostly to the work for the dead. For be it known that this great labor of temple-building, for which the Latter-day Saints are so well known and so widely famed, is very largely, though not entirely, a work in behalf of the dead. They are not giving of their substance to erect these great buildings for themselves, for aggrandizement, nor for the beautification of earth. The templebuilding spirit manifested among the Latter-day Saints is the spirit of absolute unselfishness; it is the spirit of Elijah, the spirit by which the feelings of the children are turned toward the fathers, and the feelings of the fathers are directed toward the children; for no man stands upon this earth alone. We talk of independence. No man is independent. We are all interdependent; and we shall only rise as we carry others with us, and as we are assisted by others. My own mind is led to that great subject, and I have thought of it much as I have sat through the exercises of the morning, because of the fact that it was at the glorious Easter time the work for the dead was inaugurated; it was at this season the great missionary labor in the spirit world was begun, and the doors were there opened and a means of deliverance preached unto those who had been sitting in darkness, some of them even from the days of Noah.

I feel particularly gratified in this opportunity of bearing to you a humble testimony of the divinity of this work, of the sacredness of the labor for which the Church stands. As we heard yesterday, testimony is ofttimes more effective than argument, ofttimes more potent than reasons, as man counts reasons, and lists them and collates them, and analyzes them; for, after, [sic] all he can only base the correctness of his results upon the assurance that his processes are free from error. Whereas, one who is able to stand forth and say "I know," testifies of himself, because of the knowledge that is within him; and that knowledge is given him of God. This people believe in testimonymaking, in testimony bearing, in testimony-speaking; and while they do not believe that the testimony of one man shall of itself convict or condemn another, they do believe that a man's humble, sincere testimony is entitled to respectful consideration. The Latter-day Saints tell you that they know that the Gospel is true, for that knowledge has been given unto them; and when a man is able to say, as said the chief of the apostles of old of the Christ, "Thou art the Christ, the Son of the living God," to him does the answer apply, "Flesh and blood hath not revealed this unto thee, but the Father who is in heaven." And, let that testimony come in what way it will, it has a saving power for man; this is the kind of testimony that abides and abounds in the heart of this people, and they manifest it in their lives. Jesus came with His testimony, and the people were astounded at His doctrines, not because He brought them something that was essentially new in all particulars; for He used their scriptures; He brought into service their proverbs, and referred to the things which they well knew; but He gave to all of this a new application and a new meaning; and they said: "He speaks as one having authority, and not as the scribes." His discourse was no labored compilation of passages. He did not base His doctrines upon what the prophets who had gone ahead of Him had said, though He referred approvingly to many of their inspired utterances; but He spoke from the knowledge He had within Him, and He spoke by reason of the authority that He held; and thus was He distinguished among the teachers of the day, and therefore did He compel attention.

Such, in a measure is the testimony of the Latter-day Saint Elder. He goes forth in humility. He may, perhaps, not be eloquent. He may be far from learned, as the world reckons learning; yet he is not ignorant, when he is able to stand forth and say, "I know that this Gospel is true." We look upon the scriptures of the past with reverence. We believe that they are necessary to the building up of the church in this day; but we do not depend upon them for our authority, nor for the interpretation we place upon the messages from God.

We do not believe in living wholly in the past. We believe in an up-to-date doctrine, in an up-to-date church, an up-todate religion, a religion that is ever enriched by new revelation, a church that is in direct communication with headquarters, a church that is receiving through revelation the word of God today, pertaining to the affairs of today. When the proclamation was first made, that direct revelation from God was a feature of modern times, there was consternation in the ranks of the churches of the day; for be it known that when this church was established in the nineteenth century, there was not on earth a church sacred to the name of Christ. There were churches in great variety, churches that bore the names of men, organizations as well as buildings established and erected to the name of Peter, and Paul, and Moses, and Elias, churches named after peculiarities of their worship, Presbyterian, Congregational, Episcopalian; churches named after men who had devoted themselves to their establishment—there were the Lutheran church, the Wesleyan church and the Calvinist church. But when it was proclaimed that there was now upon the earth a church sacred to the name of Christ there was fear and trembling manifest among the professors of religion. Consternation entered their souls when that banner was raised; and yet, what other name is appropriate? The profession of this church is set forth in its name. It is not the church of Joseph Smith, nor of Brigham Young, nor of Joseph F. Smith, nor of any other man or combination of men. It is not the Mormon church, though we do not object to that term which was first applied in derision, except for the possible error that may accompany its use; for it is not the church of Mormon! it is the Church of Jesus Christ. If the name, the Church of Jesus Christ, has been assumed authoritatively, it is of itself ample explanation of the phenomenal rise and development of this church; and if it has been assumed without authority, it is the most glaring instance of blasphemy the world has known. No greater challenge can be given to the world than the name borne by this church. I testify to you that this is the Church of Jesus Christ, that the power of the Christ is in it, the very Christ that lived as a man, that died as a God, the one who was ressurrected, who came forth from the tomb with the very body that had been pierced and laid there; that He has again spoken in this day and age of the world, even as had been declared He would speak, that He has again established His saving Gospel among men, and has opened the way by which men may attain salvation and eternal life in His presence and in that of the Father, the only way under heaven by which salvation and exaltation may be attained, the only name under heaven by which man may be saved.

Strange, is it not, that some have said, in their ignorance, that this Mormon Church is not a Christian church. Not Christian when it bears by authority the name of Christ, who is the author of all that is best in Christianity? Not Christian—when its great mission is the preparing of the earth for the coming of its King, that same Lord, Jesus Christ? Not Christian—when it is setting before the world an example of self-sacrifice never before known, and all in the interest of Christ and His work? The Church of Jesus Christ of Latter-day Saints is preaching the same doctrine that was preached in the church of old, and is proclaiming the same great message, Repent, repent; for the kingdom of heaven is at hand. We say that Christ will return to the earth, and literally reign here in Person, that it is His right to reign; and that the church is preparing for His coming. The testimonies to which we have listened, the testimonies to which we do listen in smaller gatherings than this, in the various stakes and wards in the Church, all have the same sound, the same truth and divinity of the Gospel of Jesus Christ and the divinity of the work of the man who was the instrument.[sic] in the hands of God, in establishing this Church on the earth in the dispensation of the fullness of times; for this is that dispensation, to which the prophets of old have been looking, for which they have yearned, toward which their desires have gone forth. It is the dispensation of fullness, it marks the ushering in of the great finale of this drama of the Lord. Right thankful should we be that we are privileged to have a name and standing in the Church in this day and to take part in this great work. I am thankful for that name and for that standing, and for the privilege of testifying to you today, as the last and the least of those who have been called to stand before the world at the present time as the special witnesses of the Lord Jesus Christ, who verily lives and who verily shall come as hath been predicted, to take His place upon the earth, amongst His people. May His spirit ever guide us, through all the scenes of life, to make us worthy of our name, worthy of our promised destiny, I ask, in His name, Amen.

{16}

"The Need for Modern Revelation,"
An Address Delivered on 6 October 1912

(from *Eighty-third Semi-Annual Conference
of the Church of Jesus Christ of Latter-day Saints*
[Salt Lake City: Published by the Deseret News, 1912],
pp. 125-29)

In common with many thousands present, I too have rejoiced in the words to which we have listened during this conference, and more than in the words have I found joy in the spirit that has been manifest in the utterances of the speakers and in the receptive condition of the hearers. We cannot be oblivious to the fact that there has been manifest amongst this vast assembly this afternoon and in the assemblies that have marked the preceding sessions of this conference, a spirit of unanimity and harmony that testifies to the presence of the Spirit of God. I have never had any fear that discord would be preferred by the Latter-day Saints to harmony, and I know that the people are standing as whole true to the faith, true to their covenants, true to their duty and obligations as Latter-day Saints,—that is to say, holy ones of the latter days. I am glad to have been present, to have heard the latest word, to be informed as to the most recent news in this great kingdom of the Lord, for it is characteristic of the spirit of this work and of this people that we are not content with the news of the past but are ever listening for the latest and newest news if you please.

Doubtless you were impressed as was I by the manner in which the article of faith relating to continuous revelation was read to you or quoted to you this morning. That is one of the fundamentals, one of the essential features of the Church of Christ, that we believe not only in what God has revealed, but in that which He does now reveal; and moreover we are living in confident assurance that He will yet reveal many great and important things pertaining to the kingdom of God. These bound volumes of scripture are necessary and essential to us,—the Bible, the Book of Mormon, and more modern records,—absolutely essential for our instruction and guidance, but we want in addition something later and more nearly adapted to the times. This book known as the Holy Bible professedly ends as a historical record about one hundred years after the birth of Christ, and there be some who say that God hath not spoken since that time, that for nearly nineteen hundred years He has never uttered a word by way of direct instruction unto His people. I cannot believe it; I cannot accept any such creed, nor have I room in my heart for any such belief, for in every other field of human thought we are ever on the alert for the new.

Not content with bound books we look eagerly for the issues of monthly magazines, weekly journals, and moreover we would not know how to get along without our daily papers, each one telling in part what God has wrought since the last issue left the press: Nor are we content with such, for here day after day I see great crowds about the bulletin boards too eager to rest contented until the next issue, too eager to know what has been done—aye, what God hath done in forwarding His plans and purposes among men during the last few hours. And in spite of that, as the prevailing spirit of the times, I say there be some who say that God hath not spoken concerning the affairs of the kingdom since about one hundred years after the birth of His Son. He has spoken much in the realm of science and discovery; He has made known many great truths through His servants, the inventors, but He has not spoken concerning the way in which His people should walk to find their way back into His presence. I say again, it is unfitting, it is unsuited, such a belief as that, to the spirit of the times, to the modern day in which we live, and I rejoice in belonging to a church that is in a measure up to date, and down to date, that gives me news of the present and that gives me the Word of God concerning the affairs of my life and the duties that lie immediately before me.

I rejoice in the progressivism of this Church and more particularly in the fact that its progressivism is of the right kind. It is not that so-called progressivism that seeks to belittle or destroy the achievements of the past; it is not a progressivism that seeks to tear down, that says our fathers were wrong and we know more than they did; that they laid a foundation which in its way was good but not sufficient for us to build upon. We have no such spirit of progressivism as that, for that is destruction. The spirit of advancement and progressivism in the Church of Christ is that which marks the progression from the seed to the blade and from the blade to the ripened ear. It is a constructive progressivism; the past is added to, and every new revelation doth but make the revelations of the past plainer and reveal their sanctity and their sacred origin the better. I ask you, have you yet discovered in this volume of modern scripture, the Doctrine and Covenants, one utterance that is in any manner opposed to the spirit of the scriptures of the past? It will be time to raise objection to modern revelation when we find that such revelation is in opposition to the spirit of the Word of God of past times; but when the modern utterances are plainly but later works of the same author, why need we complain?

I rejoice, too, in the measure of liberty which is assured us as members of this Church and I have been greatly edified and pleased in listening to what has been said respecting liberty and freedom. I believe that we should give thanks unto God for our privileges of citizenship in this great nation, for mark you, this is a nation that shall stand for liberty, for it has been so predicted. It has been prophesied and the prophecy has been proclaimed through the modern prophet, Joseph Smith, that centuries ago—aye, dating back five hundred years or more before the meridian of time,—it was declared that this land should in the latter days be a land of liberty and no king should rule here. I take it that means no king by name or by pretension; no one shall exercise imperial powers among the citizens of this great nation, until Christ, the King, shall come to rule and reign. But as I listened to my brethren expressing their joy and gratitude at this full measure of liberty which we seem to enjoy, I asked myself if we are always sure that we do not accept the imitation for the real. You know this is a day of imitations, a day of adulteration and counterfeits, a day when shoddy is palmed off for all-wool cloth, and gilded brass passes too often current for genuine gold; aye, a day when glass paste does duty as diamonds of the first water. Of all the imitators, of all the counterfeiters, Satan is the chief, for he has had the greatest experience and the longest training and he is a skillful salesman; he not only knows how to manufacture his spurious goods, but how to put them upon the market. And it is wonderfully attractive—the way in which he does up those little packages in bright-colored paper, tied with tinsel string to attract; and we are very apt to pay the price asked before we open the package. And do you know of all the counterfeits and of all the imitations that the devil has put forth on sale, I know of none that is more dangerous than his spurious brands of liberty and freedom, such as are being offered on every hand. Some of them are so rank as to be a stench in the nostrils of a normal man.

How shall we distinguish between the genuine and the imitation, you may ask? Is it necessary that we get expert advice and call in a professional chemist to make the analysis? Oh, there are simple tests by which you can determine. You can always tell after consumption whether it was the genuine or not, for the imitation leaves a wretchedly bad taste in the mouth, but that test may not be as serviceable as one that may be applied before taking. Well, you will find that true liberty always works both ways, it never works one way alone, but is of universal application. For example, I hear some men say that they claim the right to speak out and say just what they like. They make that claim that they have the right to speak out and say just what they like to say. I grant you that is true if you will let it apply the other way as well. I have the right to be safeguarded against utterances which are offensive to hear. If a man says that he under the guise of his rights as a free citizen may swear and use vile and obscene language, and may profane the name of God, I say to you that is not liberty, that is a license that is illegal. I hear some men say that they are free citizens and they are not going to be told what to do. I grant them that right, but by the same token I claim the right to seek advice if I want it and to go to whomsoever I choose for the advice and counsel which I desire. Now the men who say that they don't want to be told. [sic] usually find fault with their brothers who are willing to be told, usually criticise them because they are willing to be advised and guided. I claim the right to give advice to my brother if I do it in a manner to cause him no offense. I claim the right, if I so choose, to publish my views in magazine or newspaper or book if I can make arrangements with the publishers. I have that perfect right as long as I say nothing in my publication inimical to the rights of men nor contrary to law and order, and you have the right to read my writings or not just as you choose. I cannot force them upon you, but if there be some who do choose to read them and who are willing to be influenced and guided by them, what business is that of others who refuse so to do? I believe that we are too apt to apply these so-called rules of liberty and of freedom in a one-sided way.

There are men who say that they have the right to smoke tobacco if they want to, and in this State if they be of age they have that right legally and I know they exercise it (laughter), but I long to see the day when I shall have some rights too in that matter, and when I shall not be forced to breathe the foul emanations that come from smokers' mouths. I hope to see the day when women will no longer be offended as they board or leave street cars or as they pass along the streets, by having clouds of tobacco smoke blown into their faces. I believe we shall improve in the matter of liberty and come to see that there are rights that others have as well as rights that we claim for ourselves. The spirit of the Gospel safeguards the right of no man to the injury of another, but provides for the liberties of all; and I hope that I will never become so lifted up in egotism that I shall feel that I am the people and that I know it all. I hope that I shall ever be led to seek for those to whom I feel I can look with confidence for advice, for counsel, for guidance, and if I choose to follow the counsel and advice of those in whom I have respect, I claim that I have the right so to do as a citizen and a free man.

I trust that the spirit of charity will manifest itself in our souls and that we will be willing to allow unto others those privileges and rights that we ask for ourselves; that we may in very truth be worthy of the measure of liberty which belongs to the Church of Jesus Christ, for if it be what it professes to be, the repository of truth, there must be in it the elements of true liberty and not that false freedom of the spurious kind which is being put forth in an unceasing stream from the devil's factories. We have to scrutinize very carefully the goods that are offered in the markets today lest we be deceived. I rejoice in the fact that this people stand for the Constitution of the nation and I call to mind that the declaration of the people to that effect was made in a very early day and was reiterated at a very critical time. It was just when the Overland Telegraph wire from the east was approaching the end of the wire that was coming from the west, for you know it was within the boundaries of this state that those two ends were joined and nerve of steel that connected the east with the west was made complete. It was just at that time that the great unpleasantness was at its height between the North and the South, when brother was rising against brother, and it was rumored that Utah has seceded from the Union, or, as represented by some, Utah was to become a separate and independent government, the seat of a separate power, and that in addition to a North and a South, which had already been declared, there was to be a West also. You know the first message that was sent through the metallic nerve, went from the West to Washington, from Brigham Young to the President of the United States and this was the purport of the message, "Utah has not seceded but is firm for the Constitution and the laws of our country." That declaration has never been changed; it is as true in its application today as it was when it was flashed as the initial message across the overland telegraph wire. We stand for the Constitution and do not believe in any false notions of advancement and enlightenment and progressivism such as seeks to undermine that foundation of our liberties, for as a document we know that it was inspired and we believe that the men who framed it were raised up, as truly as was ever a prophet raised up in Israel in ancient or modern times, to frame that instrument and thereby provide for the fulfilment of prophetic utterances regarding the freedom and the liberty that should prevail in this choice land. I am pleased to add my testimony to the many to which you have listened. The testimony which I bear to you is one of knowledge and assurance beyond doubt, that God has spoken in this, the dispensation of the fulness of times, and does speak today as of old through His servants, the prophets; that in very truth Christ the Redeemer of mankind lives and that His coming is near at hand. The cry is given today as in the wilderness of old, "The kingdom of heaven is at hand, therefore repent." May the spirit of earnestness, devotion, integrity, freedom, liberty ever prevail among the Latter-day Saints, and throughout the length and breadth of the land occupied by this great nation, the nation of promise. I ask in the name of Jesus Christ. Amen.

{17}

"Our Bodies, Gifts from God,"
An Address Delivered on 6 October 1913

(from *Eighty-fourth Semi-Annual Conference*
of the Church of Jesus Christ of Latter-day Saints
[Salt Lake City: Published by the Deseret News, 1913],
pp. 116-21)

I am very grateful for the opportunity of adding my testimony to the many strong testimonies to which we have listened during this conference. As I listened to the opening address, I heard echoing through the alcoves of my mind, what I have since heard in song and quotation: "We thank Thee, O God for a Prophet;" and many times during the course of subsequent addresses I have said in my heart, "I thank Thee, O God, for prophets in Israel, who are not afraid to speak out and tell the people the needs of the hour, and preach unto them the doctrines of the day, and call attention to the things of present moment and importance." I was heartily in accord with the instruction given in that first address as indeed I have been with all the instructions given, but I have in mind particularly that relating to the neglect which we oft-times manifest in regard to spiritual things. We have been warned against giving too much attention to the things of this world, to the neglect of the things that are of greater worth. On the other hand, we have heard much concerning practical duties, practical affairs, temporal religion if you please; and we have been, by implication, warned against devoting ourselves exclusively to that other worldliness which is quite as dangerous as extereme wor[ldl]iness.

We have been told, as many of us know, and knew before, that this life is a necessary part in the course of progression designed by our Father. We have been taught, again, to look upon these bodies of ours as gifts from God. We Latter-day Saints do not regard the body as something to be condemned, something to be abhorred, and something to be subdued in the sense in which that expression is oft-times heard in the world. We regard as the sign of our royal birthright, that we have bodies upon the earth. We recognize the fact that those who kept not their first estate, in the primeval existence, were denied that inestimable blessing, the taking of mortal bodies. We believe that these bodies are to be well cared for, that they are to be looked upon as something belonging to the Lord, and that each may be made, in very truth, the temple of the Holy Ghost, the place into which the Spirit of God shall enter and where He shall delight to dwell, if He shall find there cleanliness and order and purity and uprightness of thought and conduct.

It is peculiar to the theology of the Latter-day Saints that we regard the body as an essential part of the soul. Read your dictionaries, the lexicons, the encyclopedias, and you will find that nowhere, outside of the Church of Jesus Christ, is the solemn and eternal truth taught that the soul of man is.[sic] the body and the spirit combined. It is quite the rule to regard the soul as that incorporeal part of men, that immortal part which existed before the body was framed and which shall continue to exist after that body has gone to decay; nevertheless, that is not the soul; that is only a part of the soul; that is the spirit-man, the form in which every individual of us, and every individual human being, existed before called to take tabernacle in the flesh. It has been declared in the solemn word of revelation, that the spirit and the body constitute the soul of man; (D&C 88:15) and, therefore, we should look upon this body as something that shall endure in the resurrected state, beyond the grave, something to be kept pure and holy. Be not afraid of soiling its hands; be not afraid of scars that may come to it if won in earnest effort. [sic] or in honest fight, but beware of scars that disfigure, that have come to you in places where you ought not have gone, that have befallen you in unworthy undertakings; beware of the wounds of battles in which you have been fighting on the wrong side.

I read that when our first parents were placed in the place provided for them, that at their creation, at the creation of the first man, his body was prepared; then God, the God of life, breathed into him the breath of life, and then and not before did man become a living soul. It was the advancement from the spirit state to the soul state that marked the great gift of God unto man, namely, life here upon the earth, an existence that shall prepare us for the life that lies beyond the grave. The resurrection of the body, the resurrection from the dead, is the redemption of the soul; and as Christ was the first to break the bonds of death and to take up His body, the body that had been slain, from which the spirit had temporarily departed, as by Him and through Him came the resurrection, by Him and through Him came the redemption of the soul, and hence He won for Himself the title that belongs to none other, on earth or in heaven, the Redeemer of mankind.

We have heard much in regard to the dut[i]es we owe to these bodies in keeping them from the things that are hurtful, the things that are degrading, the things that poison the tissues, the things that break down the very organism that God has created. Time has not permitted those who have spoken before me to dwell at length, any more than it permits me to dwell at length on that important revelation of God unto man, of God unto Israel in these the last days, by which man may be wise—the Word of Wisdom. This, like other revelations that have come in the present dispensation, is not wholly new. It is as old as the human race. The principle of the Word of Wisdom was revealed unto Adam. All the essentials of the Word of Wisdom were made known unto him in his immortal state, before he had taken into his body those things that made of it a thing of earth. He was warned against that very practice. He was not told to treat his body as something to be tortured. He was not told to look upon it as the fakirs of India have come to look upon it, or profess to look upon it, as a thing to be utterly contemned [sic], but he was told that he must not take into that body certain things which were there at hand. He was warned that, if he did, his body would lose the power which it then held of living for ever, and that he would become subject to death. It was pointed out to him, as it has been pointed out to you, that there are many good fruits to be plucked, to be eaten, to be enjoyed. We believe in enjoying good food. We think that these good things are given us of God. We believe in getting all the enjoyment out of eating that we can; and, therefore, we should avoid gluttony, and we should avoid extremes in all our habits of eating; and as was told unto Adam, so is it told unto us, "Touch not these things; for in the day that thou doest it thy life shall be shortened and thou shalt die." [Moses 4:9]

Here, let me say, that therein consisted the fall—the eating of things unfit, the taking into the body of the things that made of that body a thing of earth; and I take this occasion to raise my voice against the false interpretation of scripture, which in some instances has been adopted by certain people, and is current in their minds, and is referred to in a hushed and half-secret way, that the fall of man consisted in some offense against the laws of chastity and of virtue. Such a doctrine is an abomination. What right have we to turn the scriptures from their proper sense and meaning? What right have we to declare that God meant not what He said? The fall was a natural process, resulting through the incorporation into the bodies of our first parents of the things that came from food unfit, through the violation of the command of God regarding what they should eat. Don't go around whispering that the fall consisted in the mother of the race losing her chastity and her virtue. It is not true; the human race is not born of fornication. These bodies that are given unto us are given in the way that God has provided. Let it not be said that the patriarch of the race, who stood with the gods before he came here upon the earth, and his equally royal consort, were guilty of any such foul offense. The adoption of that belief has led many to excuse departures from the path of chastity and the path of virtue, by saying that it is the sin of the race, it is as old as Adam. It was not introduced by Adam. It was not committed by Eve. It was the introduction of the devil and came in order that he might sow the seeds of early death in the bodies of men and women, that the race should degenerate as it has degenerated whenever the laws of virtue and of chastity have been transgressed.

Our first parents were pure and noble, and when we pass behind the veil we shall perhaps learn something of their high estate, more than we know now. But be it known that they were pure; they were noble. It is true that they disobeyed the law of God, in eating things they were told not to eat; but who amongst you can rise up and condemn? I listened not long ago to a lesson conducted as a model lesson, in a Sunday School class; it had to deal with the fall of man. The one who was appointed to pass criticism thereon, expressed his hearty approval of the lesson as it had been rendered, and particularly complimented the teacher on having been able to conduct a lesson "on such a delicate subject as that, with a mixed class of young boys and young girls and not offend!" What is there delicate about the fall of man? The sexual element does not enter into the subject. The fall consisted in disobedience of the commands as to what things were fit for the body, and we have been falling in the same way ever since; and you have been warned about it by authoritative voices here in the several sessions of this conference. If you would live to the full measure of your days, as God intended you to, then live according to the command of God in all these things. Ye may eat of the fruits of all these good trees; you may partake to the full, within the limits of wisdom and propriety, but of that tree of the knowledge of terrible evil you ought not to partake. Oh, if you do, you will get experience that you otherwise would not get; you will know more about evil, and by contrast can perhaps estimate, in a different way, the good; but, nevertheless, you will find that you have purchased that knowledge at a very great price. We are to be judged by what we know, as much and as well as by what we do not know. For, do you remember, after they, our first parents, had undertaken to set up their own judgment above the judgment of the God who made them and who prepared the place for their abode, and who gave them commandment, they had knowledge that they did not possess before, and when next they were called by the voice of God, they hid themselves; for they had awakened to the fact that there was something vile about them, something unseemingly, something unclean, and they hid themselves; and mark you the words with which their guilt was brought home. When Adam declared that he had heard the voice of God calling him, and he had hidden himself because he had become aware of the fact that he was naked, the question was: "Who told thee that thou wast naked?" Where did Adam and Eve get that knowledge? Not by keeping the commandments of God, but by violation thereof. So I sometimes say when I find young men and young women showing by unguarded words or actions, that they know things they ought not to know, who told you that? Where have you been? What have you been doing? The time has not come for you to learn those things yet; and you never would have learned them at this stage of your advancement, and in this way, if you had not transgressed the laws of God.

What has been said concerning our duties to our bodies in this life and the strict attention we should give to spiritual things, tells us of the life that is to come and of the relation between this life and that. We hear much nowadays as to the speculative ideas of men concerning the condition beyond the grave; but the admission that there is an individual existence beyond the grave, is a declaration that there must have been an individual, intelligent creation before we came here in the flesh. Life beyond the grave postulates a pre-existent state to which reference was made yesterday. While the world admits the pre-existence of Christ and points to Him as one who before mortal birth shared with His Father in the honors of the godhead and in the powers of the Creator, they deny to the souls that are now upon the earth, and those that had lived as mortals, a pre-existent condition. I want to read to you one scripture bearing upon that subject and I read to you from the Book of Abraham, a scripture with which some of our people are better acquainted today than they were a year ago, because of the futile attempts that have been made to discredit it. By the failures that have resulted in these attempts, the strength of the faith of our people has been increased. The great patriarch says: "Now, the Lord had shown unto me, Abraham, the intelligences that were organized before the world was, and among all these there were many of the noble and great ones; and God saw these souls that they were good, and He stood in the midst of them and He said, 'These I will make my rulers:' for He stood among those that were spirits, and He saw that they were good, and He said unto me, Abraham 'Thou are one of them: thou wast chosen before thou wast born.'"[Abr. 3:22-23] Read the rest of that scripture for yourselves.

I am happy to see that the saving principles proclaimed by the prophets of this dispensation are spreading through the world, in spite of all attempts to the contrary. If the morning papers have correctly reported a lecture delivered in this city, last night, there is in our midst a scholar from London who has proclaimed not only that the scriptures prove that there is and must of necessity be an intelligent individual existence beyond the grave, but that in that state there will be opportunity for repentance and for progression. Now, that is a "Mormon" doctrine which never had been broached in the modern religious world until the voice of the Prophet Joseph Smith was heard. Sectarian ministers now tell us that no longer are the scriptures to be twisted; that by the figure which says, "Where the tree falleth there shall it be," we are not longer to understand that a man who dies can never progress. Learned divines and theologians are lifting their voices today in declaration of the fact that God has provided a means by which His sons and daughters may progress and advance through the eternities that are to come. I read further that it was declared: That there is to be a resurrection of the just as distinct from the resurrection of the unjust. Another doctrine which in the way now presented was at one time peculiar to the Church of Jesus Christ of Latter-day Saints. But, because there is hope of repentance beyond the veil, procrastinate not the day of your repentance; for, as the Prophet Alma has pointed out, you may find that the gift of repentance will be withheld from you there for a long, long time on account of your unworthiness. For repentance is a gift from God, and when man forfeits it he loses the power to repent: he can't turn away from his sins with a contrite heart and with a desire to forsake them, once and forever. O, Latter-day

Saints, ye men and women of Israel, listen unto the voices of those who speak to you under the inspiration of the power of God, and heed them; for by hearing we are condemned, if we follow not in the path that is pointed out to us as the path of our duty.

You have heard but little in the way of new doctrine in this conference, perchance,—all the more reason you should be diligent in not forgetting again, as we have forgotten from time to time the things that are most needed. We make the excuse—that is one of our weaknesses, to make excuses—we make the excuse that our memories are at fault. Our memories are all right; altogether too good to suit some of us. We would like to forget things that we cannot. Memory is the library of the mind, in which we find stored away the valuable as well as the worthless things that have come to us. Recollection is the librarian, and he is very often sluggish and sleepy, often neglectful of his duty; he doesn't know where to put his hand on the book or the document we need, just when we need it. We have had our recollections aroused in this conference, and I pray that we may ever remember the things that are most needed, the things of greatest worth; and that you and I and all of us may progress with the work of God, for it shall progress no matter what man shall do or how he may attempt to hinder its advancement. May the blessings of Israel's God be with Israel in the name of Jesus, Amen.

{18}

"A Greeting to the Missionaries"

(from the *Improvement Era* 17 [December 1913]: 172-74)

Beloved Brethren: One of the distinguishing features of the Church of Jesus Christ of Latter-day Saints is its missionary system. In proportion to numbers, no other church or sect in the world today approaches ours in the extent and scope of its missionary service, nor in the sense of importance with which that labor is regarded by the members in general.

To you who have left home and dear ones; to you who have relinquished, for a period, your material affairs; to you who have promptly and willingly responded to the call to go forth into the world as duly accredited preachers and teachers of the Gospel of Christ, without hope of pecuniary or other reward in things of earth—I write this brief greeting as one who loves you for the sacrifice you have made, for the zeal and integrity you exhibit, and for the splendid results accruing through your unselfish devotion. I write as one called and ordained to lifeservice in the same ministry in which you labor.

One of the many good gifts with which our Father requites the labors of his faithful children is the blessed boon of happiness. I know of none more truly happy than the active missionary, upon whom rests in full measure the spirit of his Divine commission. To him, no duty, no requirement, no phase of his labor is irksome or unwelcome. I commend to you for study and practice a lesson which I doubt not you have already learned in part through demonstration and test in the laboratory of experience, but which I would have you master thoroughly—the lesson that tells of the vital distinction between pleasure and *happiness*.

The present is an age of pleasure-seeking, and men are losing their sanity in the mad rush for sensations that do but excite and disappoint. In this day of counterfeits, adulterations, and base imitations, the devil is busier than he has ever been in the course of human history, in the manufacture of pleasures, both old and new; and these he offers for sale in most attractive fashion, falsely labeled, *"Happiness."* In this soul-destroying craft he is without a peer; he has had centuries of experience and practice, and by his skill he controls the market. He has learned the tricks of the trade, and knows well how to catch the eye and arouse the desire of his customers. He puts up the stuff in bright-colored packages, tied with tinsel string and tassel; and crowds flock to his bargain counters, hustling and crushing one another in their frenzy to buy.

Follow one of the purchasers as he goes off gloatingly with his gaudy packet, and watch him as he opens it. What finds he inside the gilded wrapping? He had expected fragrant happiness, but uncovers only an inferior brand of pleasure, the stench of which is nauseating.

Happiness includes all that is really desirable and of true worth in pleasure, and much beside. Happiness is genuine gold, pleasure but gilded brass, which corrodes in the hand, and is soon converted into poisonous verdigris. Happiness is as the genuine diamond, which, rough or polished, shines with its own inimitable luster; pleasure is as the paste imitation that glows only when artificially embellished. Happiness is as the ruby, red as the heart's blood, hard and enduring; pleasure, as stained glass, soft, brittle, and of but transitory beauty.

Happiness is true food, wholesome, nutritious and sweet; it builds up the body and generates energy for action, physical, mental and spiritual; pleasure is but a deceiving stimulant which, like spirituous drink, makes one think he is strong when in reality enfeebled; makes him fancy he is well when in fact stricken with deadly malady.

Happiness leaves no bad after-taste, it is followed by no depressing reaction; it calls for no repentance, brings no regret, entails no remorse; pleasure too often makes necessary repentance, contrition, and suffering; and if indulged to the extreme, it brings degradation and destruction.

True happiness is lived over and over again in memory, always with a renewal of the original good; a moment of unholy pleasure may leave a barbed sting, which, like a thorn in the flesh, is an ever-present source of anguish.

Happiness is not akin with levity, nor is it one with lightminded mirth. It springs from the deeper fountains of the soul, and is not infrequently accompanied by tears. Have you never been so happy that you have had to weep? I have.

Recently, I witnessed an instance of tearful happiness, and I shall not soon forget the experience. I had been engaged with my brethren in setting apart missionaries, who were about to leave for their several fields of labor. We had laid our hands upon their heads, one by one, and had invoked Divine blessing upon them and their work. You know the solemn procedure, for each of you has been so blessed and set apart. After the missionary assembly had closed—there in the Annex to the House of the Lord—my attention was attracted to a woman, one who had long passed the noon-tide of her life, standing with her arms about the neck of her manly son; her head rested upon his shoulder, and she was sobbing with strong emotion. He stood tenderly supporting her with his strong right arm, while his tears fell upon her whitening hair. I ventured to approach; and she, becoming aware of my presence, looked into my face through the mist of tears, and smilingly said, "He is my boy, you see; my only son; and he is going far away, across the great ocean." I asked, "Don't you want him to go?" "Want him to go?" she repeated, with beaming countenance; "oh, yes! yes! I am so thankful to have a son worthy to go out into the world as a missionary of the gospel, that I can't help crying, you know." Then, after a pause which to me was profoundly affecting, she added, "His father filled an honorable mission, and has since died; now our son goes to continue his father's good work, thank God!" And the thought of it all filled that widowed heart with such over-powering happiness that she could but weep and sob.

And now, let me tell you of another scene which I witnessed soon after the incident just described. Again I saw a loving mother with her arms about the neck of her son. She, too, was shaken with sobs, and the flood-gates of his tears were open. To my look of inquiry she replied with an explanation: "He is my son, and has just returned from his mission after nearly three years' absence. Oh, I am so happy, I just have to cry." The glad father, who stood by, wept in unison with his wife and son. The young man soon suppressed his emotion and answered my questions with proud humility and soulful gratitude in his face. His record in the mission field was good; his release was an honorable one. And as I looked upon the reunited family, I said in my heart this is happiness, indeed; while, through the inner chambers of my soul, there echoed a holy refrain, "Well done, good and faithful servant; happiness is thy reward."

Beloved brethren, may happiness be your portion, and success in the saving of souls your eternal glory.

{19}

"The Honor and Dignity of Priesthood"

(from the *Improvement Era* 17 [March 1914]: 407-11)

Many able investigators have expressed surprise and admiration over the plan of organization on which the Church of Jesus Christ of Latter-day Saints is founded. A critical observer who had devoted time and skill to the study of The Church, viewing it solely as a human institution, is credited with this expressive summary of conclusions: "The 'Mormon' Church is a magnificent organization splendidly officered."

Without caste distinction as between clergyman and layman, with no order of salaried ministers or professional preachers, The Church provides service for every member who is able and willing to labor in the ministry. The bestowal of the Priesthood is a blessing reserved for no privileged few; every worthy man in The Church may confidently aspire to some measure of this sacred investiture. Ordination to any office in the holy order of authority and power imposes responsibility, separately and individually, upon each recipient. While every holder of this Divinely-appointed commission is an officer in The Church, there are numerous official positions of specific character to which worthy members are called and appointed. Even in the several quorums, each comprising members who have been ordained to the same office in the Priesthood, there are of necessity positions of presidency and administrative service.

Priesthood is the authority delegated to man to minister in the name of Deity. It is a power such as no one can assume on his own initiative; it is an endowment from the powers of heaven; "and no man taketh this honor unto himself, but he that is called of God, as was Aaron" (Heb. 5:4).

Men may form associations for and among themselves; they may create institutions and establish authority to administer the affairs thereof; men may set up governments, as municipalities, states, and nations, and may provide for the enactment of laws and ordinances by which members of the organization are to be governed. The official acts of legally constituted authorities within all such jurisdictions are binding to the extent and for the purpose that the law may provide. Authority in all properly established institutions of men should be duly recognized and obeyed; the men in whom that authority is vested should be respected, if not for their personal merits or worthiness at least because of the office they hold. If such recognition be due to authority originated and established by man, what shall be the measure of respect rightfully attaching to the Holy Priesthood, which is the embodiment of an authority beyond all human power to create or to secure?

Concerning the Twelve who ministered with Him, our Lord specifically declared that He had chosen them; their exalted ordination was not of their own causing nor seeking. (See John 15:16, compare 6:70.) Today The Church proclaims that "a man must be called of God, by prophecy, and by the laying on of hands, by those who are in authority, to preach the Gospel, and administer in the ordinances thereof."

Appointment to office in The Church entails the ordination or setting-apart of the person so chosen; and the responsibility of faithful service is an individual requirement which he cannot evade and must not ignore. Those through whom the call came to him, those by whom he was designated and perhaps ordained, those who preside over him because of their office of broader scope and higher rank, they are as surely held answerable for their acts as is he for his; and of every one shall be demanded a strict and personal accounting for his stewardship, a report in full of service or of neglect, of use or abuse in the administration of the trust to him committed. The sense of responsibility belonging to office may be obscured in part by the honor and distinction inseparably associated therewith. Yet this should not be. The spirit of every calling in the Lord's work is that of ready service; the officer is the servant of those for whom he ministers. There are no positions of honor without service, no empty titles, no *brevet* rank, in the Church of Christ. Honorary positions, sinecures, influence dissociated from responsibility, titles that are but names, these shadows without substance are sometimes tolerated or fostered as features of human institutions; but the Divine plan of organization and government is not so belittled.

Titles expressive of rank or attainment among men are to be respected as their significance requires. Being of man's creation, they may be used as recognized propriety established by custom and as good taste may allow. There is no offense against sanctity, nor any serious impropriety, in addressing an officer of army or navy, a judge, a senator, a doctor, or a professor by his title, even in ordinary converse; though the customs of good etiquette suggest the careful and sparing use of distinguished titles. In formal and official procedure titles expressive of rank or achievement are in place.

In the use of titles pertaining to the Holy Priesthood the obligation of care is vastly greater. Remember that the higher Priesthood is described as being "after the order of the Son of God," but is designated by the name of a man—Melchizedek,—out of respect or reverence to the name of the Supreme Being, to avoid the too frequent repetition of His name (See Doc. and Cov. 107:2-4).

The presiding officer of The Church may be and should be spoken of and addressed as "President;" this is true also of the counselors in the First Presidency, for each of them is a president as the Lord hath said (Doc and Cov. 107:22, 24, 29); but it is not proper to speak commonly of the President of the Church, and even grossly incorrect to address him, as "Prophet," "Seer," or "Revelator," though each of these exalted titles is specifically his, and belongs also to each of his counselors, to each of the Twelve, and to the Presiding Patriarch of The Church. These are designations of spiritual powers and functions, and are of too sacred a character to be employed as common appellations, The title "President" is used in secular as well as in ecclesiastical application; in the latter connection it may be regarded as expressive of executive authority in the Priesthood, rather than a specific designation of Priesthood itself; it may therefore be used as occasion requires in speaking of or to the president of a stake, or the president of a quorum, council, or other organization.

The title "Bishop" is expressive of presidency; the Bishop is specifically the presiding officer over the lesser or Aaronic Priesthood in his ward, and is, moreover, president of the ward as an organization; it is, therefore, strictly within the bounds of propriety to refer to him and to address him by the title of his office: but it would be improper to make common his title of "High Priest," though none but High Priests officiate as Bishops in The Church today.

The title "Apostle" is likewise one of special significance and sanctity; it has been given of God, and belongs only to those who have been called and ordained as "special witnesses of the name of Christ in all the world, thus differing from other officers in the Church in the duties of their calling" (Doc. and Cov. 107:23). By derivation the word "apostle" is the English equivalent of the Greek *apostolos,* indicating a messenger, an ambassador, or literally "one who is sent." It signifies that he who is rightly so called, speaks and acts not of himself, but as the representative of a higher power whence his commission issued; and in this sense the title is that of a servant, rather than that of a superior. Even the Christ, however, is called an Apostle with reference to His ministry in the flesh (Hebrews 3:1), and this appellation is justified by His repeated declarations that He came to earth to do not His will but that of the Father by whom *He was sent.*

Though an apostle is thus seen to be essentially an envoy, or ambassador, his authority is great, as is also the responsibility associated therewith, for he speaks in the name of a power greater than his own—the name of Him whose special witness he is. When one of the Twelve is sent to minister in any stake, mission or other division of the Church, or to labor in regions where no Church organization has been effected, he acts as the representative of the First Presidency, and has the right to his use authority in doing whatever is requisite for the furtherance of the work of God. His duty is to preach the Gospel, administer the ordinances thereof, and set in order the affairs of the Church, wherever he is sent. So great is the sanctity of this special calling, that the title "Apostle" should not be used lightly as the common or ordinary form of address applied to living men called to this office. The quorum or council of the Twelve Apostles as existent in The Church today may better be spoken of as the "Quorum of the Twelve," the "Council of the Twelve," or simply as the "Twelve," than as the "Twelve Apostles," except as particular occasion may warrant the use of the more sacred term. It is advised that the title "Apostle" be not applied as a prefix to the name of any member of the Council of the Twelve; but that such a one be addressed or spoken of as "Brother ———," or "Elder ———," and when necessary or desirable, as in announcing his presence in a public assembly, an explanatory clause may be added, thus, "Elder ———, one of the Council of the Twelve."

The word of modern revelation expressly states that "An Apostle is an Elder" (See Doc. and Cov. 20:38; compare also paragraphs 2 and 3, same section). So also every person ordained to the higher or Melchizedek Priesthood is an Elder, whatever his special office in the Priesthood may be. We do not, and indeed should not, use the terms "High Priest" and "Seventy" as prefixed titles; the designation "Elder" is usually sufficient, and even that should be used with care and reverence. Brethren laboring in the mission field may well substitute the term "Brother" for "Elder" in common usage; though in announcements and publications involving the specification of position or authority, the title "Elder" may be wholly proper. The same care should be observed in the use of all distinguishing titles belonging to Priesthood. Though a man be ordained to the exalted and honorable office of Patriarch, he is still an Elder, and the special designation "Patriarch" is not to be used in every-day converse.

What has been said concerning the Holy Priesthood and the sanctity of names and titles associated therewith, applies in a measure to the Church as a body, and to the members thereof as individuals. The name of the Church to which we belong is of unusual significance—The Church of Jesus Christ of Latter-day Saints. It is a proclamation of the unique position claimed by the organization among the multitudinous sects and churches of the day. While this distinguishing name has been given by revelation (Doc. and Cov. 115:3, 4), it is to be employed with due respect to the sacred name of our Savior embodied in the general title. Usually it is preferable to speak of "The Church" rather than to use the full title; though, of course, in any connection in which ambiguity or uncertainty may appear, the full name of The Church may be properly used. The members are known as Latter-day Saints, and this name is of sacred import. The term "Saint," strictly applied, means "one who is holy;" that is to say, one who is set apart or has separated himself from those who profess not as he does, in sacred belief and practice. It is more appropriate to speak of those who belong as the "Members of the Church," rather than as the "Saints," except as particular and special occasion may indicate otherwise.

Every member of The Church and more especially every bearer of the Priesthood, should strive earnestly and prayerfully to be worthy of the sacred and distinguishing title belonging to his position; the title itself should be held in reverence, and the profession it signifies should be regarded as sacred.

{20}

"Latter-day Saints and the Bible," An Address Delivered on 5 April 1914

(from *Eighty-fourth Annual Conference*
of the Church of Jesus Christ of Latter-day Saints
[Salt Lake City: Published by the Deseret News, 1914],
pp. 92-95)

These great gatherings of the Church have come to be looked upon as a very remarkable phenomenon. It is indeed something to be wondered at, that men and women in such great numbers will leave their employment and at very considerable sacrifice of time and money come up from the stakes both near and afar off, twice a year, to this appointed place, the block upon which stands the great house of the Lord, and remain in session for three or more days, receiving instructions and admonition, and occasionally good and well intentioned rebuke, in order that they may be the better fitted for their duties as professing Latter-day Saints. It cannot be that curiosity brings them here, for the many decades through which this custom has continued must have abolished the element of novelty. Nor do I think the people come to be entertained, certainly not to be amused. It is true we have the privilege of listening to music of the very highest order—music of prayer and praise; and great shall be the blessing that shall come to every one of our talented singers and musicians who are so ready and willing to use their God-given gift in praise and worship. We do not come to be impressed by pulpit oratory. There is none of the attractiveness of oratorical display about the addresses that are delivered from this stand. I have rejoiced many times and do now rejoice, that our public speaking in the Church of Jesus Christ is devoid of those characteristics usually classed under the name of oratory. Oratory too often means little more than the sounding of brass and the tinkling of cymbals to tickle the ears. I do rejoice, however, in the eloquence of those who speak under the influence of the Spirit of God. Oratory is addressed to the ears; eloquence given of God, to the heart. I cannot conclude otherwise than that our people thus come together so willingly and so eagerly because they receive something worth the coming. They find it pays them to come; they go away satisfied. If they went otherwise they would be less inclined to come back again, and we know that every recurrence of the conference, both at the April and at the October season is marked by the gathering of these great concourses of people who have come up from all parts of the land of Israel. I feel that they come to hear the word of God, proclaimed in its simplicity; and it is the simplicity of the word that pleases the people, and that carries it home to their hearts. I call to mind that it was predicted by the inspired apostle of old that the day would come when people would tire of simplicity, and would look for something other than the eloquence of truth. Paul in writing to his beloved son in Christ, as he called him, Timothy, admonished him as to his duties; and as I read in the fourth chapter of the second epistle that passed between these two worthy ministers of Christ, Paul said:

"I charge thee therefore before God, and the Lord Jesus Christ, who shall judge the quick and the dead at His appearing and His kingdom, Preach the word; be instant in season, out of season; reprove, rebuke, exhort with all long suffering and doctrine.

"For the time will come when they will not endure sound doctrine; but after their own lusts shall they heap to themselves teachers, having itchy ears;

"And they shall turn away their ears from the truth, and shall be turned unto fables.

"But watch thou in all things, endure afflictions, do the work of an evangelist, and make full proof of thy ministry."

Who can doubt that this prediction has seen fulfillment and that the fact of its fulfillment is apparent today? Many there be who will no longer endure sound doctrine, but turn away after fables that tickle their ears and please their fancy, and demand of them none of that self-denial, sacrifice and earnest effort so characteristic of the requirements made of those who have taken upon themselves the name of Christ.

Our attention was called in the opening session of this conference to the dangers of our being led astray by those who would make believe that the very word of God itself is a fable, a collection of myths and legends, meaning not what it says but what men may fancy or would suppose. There be men who have arrogated to themselves the claim of superiority, who pronounce themselves higher critics of the scriptures of Almighty God, and proclaim that the scriptures mean not what they say. Right glad am I that my people are pleased with sound doctrine; that the wholesome food of the Gospel is still sweet in their mouths. There are some who would make it appear that it is today an evidence of inferior perception to accept the word of God for just what it professes to be, and that one is not up with the times unless he can read between the lines and unless he can perceive the metaphorical and the figurative in the Holy Scriptures. There are parts of the Bible that are plainly figurative; but no one who can read can be in doubt as to when a figure is used, and as to when the plain truth is declared in the simplest of language. Parables there are, and of great value are the lessons set forth thereby. But there is no parable, there is no metaphor in the plain declarations of the scriptures as to what is the price of salvation.

I don't believe the Latter-day Saints are influenced by these vagaries of the so-called higher criticism of the s[c]riptures. I believe our people stand upon the platform of the word of God as it has been delivered unto them through the mouths of men who have been empowered and directed to declare it unto them. But there are some, particularly of our younger people, who perhaps are inclined to believe that it is a little superior to profess doubt as to the truth and plain meaning of the Holy Scriptures. To them let me say, it is not the leaders in thought in the world today who are doubting the scriptures, and reading into them a meaning that was never intended. The majority of the really great men, great thinkers, men who have influence amongst their fellows, accept the scriptures in their literalness and simplicity.

There is now in existence a society known as the Philosophical Society of Great Britain. It embraces not only subjects of the King of England, but men in many other nations. It is known also by another name, given in honor of the late Empress Queen who was its patron for many years, The Victoria Institute. Upon its rolls you will find the names of many of the leading scientists of the world, philosophers, literary men, theologians. The conditions attendant upon membership in that great association are precise. The first is that the candidate shall be a man or woman of recognized ability. The second is that he shall be without reservation a Christian, believing that Jesus Christ was in very truth the Son of God, that He was born of the Virgin Mary, that He lived as the scriptures declare He did, that He did suffer death and that He did literally come forth from the tomb, an immortalized Being. And that society whose president today is the Lord Chancellor of

England, whose honorary president and patron is the King, declares that it has no time to go over the ground again and thresh the old straw and winnow the old chaff of infidelity, or of questions that arise respecting the integrity of the Holy Scriptures. Men who will not accept Christ as the Redeemer of mankind can have no place there; and yet I am told that it belittles one in the eyes of learned men to accept the plain and simple declarations of the scriptures with respect to the mission of the divine Son of God.

I have been told that no really great mind can believe for a moment in the actuality of the miracles recorded in the New Testament, particularly those attributed to the Christ Himself. Yet that body of men, amongst whom are some of the most prominent of the leaders of men in the world, have but recently put themselves upon record. The subject of the miracles of the New Testament has been investigated scientifically, and according to the accepted canons of analysis, and the report unanimously adopted and put upon record by the Philosophical Society of Great Britain, is that the miracles of the New Testament from that of Cana in Galilee to the greatest miracle of all, the coming forth of the Christ from the tomb on the resurrection morn, are attested by evidence that is as trustworty and in every way as acceptable as the evidence attesting any event of past history; and the Philosophical Society of Great Britain declares its acceptance of the miracles of the Bible as the very manifestation of the power of God. Those men are not above saying that because they can't perform such miracles, no such miracles were ever performed; but they proclaim that to say they cannot understand them is no argument that they did not take place. I am inclined to accept the opinions of such men as those before the opinions of little-great men who seek to stir up doubt in the minds of those who believe in God and in His Son Jesus Christ. Most pernicious is the effect that such have upon children and young people of immature powers who cannot analyze for themselves and who follow their teachers and are impressed by those who instruct them in more things than the mere subjects which are set down on the program.

Young Latter-day Saints, I say unto you as I have said before, it is not unscientific to believe in God, the very Eternal Father, nor in Jesus Christ as the one and only Redeemer of mankind. It is not unphilosophical to accept the scriptural record of His birth, of His life, of His death, of His resurrection. I have met men of science and philosophy in many lands, and have discussed the scriptures with them, and I testify to you I never yet have had to take a back seat nor to bow my head because of the principles which I profess to believe, nor because I was a Latter-day Saint. I have found the teachings of my Church, which is your Church and the Church of Jesus Christ, to be abreast of the very best of scientific conception, discovery and teaching of the day. Beware of these who come telling you that you are behind the times in accepting the faith of your fathers.

I am most happy to add my testimony to those to which we have listened in the course of this conference, most grateful that the Lord has been with us in these meetings, and I recognize in it a fulfillment of His glorious promise while He lived in the flesh when he declared: "Where two or three are gathered together in my name, there am I in their midst." [Matt. 18:20] He has been in the congregations of the Saints who have assembled here, and the result is inspiration in the words of those who have spoken and who have instructed us. While perchance we have heard nothing that is strictly novel or new, nothing that we may not have heard before, we have been reminded of those things that are most precious pertaining to the duties that shall save—the neglect of which shall condemn. I rejoice with my brethren who have already expressed their joy that the Gospel revealed unto man fits man to his environment and enables him to meet the exigencies of the present day. Its scriptures are not alone the scriptures of the past but those of the very day in which we live.

Is it not strange that this people who a few years ago were severely arraigned and criticized because in their declaration of faith they said, "We believe the Bible to be the word of God as far as it is translated correctly," should now be criticized because of their literal acceptance of that volume of holy writ. We accept it for what it is. We believe that other scriptures are necessary, and we affirm that other scriptures have been written, and that yet others shall be written; but the Church of Jesus Christ stands for the integrity of the Holy Bible, and defends it against the attacks and the assaults of those who would make you believe that it is but a compilation of fairy stories that pleased the people in bygone centuries, but that are not adapted to the greater and higher development of the present day. The Bible and other scriptures given of God will always be up to date in their fundamental principles, and other scriptures will be given as occasion may require, to meet the condition of the advancing years. Let us go hence with the spirit of the conference burning in our hearts, that we may shed light and warmth in our homes and impart it unto those who have not been privileged to meet with us here. We are simple minded enough, child-like enough, thank God, to believe that He meant what He said when He spoke of old, and that He means what He says when He speaks today. God be with you. Amen.

"The Eternity of Sex"

(from the *Young Woman's Journal*
25 [October 1914]: 600-604)

The Church of Jesus Christ of Latter-day Saints affirms as reasonable, scriptural, and true, the doctrine of the eternity of sex among the children of God. The distinction between male and female is no condition peculiar to the relatively brief period of mortal life; it was an essential characteristic of our pre-existent state, even as it shall continue after death, in both the disembodied and resurrected states.

That birth or even its antecedent, conception, in no wise marks the creation of a being who before that event did not exist, is abundantly attested by the revealed word; it is positively declared that every child born to earth lived as an individual spirit, male or female, in the primeval world. There is no accident or chance, due to purely physical conditions, by which the sex of the unborn is determined; the body takes form as male or female according to the sex of the spirit whose appointment it is to tenant that body as a tabernacle formed of the elements of the earth, through which means alone the individual may enter upon the indispensable course of human experience, probation, and training.

That the vital distinction of sex characterizes life on earth cannot be questioned; its antemortal and postmortal existence may be thought by some to require demonstration.

In the first chapter of Genesis, verse 27, we read:

"So God created man in his own image, in the image of God created he him; male and female created he them."

The next chapter makes plain the fact that the placing of man upon the earth, clothed with a body of earthly material, was a subsequent event; thus as stated in verses 4-7:

"These are the generations of the heavens and of the earth when they were created, in the day that the Lord God made the earth and the heavens, and every plant of the field before it was in the earth, and every herb of the field before it grew: for the Lord God had not caused it to rain upon the earth, and there was not a man to till the ground.

But there went up a mist from the earth, and watered the whole face of the ground. And the Lord God formed man of the dust of the ground, and breathed into his nostrils the breath of life; and man became a living soul."

As shown to Moses in vision, and as subsequently revealed to Joseph Smith, the essential facts comprised in the scriptures above quoted are set forth with somewhat greater plainness as follows:

"And I, God, created man in mine own image, in the image of mine Only Begotten created I him; male and female created I them." (Pearl of Great Price, Moses 2:27.)

Further:

"And now, behold, I say unto you, that these are the generations of the heaven and of the earth, when they were created, in the day that I, the Lord God, made the heaven and the earth. And every plant of the field before it was in the earth, and every herb of the field before it grew. For I, the Lord God, created all things, of which I have spoken, spiritually, before they were naturally upon the face of the earth. For I, the Lord God, had not caused it to rain upon the face of the earth. And I, the Lord God, had created all the children of men; and not yet a man to till the ground; for in heaven created I them; and there was not yet flesh upon the earth, neither in the water, neither in the air; but I, the Lord God, spake, and there went up a mist from the earth, and watered the whole face of the ground. And I, the Lord God, formed man from the dust of the ground, and breathed into his nostrils the breath of life, and man became a living soul, the first flesh upon the earth, the first man also; nevertheless, all things were before created; but spiritually were they created and made according to my word." (Moses 3:4-7.)

These scriptures attest a state of existence preceding mortality, in which the spirit-children of God lived, doubtless with distinguishing personal characteristics, certainly with the distinction of sex, for "male and female created He them" spiritually, even "before they were [created] naturally upon the face of the earth." It is plain that this spiritual creation of mankind embraced the entire human family and not alone the pair ordained to be the first mortal parents of men; for it is expressly stated that "the Lord God had created all the children of men" before a man had been placed upon the earth "to till the ground;" yea, even before the earth was tillable, or capable of support-ing the vegetation necessary for human food.

In passing, one may inquire: Is it not in harmony with the genius of these scriptures to infer that the spirits, since known in their embodied state as the human family, lived, developed, and progressed, as sentient beings of varied degrees of intelligence and capability, within the limitations of that primeval sphere of activity: and that in due time they have been and are yet being sent to earth to gain the experiences incident to mortality? For scriptural affirmation supporting this inference, cons[i]der that marvelous revelation given to Abraham, wherein the Lord God declared that the Divine purpose in forming the earth, from materials before existent but unorganized, was to provide a place whereon His children, then existing as spirits, could dwell, that they might be proved as to integrity and righteous effort; that among those spirit children there were many who were relatively noble and great, and that these were chosen and fore-ordained to labors of special importance in the course of their mundane life. (See Abraham 3:21-26. For special study of the antemortal existence of the human family see the author's "Articles of Faith," pp. 195-199.)

The continuation of individual existence beyond the grave is even more abundantly declared, though perhaps not more specifically attested, in scripture, than is the fact of antemortal life. All Christendom professes belief in life after death, and accepts to some degree, though not infrequently in distorted form, the doctrine of the resurrection. The Church of Jesus Christ of Latter-day Saints proclaims the plain, simple, uncorrupted, scriptural truth of a literal resurrection of the body, by which the spirit that had been disembodied by death will again be clothed with a tabernacle of flesh and bones identical in form with the body that was laid down. This comprises as a necessary condition the continuation of the individual existence of the spirit, as a separate and distinct being, intelligent and progressive, during the interval between death and the resurrection. The literalness of the resurrection is explicitly taught by Alma, a Nephite prophet, in the forceful declaration that in the resurrected body every limb and joint shall be restored to the possession of the spirit, and that "even a hair of the head shall not be lost, but all things shall be restored to their proper and perfect frame. (Alma 40:23; read the entire chapter. For a special treatment of the "Resurrection of the Body," and the literalness thereof, see the author's "Articles of Faith," pp. 391-403.)

With such definite word as to the actuality of a bodily resurrection, which shall come to all, righteous and sinner alike, is it conceivable that the essential differences of sex shall be eliminated? Children of God have comprised male and female from the beginning. Man is man and woman is woman, fundamentally, unchangeably, eternally. Each is indispensable to the other and to the accomplishment of the purposes of God, the crowning glory of which is "to bring to pass the immortality and eternal life of man." (Moses 1:39).

The status of woman in the world is a subject of present-day discussion and an element of current social unrest; it is, however, by no means a new topic. The female sex is not infrequently referred to as the weaker of the two. As gauged by physical standards this classification may be essentially correct. And be it said to the discredit and shame of the stronger sex, man through the centuries gone has been prone to use his superior strength to the oppression of woman. She has suffered the greatest humiliation during periods of spiritual darkness, when the Gospel of Christ was forgotten. Woman occupies a position all her own in the eternal economy of the Creator; and in that position she is as truly superior to man as is he to her in his appointed place. Woman shall yet come to her own, exercising her rights and her privileges as a sanctified investiture which none shall dare profane.

It is part of woman's mission in this life to occupy a secondary position of authority in the activities of the world, both in the home and in the affairs of public concern. Of this condition, explanation and justification may be found in the fact that in every organization, however simple or complex, there must needs be a centralization of authority, in short, a head. The secular law recognizes the husband as the head of the household, and theoretically at least holds hi[m] accountable for his administration. That many men fail in their station, that some are weak and unfit, that in particular instances the wife may be the more capable and in divers ways the better of the pair, should not be considered as evidencing impropriety or unrighteousness in the established order as a general condition. Woman should be regarded, not in the sense of privilege but of right, as the associate of man in the community of the home, and they two should form the governing head of the family institution, while to each separately pertain duties and functions which the other is less qualified to discharge. Weakness or inefficiency on the part of either in specified instances must not be taken to impugn the wisdom by which the organization of the home and of society has been planned.

In the restored Church of Jesus Christ, the Holy Priesthood is conferred, as an individual bestowal, upon men only, and this in accordance with Divine requirement. It is not given to woman to exercise the authority of the Priesthood independently; nevertheless, in the sacred endowments associated with the ordinances pertaining to the House of the Lord, woman shares with man the blessings of the Priesthood. When the frailities and imperfections of mortality are left behind, in the glorified state of the blessed hereafter, husband and wife will administer in their respective stations, seeing and understanding alike, and co-operating to the full in the government of their family kingdom. Then shall woman be recompensed in rich measure for all the injustice that womanhood has endured in mortality. Then shall woman reign by Divine right, a queen in the resplendent realm of her glorified state, even as exalted man shall stand, priest and king unto the Most High God. Mortal eye cannot see nor mind comprehend the beauty, glory, and majesty of a righteous woman made perfect in the celestial kingdom of God.

Through the sure word of revealed truth we learn of the actual relationship between God and man, and that this is the literal relationship of parent to child. The spirits of men are the offspring of Deity, born in the antemortal world and endowed with the Divine birthright of eternal development and progression, in which course of advancement the life on earth is but a stage. The glorious possibilities of man's attainment are indicated in the admonition of the Lord Jesus: "Be ye therefore perfect, even as your Father which is in heaven is perfect." (Matt. 5:48)

To become perfect as God is perfect is to attain the state, power, dignity, and authority of godship. Plainly there is a way provided by which the child of God may follow the footsteps of the Father, and in time—sometime in the distant eternities—be as that Divine Father is. Even as Christ, the Only Begotten Son of God in the flesh, endured the experiences of mortality, passed the portals of death and became a resurrected Being, so the Father before Him had trodden the same path of progression from manhood to Godhood, and today sits enthroned in the heavens by right of achievement. He is the Eternal Father and with Him, crowned with glory and majesty, is the eternal Mother. They twain are the parents of the spirit-children for whose schooling in the lessons of mortality this earth was framed. When God said, "Let us make man in our image, after our likeness," "male and female created He them;" and male and female shall they be, to and beyond the resurrection, forever.

Eternal exaltation is the assured attainment of those who obey in its fulness the whole law of the Gospel of Christ; theirs it is to become like unto their Celestial Parents.

"Then shall they be Gods, because they have no end; therefore shall they be from everlasting to everlasting, because they continue; then shall they be above all, because all things are subject unto them. Then shall they be Gods, because they have all power, and the angels are subject unto them." (Doctrine and Covenants 132:20).

Is there anything inconsistent, unnatural, or even surprising in the fact that offspring may develop to the status and spiritual stature of the parents? Would not the contrary be an exception to the recognized order of life? Such complete achievement, however, is possible only to children who pursue the course of development that the parents have followed,—to those only who resolutely advance, ever obedient, through struggle and strife, endurance and suffering, denial and conquest, as those who went before had to do.

The association of man and woman in marriage may be a union for mortality only, or for this life and the hereafter, according to the authority by which the relationship is sanctioned and solemnized. A marriage contracted under human law alone, while legally binding and valid on earth, is terminated by the death summons. This condition is expressly recognized and specified in the ordinary ritual of marriage, in the pronouncement of the officiating authority to the contracting parties, *"Until death do you part."*

To be effective and binding in the eternal worlds, the union of man and woman in marriage must be solemnized by an authority greater than any that can be established or invoked through human institutions. This superior authority must of necessity be given from the heavens, wherein its administration is to be recognized. Such is found in the Holy Priesthood only. Marriage covenants authorized and sealed by that God-given power endure, if the parties thereto are true to their troth, not through mortal life alone, but through time and all eternity. Thus the worthy husband and wife who have been sealed under the everlasting covenant shall come forth in the day of the resurrection to receive their heritage of glory, immortality, and eternal lives.

It is the blessed privilege of resurrected beings who attain an exaltation in the celestial kingdom to enjoy the glory of endless increase, to become the parents of generations of spirit-offspring, and to direct their development through probationary stages analogous to those through which they themselves have passed.

Eternal are the purposes of God; never-ending progression is provided for His children, worlds without end.

{22}

"The Son of Man,"
An Address Delivered on 6 April 1915

(from the Journal of James E. Talmage, 10 May 1915,
Archives and Manuscripts, Harold B. Lee Library,
Brigham Young University, Provo, Utah;
and *Eighty-fifth Annual Conference
of the Church of Jesus Christ of Latter-day Saints*
[Salt Lake City: Published by the Deseret News, 1915],
pp. 120-24)

May 10, 1915—The usual publication containing report of the addresses delivered at the annual conference of the Church was issued from the press today. This issue comprising proceedings of the Eighty-Fifth Annual Conference held last month. The publication has been delayed owing to a consultation regarding my own brief address. I incorporate herewith the press sheets of the address as actually delivered, and the slightly curtailed form of the same in which it appears in the booklet. It will be observed that part of the paragraph relating to the significance of the title "The Son of Man" is omitted from the official publication,—the part being that which most distinctly interprets the title as having reference to Christ's being the Son of the only supremely glorified Man known to Him during His mortal existence—namely the Eternal Father. By way of explanation it should be said that this conception of the title "The Son of Man" has been incorporated in my forthcoming book "Jesus the Christ", and that it was submitted to and approved by President Joseph F. Smith. Further, the President of the Church heartily approves the doctrine as set forth in the conference address, and personally desired its publication in full. President Charles W. Penrose, however, is of the opinion that the wide spread publication of this doctrine would cause difficulty to the elders in the field, who he thinks would be confronted with the charge that we as a people worship a Man. Under the circumstances it was deemed advisable to omit a few sentences from the official report. I think it proper, however, to incorporate here the full report and the slightly abbreviated publication, and particularly so as President Joseph

135

F. Smith desired that the full and original report be preserved—The doctrine that the true significance of the title "The Son of Man" lies in the fact that Jesus the Christ was the Son of the Eternal Father both in spirit and in body, and that God the Eternal Father has passed through experiences analogous to those of our present mortality, and that the Eternal Father is a resurrected Being, and was to Christ while he dwelt in the flesh the only Being known who had attained supreme glorification as a Man. Christ Himself has now been glorified with the glory of the Father, nevertheless even in modern revelation He acknowledges His filial relationship to the Father in the perpetuated title as used by Christ "The Son of Man".

[For the reader's convenience, those portions of the address that were omitted from the published version have been italicized. In a couple of instances words have been added to the published version, different from the first proof; these additions are indicated by brackets.]

Knowledge concerning God's attributes essential to intelligent worship—The relationship of Jesus Christ to God the Eternal Father, spiritually and bodily—*Significance of the title "The Son of Man"*—Relationship of mankind to Deity.

In common with my brethren and sisters who make up these assembled thousands of modern Israel, I have been fed with good food and made glad in each meeting of this conference. I have felt that the Spirit of the Lord has been present with us in great abundance. We have heard much concerning our temporal duties, and much relating to our spiritual welfare. It has been made plain unto us that these two classes of things differ in degree rather tha[n] in kind, and that we cannot serve God acceptably by devoting ourselves wholly to scripture study, for there are many things pertaining to temporalities which enter into and our appointed experiences here upon the earth. On the other hand, we have been assured, not for the first time, by any means, that we cannot please the Lord by wholly devoting ourselves to temporal affairs, to the exclusion of the consideration of the great spiritual principles and truths that have been given us.

We belong to the Church of Jesus Christ, and much has been said of His proprietorship, His mastership, in the Church, the Church that bears His name. I take it to be a plain and simple principle that we cannot worship intelligently, and therefore acceptably unto the Lord, unless we know something of the attributes and of the will of Him whom we profess to worship. The relationship of the Christ to the

Eternal Father has been set forth in such plainness that I do not think any wayfaring man amongst us can fail to understand. We recognize in Jesus Christ, the Son of the Eternal Father, both in spirit and in body. There is no other meaning to attach to that expression, as used by the Eternal Father Himself—"Mine Only Begotten Son." Christ combined within His own person and nature the attributes of His mortal mother, and just as truly the attributes of His immortal Sire. By that fixed and inexorable law of nature, that every living organism shall follow after his kind, Jesus Christ had the power to die, for He was the offspring of a mortal woman; and He had the power to withstand death indefinitely, for He was the son of an immortal Father. This simplicity of doctrine has shocked many, but the truth is frequently shocking just because of its simplicity and consequent grandeur. We must know something of the attributes of the Eternal Father, that we may the more fully comprehend His relationship to His Only Begotten Son.

Did not Christ declare again and again that He possessed in His own person such power over life that no man could take His life from Him—in plain words, that no one could kill Him--until He would voluntarily surrender Himself, and permit mortal and infernal powers to prevail for the time being? How could it be otherwise for the Son of an immortal Father, who inherited the power to keep death in abeyance? Death could not touch Him until He willed and permitted it so. Did He not say also, not once but many a time, that He did what He had seen His Father do? Did He not declare that He did only what He had seen His Father do, or what His Father had done? And did He not make it plain that He was following in the footsteps of His immortal Father, the very Eternal Father to whom we pray in the name of His Son? It necessarily follows that the Eternal Father once passed through experiences analogous to those which His Son, the Lord Jesus, afterward passed through, and through which we are now passing. The Eternal Father, therefore, is a Being who has had experiences incident to the mortal state. He is a resurrected Being; He conquered death; and He gave power unto His Son to conquer death, through whom power shall be given unto the Saints, yea, unto all who will accept the boon of eternal life, to be redeemed from death.

On an early occasion in the earthly ministry of Christ when He first met Nathanael, Jesus recognized in the man at once an Israelite in whom was no guile. In His conversation with Nathanael Jesus the Christ called Himself for the first time, as far as our scripture records show, "The Son of Man." (John 1:51) [In the published version, the title "The Son of Man" does not contain quotation marks.] Then, in an interview with Nicodemus, that renowned teacher in Israel and learned doctor of the law, Jesus called Himself again The Son of Man (John 3:13); and you will find the same expression used in the four gospels approximately eighty times. Eliminating all parallel passages, or sayings that are reported by more than one of the writers, there are approximately forty separate instances in which Jesus Christ called Himself The Son of Man; but nowhere in the four gospels do you find the title used by any other than the Christ, nor applied by the Christ to any other than Himself. *That expression has puzzled theologians, and has taxed the ingenuity of such interpreters of scripture as try to make the scriptures conform to their own conceptions and views.*

It may be remarked, in passing, that you will find a somewhat similar expression used in the Old Testament, [not "The Son of Man", but "Son of man",] in the form of address; and in these instances it is plainly used in its literal and ordinary or common meaning—the son of a mortal man. It is so used approximately ninety times in the Book of Ezekial; in each instance, however, Jehovah applies it to His prophet, addressing him as "Son of man", as the context of the several passages plainly shows, to impress upon Ezekial the fact that though he was permitted to voice and write the very words of Jehovah, he was nevertheless but a man. So also in the Book of Moses you will find that Satan blasphemously assumed to establish, or to make it appear that there existed a similar difference between him and Moses, when he said "Moses, son of man, worship me". (Pearl of Great Price, Moses 1:12).

But the distinctive title "The Son of Man" occurs only once in the Old Testament. It is in the seventh chapter of Daniel, wherein is given an account of a wonderful manifestation from God, in which Daniel saw, in the vision of the night, the scenes that shall take place in a time yet future, when the Ancient of Days, Adam, who is the patriarch of the race, shall sit to judge his posterity, and they shall come before him, or as Daniel saw it, they came before him, in their order; and among them there came one like unto the Son of Man who appeared in the clouds in heaven; and when He came all power and dominion were given unto Him, and His kingdom was declared to be an all embracing and an everlasting kingdom. Thus is shown the superiority of the Son of Man over the Ancient of Days, or in other words, the supremacy of Jesus the Christ over Adam, the patriarch of the race (see Dan. 7:9-14).

Now, in the New Testament, outside the four gospels, you will find the title "The Son of Man" occurring about three times, and in each instance it is applied to the Christ in His then glorified state (see Acts 7:56; Rev. 1:13, and 14:14). When Stephen stood before his unrighteous judges, the heavens were opened to him, and he could not keep within his soul what he saw. He said, "Behold I see The Son of Man, standing on the right hand of God"; and for that testimony they took Stephen out and stoned him, as for the testimony of the Father they had before crucified the Christ.

Now, our learned biblical scholars and theologians, or, at least those of them who reject the light of modern revelation, which throws such wonderfully illuminating rays upon the ancient scriptures, claim that the expression, "The Son of Man", is applied to Christ to express His unique relationship to the human family, that it was an appellation of humility, a title of abject lowliness; while on the contrary, it was one of the highest titles that He could assume. And yet you will find, in what we call the authorized version, or the King James version, and in the revised version, and in other versions of the New Testament, as well as in the commentaries and in the learned disquisitions that have been published pertaining thereunto, that the writers with scrupulous care write "Son" with a capital "S", and "man" with a small "m." Now, I ask you, who is that small-m-man whose son was Jesus the Christ? Jesus Christ was the only male human being that has ever walked the earth since Adam who was not the son of a mortal man, and to think that He should take upon Himself a title, a distinguishing and exclusive title, connoting the son of a mortal man when He is the only male descendant of Adam who has ever tabernacled in the flesh, who was not the son of a mortal man, is to assume misrepresentation of fact.

The word of revelation, given in this day, makes plain the meaning as to who was the one and only supremely glorified Man, whom Christ knew—God, the Eternal Father, the Father of the spirit of Jesus, and literally, the Father of His body. Therefore the title "The Son of Man" is an appellation of glory, authority and power among all sons of men. The Son of Man is the Only Begotten of the one and only supremely glorified Man at that time. God *has since glorified His Son; but though the Son is glorified with the glory of the Father, you can't change the fact that He is the Son of that Father, and that Father, the Eternal Father, not Jesus Christ, but the Father of Jesus Christ, the Father of His spirit and the Father of His body, was a Man, and has progressed, not by any favor but by the right of conquest over sin, and over unrighteousness, to His present position of priest-*

hood and power, of Godship and Godliness, as the Supreme Being whom we all profess to worship. The title "The Son of Man" therefore is in a great measure synonymous with "The Son of God". We are all spirit sons and daughters of God; but Jesus Christ was and is The Son of God in a superlative and distinctive sense, God the Eternal Father being His Father both in spirit and in flesh.

We believe in the more than imperial status of the human race. We believe that our spirits are the off-spring of Deity, and we hold that when Christ said to His apostles, "Be ye therefore perfect, even as your Father which is in heaven is perfect," He was not talking of a merely idealistic yet impossible achievement; but that on the contrary He meant that it was possible for men to advance until they shall become like unto the Gods in their powers and in their attainments, through righteousness.

According to the spirit of the revealed word, perfection is rather relative than absolute. Though a man become perfect in his mortal sphere of activity, he is by no means perfect as gauged by the standard prevailing in heaven. As the Prophet Joseph Smith said to the Church in early days, so now says the Church unto the world—if the heavens could be rent, and you could see the Eternal Father sitting upon His throne, you would see *a glorified, perfect Man* [the published version reads "you would see Him like a man in form"]. That the Eternal Father has called Himself a Man is plainly apparent in the testimony of Enoch the Seer; and in the same scripture Jesus Christ is designated "The Son of Man" even before the time of the flood; "For in the language of Adam, Man of Holiness is His name, and the name of His Only Begotten is the Son of Man, even Jesus Christ", (Moses 6:57; compare 7:24, 47 and 54). In a certain revelation to Enoch, the Eternal Father thus spake: "Behold I am God; Man of Holiness is my name, Man of Counsel is my name; and Endless and Eternal is my name, also." (Moses 7:35). Thus does the light of modern revelation illuminate the dark passages of old.

The doctrine of the relationship between God and men, as made plain through the word of revelation, is today as it was of old, though in the light of later scripture we are enabled to read the meaning more clearly. It is provided that we, the sons and daughters of God, may advance until we become like unto our Eternal Father and our Eternal Mother, in that we may become perfect in our spheres as they are in theirs. That grand truth taught by the Prophet Joseph, and ridiculed

for the time, has now gripped the minds of the thinkers and philosophers of the age. You will find it hinted at and timidly expressed in the
writings of many recent and learned publications in the theological
field. That great truth is finding its way into the literature of the world.
It was crystallized into what we may call an aphorism, by President
Lorenzo Snow: "As man is God once was; as God is man may be". We
know that Christ is God, and that He lived upon the earth as a Man.
In the sense in which Christ was perfect in His sphere, we may become
perfect in ours. We may progress, not to become each one a savior of
the world in the particular sense in which Christ was the Savior of the
world, but we may follow Him to eternal glory, and to eternal life,
which may our Father grant, in the name of Jesus. Amen.

{23}

"The Philosophical Basis of 'Mormonism'"
An Address Delivered at the Congress of
Religious Philosophies, San Francisco, California,
on 29-31 July 1915

(from *The Philosophical Basis of "Mormonism"*
[Independence, MO: Zion's Printing
and Publishing Company, 1915])

Permit me to explain that the term "Mormon," with its several derivatives, is no part of the name of the Church with which it is usually associated. It was first applied to the Church as a convenient nickname, and had reference to an early publication, "The Book of Mormon;" but the appellative is now so generally current that Church and people answer readily to its call. The proper designation of the so-called "Mormon" Church is The Church of Jesus Christ of Latter-day Saints. The philosophy of its religious system is largely expressed in its name.

The philosophical foundation of "Mormonism" is constructed upon the following outline of facts and premises:

1. The eternal existence of a living personal God; and the preexistence and eternal duration of mankind as His literal offspring.

2. The placing of man upon the earth as embodied spirit to undergo the experiences of an intermediate probation.

3. The transgression and fall of the first parents of the race, by which man became mortal, or in other words was doomed to suffer a separation of spirit and body through death.

4. The absolute need of a Redeemer, empowered to overcome death, and thereby provide for a reunion of the spirits and bodies of mankind through a material resurrection from death to immortality.

5. The providing of a definite plan of salvation, by obedience to which man may obtain remission of his sins, and be enabled to advance by effort and righteous achievement throughout eternity.

6. The establishment of the Church of Jesus Christ in the "meridian of time," by the personal ministry and atoning death of the foreordained Redeemer and Savior of mankind, and the proclamation

of His saving Gospel through the ministry of the Holy Priesthood during the apostolic period and for a season thereafter.

7. The general "falling away" from the Gospel of Jesus Christ, by which the world degenerated into a state of apostasy, and the Holy Priesthood ceased to be operative in the organization of sects and churches designed and effected by the authority of man.

8. The restoration of the Gospel in the current age, the reestablishment of the Church of Jesus Christ by the bestowal of the Holy Priesthood through Divine revelation.

9. The appointed mission of the restored Church of Jesus Christ to preach the Gospel and administer in the ordinances thereof amongst all nations, in preparation for the near advent of our Savior Jesus Christ, who shall reign on earth as Lord and King.

1.

The eternal existence of a living personal God; and the preexistence and eternal duration of mankind as His literal offspring.

As its principle cornerstone "Mormonism" affirms the existence of the true and living God; the Supreme Being, in whose image and likeness man has been created in the flesh.

We hold it to be reasonable, scriptural and true, that man's period of earth-life is but one stage in the general plan of the soul's progression; and that birth is no more the beginning than is death the close of individual existence. God created all things spiritually before they were created temporally upon the earth; and the spirits of all men lived as intelligent beings, endowed with the capacity of choice and the rights of free agency, before they were born in the flesh. They were spirit-children of God. It was their Divine Father's purpose to provide a means by which they could be trained and developed, with opportunity to meet, combat, and overcome evil, and thus gain strength, power and skill, as means of yet further development through the eternities of the endless future. For this purpose was the earth created, whereon, as on other worlds, spirits might take upon themselves bodies, living in probation as candidates for a higher and more glorious future.

These unembodied spirits were of varied qualifications, some of them noble and great, fit for leadership and emprise of the highest order, others suited rather to be followers, but all capacitated to advance in righteous achievement if they would.

No one professing a belief in Christianity can consistently accept the Holy Scriptures as genuine and deny the preexistence of the Christ, or doubt that before the birth of the Holy One as Mary's Babe in Bethlehem of Judea, He had lived with the Father as an unembodied spirit, the Firstborn of the Father's children. So lived or live the hosts of spirits who have taken or yet shall take bodies of flesh and bones. Christ while a man among men repeatedly affirmed the fact of His antemortal life—that He came forth from the Father, and would return to the Father on the completion of His mission in mortality.

John the Revelator was shown in vision some of the scenes that had occurred in the world of unembodied spirits even before the beginning of human history. He saw the spirits that rebelled against God, under the leadership of Lucifer, a son of the morning, later known as Satan, the dragon; and he witnessed the struggle between those rebellious hosts and the army of loyal and obedient spirits who fought under the banner of Michael the archangel. We read that there was war in heaven; Michael and his angels fought, and the dragon and his angels fought. The victory was with Michael and his hosts, who by their allegiance and valor made good their title as victors in their "first estate," referred to by Jude, [Jude 1:6] while Satan and his defeated followers, who "kept not their first estate" were cast out upon the earth and became the devil and his angels, forever denied the privileges of mortal existence with its possibilities of eternal advancement.

The cause of the great antemortal "war in heaven" was the rebellion of Lucifer following the rejection of his plan whereby it was proposed that mankind be saved from the dangers and sins of their future mortality, not through the merit of struggle and endeavor against evil, but by compulsion. Satan sought to destroy the free agency of man; and in the primeval council of the angels and the Gods he was discredited; while the offer of the Well Beloved Son, Jehovah, afterwards Jesus the Christ to insure the free agency of man in the mortal state, and to give Himself a sacrifice and propitiation for the sins of the race, was accepted, and was made the basis of the plan of salvation.

The spirits who kept their first estate were to be advanced to the second, or mortal state, to be further tested and proved, withal, and to demonstrate whether they would observe and keep the commandments which the Lord their God should give them, with the assurance and promise that all who fill the measure of their second estate "shall have glory added upon their heads forever and ever." [Abr. 3:25-26]

2.

The placing of man upon the earth as an embodied spirit to undergo the experiences of an intermediate probation.

The advancement of the spirit-children of God from their first to their second estate was inaugurated by the creation of man upon the earth, whereby the individual spirit was clothed in a body of flesh and bones, consisting of the elements of the earth, or as stated in Genesis, made of the dust of the earth. With the ways and means by which this creation was wrought we are not especially concerned at this point. The spirit of the first man, Adam, was tabernacled in a body of earthly material; and his remembrance of an earlier existence and of his former place amongst the unembodied was suspended, so that a thick veil of forgetfulness fell between his earth-life and his past. Man and women thus became tenants of earth, and received from their Creator power and dominion over all inferior creations.

They were given commandment and law, with freedom of action and agency of choice. In a measure, they were left to themselves to choose the good or the evil, to be obedient or disobedient to the laws governing their second estate, or embodied condition. Experiences unknown in the preexistent state crowded upon the first parents of the race in their changed condition and new environment; and they were subjected to test and trial. Such was the purpose of their existence on earth. To them as also their unnumbered posterity—the entire race of mankind—this present life is a connecting link, an intermediate and probationary state, uniting the eternity of the past with that of the future. We, the human family, literally the sons and daughters of Divine Parents, the spiritual progeny of God our Eternal Father, and of our God Mother, are away from home for a season, studying and working as pupils duly matriculated in the University of Mortality, honorable graduation from which great institution means an exalted and enlarged sphere of activity and endeavor beyond.

3.

The transgression and fall of the first parents of the race, by which man became mortal, or in other words was doomed to suffer a separation of spirit and body through death.

Prominent among the commandments given to the parents of the race in Eden was that forbidding their eating of food unsuited to their condition. The natural and inevitable result of disobedience in this particular was set before them as a penalty—that, should they incorporate into their bodies the foreign substances of earth contained in the food against which they were solemnly cautioned, they would surely die. True, they could not fail by violation of this restriction to gain experience and knowledge; and the forbidden food is expressively designated as the fruit "of the tree of the knowledge of good and evil."

They disobeyed the commandment of God, and thus was brought about the Fall of Man. The bodies of both woman and man, which when created were perfect in form and function, now became degenerate, liable to the ever physical ailments and weaknesses to which flesh has since been heir, and subjects for eventual dissolution or death.

The arch-tempter through whose sophistries, half-truths, and infamous falsehoods Eve had been beguiled, was none other than Satan, or Lucifer, that rebellious and fallen "son of the morning," whose proposal involved the destruction of man's liberty had been rejected in the council of the heavens, and who had been "cast out into the earth," he and all his angels as unembodied spirits, never to be tabernacled in bodies of their own. As an act of diabolic reprisal following his rejection, his defeat by Michael and the heavenly hosts, his ignomminious [sic] expulsion from heaven, Satan planned to destroy the bodies in which the faithful spirits—those who had kept their first estate—would be born; and his beguilement of Eve was but an early stage of that infernal scheme.

Death has come to be the universal heritage; it may claim its victim in infancy or youth, in the period of life's prime, or its summons may be deferred until the snows of age have gathered upon the hoary head; it may befall as the result of accident or disease, by violence, or as we say, through natural causes; but come it must, as Satan well knows; and in this knowledge is his present though but temporary triumph. But the purposes of God, as they ever have been and ever shall be, are infinitely superior to the deepest designs of men or devils; and the Satanic machinations to make death inevitable, perpetual and supreme were provided against even before the first man had been created in the flesh. The Atonement to be wrought by Jesus the Christ was ordained to overcome death and to provide a means of ransom from the power of Satan.

4.

The absolute need of a Redeemer empowered to overcome death and thereby provide for a reunion of the spirits and bodies of mankind through a material resurrection from death to immortality.

From what has been said it is evident that "Mormonism" accepts the scriptural account of the creation of men and that of the Fall. We hold that the Fall was a process of physical degeneracy, whereby the body of man lost its power to withstand malady and death, and that with sin death entered into the world. We hold that the Fall was foreseen of God, and that it was by Divine wisdom turned to account as the means by which His embodied children would be subjected to the foreappointed test and trial through which the way to advancement, otherwise impossible, would be opened to them.

Let it not be assumed, however, that the fact of God's foreknowledge as to what *would be* under any given conditions, is a determining cause that such *must be*. Omnipotent though He be, He permits much that is contrary to his will. We cannot believe that vice and crime, injustice, intolerance, and unrighteous domination of the weak by the strong, the oppression of the poor by the rich, exist by the will and determination of God. It is not His design or wish that even one soul be lost; on the contrary, it was and is His work and glory "to bring to pass the immortality and eternal life of man." So also, it is not God's purpose to interfere with, far less to annul, the free agency of His children, even though those children prostitute their Divine birthright of freedom to the accomplishment of evil and the condemnation of their souls.

Before man was created in the flesh the Eternal Father foresaw that in the school of life some of His children would succeed and others fail, some would be faithful and others false; some would elect to tread the path of righteousness while others would follow the road to destruction. He further foresaw that death would enter the world, and that the possession of bodies by, His children would be of but brief individual duration. He saw that His commandments would be disobeyed and His law violated; and that men, shut out from His presence and left to themselves, would sink rather than rise, would retrograde rather than advance, and would be lost to the heavens. It was necessary that a means of redemption be provided, whereby erring man might make amends, and by compliance with established law achieve salvation and eventual exaltation in the eternal worlds. The power of death was to be overcome, so that, though men would of necessity die, they would live anew, their spirits clothed with immortalized bodies over which death could not again prevail.

While recognizing the transgression of Adam as an event by which the race has been brought under the penalty of death we hold that none but Adam shall be held accountable for his disobedience. True, the penalty incident to that transgression is operative upon all flesh, and upon the earth and all the elements thereof; but in the great reckoning, which men call the judgment, the environment and determining conditions under which each soul has lived, the handicap in the race of mortal strife and endeavor shall be taken into due account. "Wherefore, as by one man sin entered into the world, and death by sin; and so death passed upon all men, for that all have sinned: * * * Therefore as by the offense of one, judgment came upon all men to condemnation; even so by the righteousness of one the free gift came upon all men unto justification of life." (Romans 5:12,18.)

We affirm that man stands alone in absolute need of a Redeemer, for by self-effort alone he is utterly incapable of lifting himself from the lower to a higher plane. Even as lifeless mineral particles can be incorporated into the tissues of plants only as the plant reaches down into the lower world and through its own life processes raises the mineral to its own plane, or as vegetable substance may be woven into the body of the animal only as the animal by the exercise of its own vital functions assimilates the vegetable, so man may be lifted from his fallen earthly state characterized by human weaknesses, bodily frailties, and a persistent tendency to sink into the quagmire of sin, only as a power above that of humanity reaches down and helps him to rise. We affirm as a fundamental principle of Christian philosophy the *Atonement wrought by Jesus Christ;* and we accept in its literal simplicity the scriptural doctrine thereof. Through the Atonement the bonds of death are broken, and a way is provided for the annulment of the effects of individual sin. We hold that Jesus Christ was the one and only Being fitted to become the Savior and Redeemer of the world, for the following reasons:

(1) He is the only sinless Man who has ever walked the earth.

(2) He is the Only Begotten of the Eternal Father in the flesh, and therefore the only Being born to earth possessing in their fulness the attributes and powers of both Godhood and manhood.

(3) He is the One who has been chosen in the primeval council of

148

the Gods and foreordained to this service.

No other man has lived without sin, and therefore wholly free from the domination of Satan. Jesus Christ was the one Being to whom death, the natural wage of sin, was not due. Christ's sinlessness rendered Him eligible as the subject of the atoning sacrifice whereby propitiation could be made for the sins of all men.

No other man has possessed the power to hold death in abeyance and to die only as he willed so to do. We accept in their literalness and simplicity the scriptural declarations to the effect that Jesus Christ possessed within Himself power over death. "For as the Father hath life in himself; so hath he given to the Son to have life in himself" we read (John 5:26); and again "Therefore doth my Father love me, because I lay down my life, that I may take it again. No man taketh it from me, but I lay it down of myself. I have power to lay it down, and I have power to take it again." (John 10:17,18).

This unique condition was the natural heritage of Jesus the Christ, He being in His embodied state the Son of a mortal mother and of an immortal Sire. No mortal man was His father. From Mary He inherited the attributes of a mortal being, including the capacity to die; from His immortal Father He derived the power to live in the flesh indefinitely, immune to death except as He submitted voluntarily thereto.

No other being has been born to earth with such investiture of preappointment and foreordination to lay down his life as a propitiatory atonement for the race. Prominent among the teachings of Jesus Christ in the course of His earthly ministry was the reiterated avowal that He had come down from heaven not to do His own will but the will of Him by whom He had been sent.

The Atonement accomplished by the Savior was a vicarious service for mankind, all of whom had become estranged from God through sin; and by that sacrifice of propitiation, a way had been opened for reconciliation whereby man may be brought again into communion with God, and be made able to live and advance as a resurrected being in the eternal worlds. This fundamental conception is strikingly expressed in our English word "atonement," which, as its syllables attest is "at-one-ment," "denoting reconciliation, or the bringing into agreement of those who had been estranged."

As already indicated the effect of the Atonement is twofold:

(1) The universal redemption of the human race from death, which was invoked by the transgression of our first earthly parents; and

(2) Salvation, whereby relief is offered from the effects of individual sin.

The victory over death was inaugurated by the resurrection of Jesus Christ, who had been crucified and slain. He was the first to rise from death to immortality and is therefore rightly called "the first fruits of them that slept" (I Cor.15:20); "the firstborn from the dead" (Col. 1:18); "the first begotten of the dead" (Rev. 1:5). Instances of the raising of the dead to life are of record as antedating the death and resurrection of Christ; but such were cases of restoration to mortal existence; and that the subjects of such miraculous reanimation had to die again is certain.

Immediately following the resurrection of Jesus Christ, many of the righteous dead were resurrected, and appeared in their material bodies of tangible flesh and bones. The Holy Bible affirms such instances on the eastern hemisphere, and the Book of Mormon records analogous occurrences in the western world. The resurrection of the dead is to be universal, extending alike to all who have tabernacled in the flesh upon the earth, irrespective of their state, whether of righteousness or of sin; but all shall be called from the state of death in order, according to their condition. So taught the Master, when He said, following His avouchment that the Gospel should be preached even to those already dead. "Marvel not at this. for the hour is coming, in the which all that are in the graves shall hear his voice, And shall come forth; they that have done good, unto the resurrection of life; and they that have done evil, unto the resurrection of damnation." (John 5:28,29.) As part of a Divine revelation given in modern times we read: "They who have done good in the resurrection of the just, and they who have done evil in the resurrection of the unjust." (Doctrine and Covenants 76:17.)

The assured resurrection of all who have lived and died on earth is a foundation stone in the structure of "Mormon" philosophy. "Blessed and holy is he that hath part in the first resurrection: on such the second death hath no power, but they shall be priest of God and of Christ, and shall reign with him a thousand years." (Rev. 20:6).

5.

The providing of a definite plan of salvation by obedience to which man may obtain remission of his sins, and be enabled to advance by effort and righteous achievement throughout eternity.

In addition to the inestimable boon of redemption from death and the grave, the Atonement effected by Jesus Christ is universally operative in bringing a measure of salvation—what may be called general salvation—to the entire posterity of Adam, in that all men are thereby exonerated from the direct effects of the Fall in so far as such effects have been the cause of evil in their lives. Man is individually answerable for his own transgressions alone—the sins for which he, as a free agent, capacitated and empowered to choose for himself, commits culpably and on his own account or volition.

As an essential corollary to this fundamental principle, it follows that all children who die before they reach the age of accountability are not alone redeemed from death through resurrection to an endless life, with spirits and bodies inseparably united, but also from any possible effect of inherited tendency to sin. It will be admitted, without disputation, I take it, that children are born heirs to the inescapable birthright of heredity. Tendencies either good or evil, blessings and curses are transmuted from generation to generation. While heredity is to be regarded as tendency or capability only, and not as assurance and absolute predestination, nevertheless all children are born subject to the algebraic sum of the traits and tendencies of their ancestors, combined with their own specific and personal characteristics by which they were distinguished while yet unembodied spirits. From this heritage of sinward tendency all children are redeemed through the Atonement of Christ; and justly so, for the debt came to them as a legacy and is paid for them. They require no baptismal cleansing nor other ordinance of admittance into the Kingdom of God; for being incapable of repentance, and not having attained unto the condition of accountability, they are innocent in the sight of God, and will be counted among the redeemed and sanctified.

But there is a specific or individual effect of the Atonement, by which every soul that has lived in the flesh to the age and condition of responsibility and accountability may place himself within the reach of Divine mercy, and obtain absolution for personal sin by compliance with the laws and ordinances of the Gospel, as prescribed and decreed by the Author of the plan of salvation. The indispensable conditions of individual salvation are: (1) Faith in the Lord Jesus Christ; that is, acceptance of His Gospel and allegiance to His commandments, and to Him as the one and only Savior of men. (2) Repentance, embracing genuine contrition for the sins of the past, and a resolute turning away therefrom, with a determination to avoid, by all possible effort, future sin. (3) Baptism by immersion in water, for the remission of sins, the ordinance to be administered by one having the authority of the Priesthood, that is to say the right and commission to thus officiate in the name of Diety. (4) The higher baptism of the Spirit or bestowal of the Holy Ghost by the authorized imposition of hands by one holding the requisite authority—that of the Higher or Melchizedek Priesthood. To insure the salvation to which compliance with these fundamental principles of the Gospel of Jesus Christ makes the repentant believer eligible, a life of continued resistance to sin and observance of the laws of righteousness is requisite.

We hold that salvation from sin is obtainable only through obedience, and that while the door to the Kingdom of God has been opened by the sacrificial death and resurrection of our Lord the Christ, no man may enter there except by his personal and voluntary application expressed in terms of obedience to the prescribed laws and ordinances of the Gospel. Christ "became the author of eternal salvation to all them that obey him" (Heb.5:9). And further: God "will render to every man according to his deeds: to them who by patient continuance in well doing seek for glory and honour and immortality, eternal life: But unto them that are contentious, and do not obey the truth, but obey unrighteousness, indignation and wrath, tribulation and anguish, upon every soul of man that doeth evil, ★★★ For there is no respect of persons with God." (Romans 2:6-11.)

"Mormon" philosophy holds that salvation, thus made accessible to all through faith and works, implies no uniformity of condition as to future happiness and glory, any more than does condemnation of the soul mean the same state of disappointment, remorse and misery to all who incur that dread but natural penalty. We reject the unscriptural dogma that for resurrected souls there are but two places or states of eternal existence—heaven and hell—to the one or the other of which each shall be assigned according to the record of his deeds, whether good or bad, and however narrow the margin may appear on the balance sheet of his mortal life. "In my father's house are many mansions:" said the embodied Christ to His apostles, and "if it were not so, I would have told you. I go to prepare a place for you." (John 14:1, 2.)

The life we are to experience hereafter will be in righteous strictness the result of the life we lead in this world; and as here men exhibit infinite gradations of faithful adherence to the truth, and of servility to sin, so in the world beyond the grave shall gradations exist. Salvation grades into exaltation, and every soul shall find place and conditions as befits him, "Mormonism" affirms, on the basis of direct revelation from God, that graded degrees of glory are prepared for the souls of men, and that these comprise in decreasing order the Celestial, the Terrestrial and the Telestial kingdoms of glory, within each of which are orders or grades innumerable. These several glories—Celestial, Terrestrial, and Telestial—are comparable to the sun, the moon and the stars, in their beauty, worth and splendor. Such a condition was revealed to an apostle of olden time: "there are also celestial bodies, and bodies terrestrial; but the glory of the celestial is one, and the glory of the terrestrial is another. There is one glory of the sun, and another glory of the moon, and another glory of the stars: for one star differeth from another in glory. So also is the resurrection of the dead." (I Cor. 15:40-42.) Thus is it provided in the economy of God, that to progression there is no end.

As a necessary consequence, man may advance by effort and by obedience to higher and yet higher laws as he may learn them through the eternities to come, until he attains the rank and status of Godship. "Mormonism" is so bold as to declare that such is the possible destiny of the human soul. And why not? Is this possibility unreasonable? Would not the contrary be opposed to what we recognize as natural law? Man is the lineage of the Gods. He is the spirit-offspring of the Eternal One, and by the inviolable law that living things perpetuate after their kind, the children of God may become like unto their Parents in kind if not degree. The human soul is a God *in embryo;* even as the crawling caterpillar or the corpse-like chrysalis embodies the potential possibilities of the matured and glorified imago. We assert that there was more than figurative simile, and instead thereof the assured possibility of actual attainment in the Master's words: "Be ye therefore perfect, even as your Father which is in heaven is perfect." (Matt. 5:48.)

The fact of man's eternal progression in nowise indicates a state of eventual equality on however exalted a plane; nor does it imply that the progressive soul must in the eternal eons overtake those once far ahead of him in achievement. Advancement is not a characteristic of inferior status alone; indeed, the increment of progress may be vastly greater in the higher spheres of activity. This conception leads to the inevitable deduction that God Himself, Elohim, the Very Eternal Father, is a progressive Being, eternally advancing from one perfection to another, possessed as He is of that distinguishing attribute, which shall be the endowment of all who attain eternal exaltation—the power of eternal increase.

6.

The establishment of the Church of Jesus Christ in the "meridian of time," by the personal ministry and atoning death of the foreordained Redeemer and Savior of mankind, and the proclamation of His saving Gospel through the ministry of the Holy Priesthood during the apostolic period and for a season thereafter.

"Mormonism" incorporates as an essential part of its philosophy the scriptural account of the earthly birth, life, ministry, and death of Jesus Christ; and affirms the fulfillment of prophecy in all the events of the Savior's earthly existence and works. The time of His birth has been made a dividing line in the history of the ages; it was veritably the "meridian of time." Early in His ministry on earth He declared, and throughout His subsequent years repeatedly affirmed that He had come in pursuance of foreordained plan and purpose—not to do His own will but that of the Father who sent Him.

From the days of Moses down to the advent of Christ the people of Israel, who constituted the only nation professing to know and worship the true and the living God—"Jehovah worshippers" as they were distinctively called—had lived under the law of carnal commandments comprised in the Mosaic code. To Israel the law and prophets were the scriptures of life, however much the people may have departed therefrom through traditional alterations and misconstruction. Christ came not to destroy the Law—for it was He who gave the Law—amidst the awful glory of Sinai—but to fulfill and supersede the Law by the Gospel. Aside from the transcendent work of Atonement, Jesus Christ taught the principles of the Gospel, and laid down in plainness the laws and ordinances essential to the salvation of mankind. He made clear the fact that the Law of Moses had been given as a preparation for the Gospel which he gave to Israel.

He chose men for work in the ministry; in a special sense He chose twelve, whom He ordained and called Apostles. To them He committed power and authority not alone to preach and teach, to heal the sick, rebuke and cast out demons, but to build up the Church as a divinely established institution. These men were assured that through the Holy Ghost even after the Lord's ascension they would be kept in communion and communication with Christ and the Father; and that upon the foundation of such close relationship, *viz.,* direct revelation from God to man, would the Church of Jesus Christ be reared. That the apostles realized the actuality of their authority, and that of the responsibility resting upon them by virtue of their ordination to the Holy Priesthood, is evidenced by their prompt action following the Ascension, in filling the vacancy existing in the body as a consequence of Iscariot's apostasy and suicide, and other administrative acts.

When the Holy Ghost was given unto the Twelve, at the memorable time of Pentecost, the gifts, graces and powers of the Holy Priesthood were manifested through those men as never had been before; and the proof of their wondrous investiture of actual power and inherent authority continued throughout their lives. The apostles carried the Gospel of Jesus Christ to every known nation establishing church communities or branches of the church wherever possible. For each of these branches, the requisite officers were chosen and ordained, such as high priests, elders, bishops, priests, teachers and deacons; while for more general supervision evangelists and pastors were commissioned with the powers of priesthood. So zealous and efficient were the apostles in their particular ministry, that the Gospel of salvation was known to Jew and Gentile. Paul, writing approximately thirty years after the Ascension, declared then the Gospel had been preached to every creature under heaven (Col. 1:23), which assertion we may reasonably construe as meaning that the Gospel message had been proclaimed so widely that all who desired might learn of it.

The purpose of establishing the several graded offices of authority in the Church, and if installing therein men duly ordained to the requisite order of priesthood, has been impressively stated as "for the perfecting of the saints, for the work of the ministry, for the edifying of the body of Christ." (Eph. 4:12.) So necessary were the several offices to the proper administration of the affairs of the Church, that they were aptly compared to the several organs of a perfect human body (see I Cor. 12), all essential to a fulness of efficiency, and no one justified in saying to the other, "I have no need of thee."

7.

The general "falling away" from the Gospel of Jesus Christ, by which the world degenerated into a state of apostasy, and the Holy Priesthood ceased to be operative in the organizations of sects and churches designed and effected by the authority of man.

The apostolic ministry continued in the Primitive Church for about sixty years after the death of Christ, or nearly to the end of the first century of the Christian era. For some time thereafter the Church existed as a unified body, officered by men duly invested by ordination in the authority of the Holy Priesthood, though, even during the lifetime of some of the apostles, the leaven of apostasy and disintegration had been working. Indeed, hardly had the Gospel seed been sown when the enemy of all righteousness had started assiduously to sow tares in the field; and so closely intimate was the growth of the two that any forcible attempt to extirpate the tares would have imperiled the wheat. The evidences of spiritual decline were observed with anguish by the apostles who, however, recognized the fulfilment of earlier prophecy in the declension, and added their own inspired testimony to the effect that even a greater falling away was impending.

The apostasy progressed rapidly, in consequence of a cooperation of disrupting forces without and within the Church. The dreadful persecution to which the early Christians were subjected, particularly from the reign of Nero to that of Diocletian, both inclusive, drove great numbers of Christians to renounce their allegiance to Christianity, thus causing a widespread *apostasy from the Church.* But far more destructive was the contagion of evil that spread within the body, manifesting its effects mainly in the following developments:

(1) The corrupting of the simple principles of the Gospel of Christ by admixture with the so-called philosophical systems of the times.

(2) Unauthorized additions to the rites of the Church, and the introduction of vital changes in essential ordinances.

(3) Unauthorized changes in Church organization and government.

The result of the degeneracy so produced was to bring about an actual *apostasy of the entire Church.*

In the early part of the fourth century, Constantine cast about the Church the mantle of state recognition and government protection. Though unbaptized and therefore no member of the Church, he proclaimed himself the head of the Church of Christ, and distributed at his pleasure the titles and office in the Holy Priesthood. Churchly dignity was more sought after than military distinctions or honors of state. A bishop was more esteemed than a general, and an archbishop than a prince. Soon the Church laid claim to temporal power, and in the course of the centuries became the supreme potentate over all earthly governments.

Revolt was inevitable, and early in the sixteenth century the Reformation was begun. One notable effect of this epoch-making movement was the establishment of the Church of England as an immediate result of a disagreement between Henry VIII and the Pope. By Act of Parliament the king was proclaimed the supreme head of the Church within his realm. The Church as an organization, whether Papal or Protestant, had become an institution of men. The Holy Priesthood, to which men of old were called of God and ordained thereto by those having authority through prior ordination, no longer existed among men. The name but not the authority of priesthood and priestly office remained. Bishops, priests, and deacons—so called— were made or unmade at the will of kings. The awful fact of the universal apostasy, and the absence of Divine authority from the earth was observed and frankly admitted by many earnest and conscientious theologians. The Church of England, in her "Homily Against Peril of Idolatry" (Homily xiv) officially affirmed the state of general degeneracy as follows: "So that laity and clergy, learned and unlearned, all ages, sects, and degrees of men, women and children of whole Christendom—an horrible and most dreadful thing to think—have been at once drowned in abominable idolatry; of all other vices most detested of God, and most damnable to man; and that by the space of eight hundred years and more." The Book of Homilies dates from about the middle of the sixteenth century, and in it is thus officially set forth, that the so-called Church and in fact the entire religious world had been utterly apostate for eight centuries or more prior to the establishment of the Church of England.

The apostasy had been divinely predicted; its actuality is attested by a reasonable interpretation of history.

8.

The restoration of the Gospel in the current age, and the reestablishment of the Church of Jesus Christ by the bestowal of the Holy priesthood through Divine revelation.

From the time of the Reformation, sects and churches have multiplied apace. On every side there has been heard the cry "Lo, here is

Christ," or "Lo, there." As the present speaker has written elsewhere: There are churches named from the circumstances of their origin—as the Church of England; others after their famous founders or promoters—as Lutheran, Calvinist, Wesleyan; some are known by the peculiarities of doctrine or plan of administration—as Methodist, Presbyterian, Baptist, Congregationalist; but down to the third decade of the nineteenth century there was no church on earth affirming name or title as the Church of Jesus Christ. The only organization called a church existing at that time and venturing to assert claim to authority by succession was the Catholic Church, which for centuries had been apostate, and wholly bereft of Divine authority or recognition. If the "Mother Church" be without a valid priesthood, and devoid of spiritual power, how can her offspring derive from her the right to officiate in the things of God? Who would dare to affirm that man can originate a priesthood which God is bound to honor and acknowledge?

Granted that men may and do create among themselves societies, associations, sects, and even "churches" if they choose so to designate their religious organizations; granted they may prescribe rules, formulate laws, and devise plans of operation, discipline, and government, and that all such laws, rules, and schemes of administration are binding upon those who assume membership—granted all these rights and powers—whence can such human institutions derive the authority of the Holy Priesthood, without which there can be no Church of Christ? [see *Jesus the Christ* p. 752.]

But the world was not to be forever bereft of the Church of Jesus Christ, nor of the authority of the Holy Priesthood. As surely as had been predicted the birth of the Messiah, and the great falling away from the Church of His founding, was the restoration of the Gospel foretold as a characteristic feature of the last days, the dispensation of the fulness of times. John, the apostle and revelator, saw in vision the foreappointed reopening of the windows of heaven in the last days, and thus affirmed: "And I saw another angel fly in the midst of heaven, having the everlasting gospel to preach unto them that dwell on earth, and to every nation, and kindred, and tongue, and people, Saying with a loud voice, Fear God, and give glory to him; for the hour of his judgment is come: and worship him that made heaven, and earth, and the sea, and the fountains of waters." (Rev. 14:6, 7.)

The Church of Jesus Christ of Latter-day Saints is founded upon the literal fulfilment of this prediction—for prophecy it was, though worded as a record of what the prophet and revelator saw—an event of a then future but now past time.

"Mormonism" as a religious system would be incomplete, inconsistent, and consequently without philosophical basis, but for its solemn avouchment that the Gospel had been restored to earth and that the Church of Jesus Christ has been reestablished among men. The Church today affirms to the world, that in A.D. 1820 there was manifested to Joseph Smith a theophany such as never before had been vouchsafed to man. He was but a youth at the time, living with his parents in the State of New York. Being confused and puzzled by the "war of words and tumult of opinions" by which the many contending sects were divided, and realizing that not all could be right, he acted upon the admonition of James: "If any of you lack wisdom, let him ask of God, that giveth to all men liberally, and upbraideth not; and it shall be given him." (James 1:5.)

In answer to the young man's earnest prayer as to which, if any, of the discordant sects of the day was the Church of Christ, as he solemnly avows, both the Eternal Father and His Son Jesus Christ appeared to him in visible form as distinct and glorified Personages; and the One, pointing to the Other, said: *"This is my Beloved Son, hear Him!"* The Son of God, Jesus Christ, directed the young man to ally himself with none of the sects or churches of the day, for all of them were wrong and their creeds were an abomination in His sight, in that they drew near to Him with their lips while their hearts were far from Him, and because they taught for doctrines the commandments of men, having a form of godliness but denying the power thereof. Thus was broken, by the voices of Eternal Beings, the long silence that had lain between the heavens and the earth incident to the apostasy of mankind. In 1820 there stood upon this globe one person who knew beyond doubt or peradventure, that the "orthodox" conception of Deity as an incorporeal essence devoid of definite shape and tangible substance, was utterly false. Joseph Smith knew that both the Eternal Father and His glorified Son, Jesus Christ, were in form and stature like unto perfect men; and that in Their physical image and likeness mankind had been created in the flesh. He knew further that Father and Son were individual Personages—a fact abundantly averred by the Lord Jesus during His life on earth, but which had been obscured by the sophistries of men.

Somewhat more than three years after the glorious appearing of the Father and the Son to Joseph Smith, the young revelator was visited by a heavenly personage, who revealed to him the place where lay the ancient record which since has been translated through the gift and power of God and published to the world as the Book of Mormon. This volume contains a history of a division of the House of Israel, which had been led to the western continent centuries before the time of Christ. It is the ancient scripture of the western continent as the Holy Bible is the record of the dealings of God with His people on the eastern hemisphere. The Book of Mormon contains the Gospel of Christ in its fulness as given to the ancient inhabitants of this continent; and in its restoration, through the personal ministry of an angel sent from the presence of God, was fulfilled in part the vision-prophecy of John the Revelator of old.

The Holy Priesthood, having been lost to mankind through the universal apostasy, could be made again operative and valid only by a restoration or rebestowal from the heavens.

We affirm that the Lesser or Aaronic Priesthood, including the Levitical order, was conferred upon Joseph Smith and his companion in the ministry, Oliver Cowdery, through personal ordination under the hands of John, known of old as the Baptist, who appeared to the two men as a resurrected being, and transmitted to them the authority by which he had ministered while in mortality. That order of the Priesthood—the Aaronic—as John the Baptist declared, holds the keys of the Gospel of repentance for the remission of sins.

We affirm that the Higher or Melchizedek Priesthood was conferred upon Joseph Smith and Oliver Cowdery by ordination under the hands of those who, in the ancient apostolic period, held the keys of the Holy Apostleship, *viz.,* Peter, James and John.

Under the authority so bestowed, the Church of Jesus Christ has been reestablished upon the earth. To distinguish it from the Church as it existed in ancient apostolic days it has been named—and this also through direct revelation—*The Church of Jesus Christ of Latter-day Saints.*

As an institution among men, as a body corporate, it dates from April 6, 1830, on which day the Church was legally organized at Fayette, Seneca County, New York, under the laws of the State. Only six persons figured as actual participants in the formal procedure of organization and incorporation, that number being the minimum required by law in such an undertaking.

Whatever may be the opinions of individuals, or the consensus of belief, respecting the genuineness and validity of the claims set forth by the restored Church as to the source of the Priesthood it professes to hold, none can reasonably prefer the charge of incongruity or inconsistency on scriptural grounds. It is axiomatic to say that no man can give or transmit an authority he does not himself possess. The authority of the Priesthood of Aaron was restored to earth by the being who held the keys of that power in the earlier dispensation—John the Baptist. The Holy Apostleship, comprising all the powers inherent in the Priesthood after the order of Melchizedek, was restored by those who held the presidency of that Priesthood prior to the apostasy, *viz.,* Peter, James and John.

We further affirm, that in 1836 there appeared to Joseph Smith and Oliver Cowdery in the Temple at Kirtland, Ohio, other ancient prophets, each of whom authoritatively bestowed upon the two mortal prophets, seers, and revelators, the keys of the power by which he had ministered in the long past dispensation in which he had officiated. Thus came Moses and committed to the modern prophets the keys of the gathering of Israel after their long dispersion. Elias came, and gave the authority that had been operative in the dispensation of the Gospel of Abraham. Elijah followed, in literal fulfilment of Malachi's porten-tous prediction, and committed the authority of vicarious labor for the dead, by which the hearts of the departed fathers shall be turned toward their yet living descendants, and the hearts of the children be turned toward the fathers, which labor, as affirmed by Malachi, is a necessary antecedent to the dawn of the great and dreadful day of the Lord, as otherwise the earth would be smitten with a curse at His coming.

9.

The appointed mission of the restored Church of Jesus Christ to preach the Gospel and administer in the ordinances thereof amongst all nations, in preparation for the near advent of our Savior Jesus Christ, who shall reign on earth as Lord and King.

The Church of Jesus Christ of Latter-day Saints, claiming to be all that its name expresses or logically implies, holds that its special mission in the world is to officiate in the authority of the Holy Priesthood by proclaiming the Gospel and administering in the ordi-nances thereof amongst all nations, and this in preparation for the advent of the Lord Jesus Christ, who shall soon appear and assume His rightful place as King of kings and Lord of lords.

Besides its missionary labor among the living, the Church, true to the commission laid upon it through Elijah, is continuously engaged in vicarious service for the dead, administering the ordinances of salvation to the living in behalf of their departed progenitors. Largely for this purpose the Church constructs Temples, and maintains therein the requisite ministry in behalf of the dead.

In carrying out the work committed to it, the Church is tolerant of all sects and parties, claiming for itself no right or privilege which it would deny to individuals or other organizations. It affirms itself to be *The Church* of old established anew. Its message to the world is that of peace and good will—the invitation to come and partake of the blessings incident to the new and everlasting covenant between God and His children. Its warning voice is heard in all lands and climes:

Repent ye! Repent! For the kingdom of Heaven is at hand.

Such in scant outline is the philosophical basis of "Mormonism".

{24}

Jesus the Christ

(Entries from the Journal of James E. Talmage, 1904-22,
Archives and Manuscripts, Harold B. Lee Library,
Brigham Young University, Provo, Utah)

Sept. 18, 1904—Sunday: Forenoon committee meeting and afternoon consultation regarding University Sunday School. Decided to conduct the work this year as lecture courses, of which there will be one on the Book of Mormon by Brother John M. Mills, and one on the subject "Jesus The Christ" by myself. . . .

Aug. 9, 1905— . . . In the course of the interview with the First Presidency, I was handed the attached letter, which has been awaiting me since the date thereof. Compliance with the request will require much time as not half the lectures have been delivered and not a line of one of them written, except as class notes.

The First Presidency
    of the
Church of Jesus Christ
    of
Latter-day Saints
P.O. Box B
    Salt Lake City, Utah

July 18th, 1905

Dr. James E. Talmage,
City.

Dear Brother:—

We should be pleased to have you print and publish in book form the course of lectures being delivered by you before the University Sunday School on the subject, Jesus the Christ, believing they will prove a valuable acquisition to our Church Literature, and that the proposed work should be placed within the reach of Church members and general readers.

Your Brethren,
Joseph F. Smith
John R. Winder
Anthon H. Lund . . .

Sept. 14, 1914—During the school periods of 1904-1905, and 1905-1906, I delivered a series of lectures entitled "Jesus The Christ" under the auspices of the University Sunday School. The sessions were held during Sunday forenoons in Barratt Hall. I received written appointment from the First Presidency to embody the lectures in a book to be published for the use of the Church in general. Work on this appointment has been suspended from time to time owing to other duties being imposed upon me. Lately, however, I have been asked to prepare the matter for the book with as little delay as possible. Experiences demonstrated that neither in my comfortable office nor in the convenient study room at home can I be free from visits and telephone calls. The consequence of this condition and in view of the importance of the work, I had been directed to occupy a room in the Temple where I will be free from interruption. I began the work in the Temple today and hope that I shall be able to devote the necessary time thereto. . . .

Nov. 19, 1914—Spent some time at the office of the First Presidency. During the afternoon attended a meeting of the First Presidency and certain invited members of the Deseret Sunday School Union Board. At this meeting I read aloud several chapters of the book, "Jesus The Christ" now in process of preparation. The purpose being to ascertain whether the book would be properly suited for the lower or higher grades in the theological department. As was intended the work is being prepared for our people in general and is not adapted for use as a textbook for immature students. It was decided by the First Presidency that the work be completed of the same scope and plan as here-to-fore followed, and that the theological department of the Deseret Sunday School Union provide their own outline of the students of the first years work in said departments. In connection with the matter of the book, it may be well to record here that since my beginning on the writing September 14th last, I have devoted every spare hour to that labor and have at present in written form though not all in revised condition, twenty chapters. According to present indications, the work of the book will be interrupted through other appointments already made. The purpose is, however, to bring it to completion at the earliest possible time, though with some relief from the intense pressure under which the writing has been here-to-fore done. . . .

Dec. 22, 1914—Sunday. Devoted a greater part of the tight day to study in the Temple. . . .

Jan. 1, 1915—I spent the greater part of this day in the Temple engaged in study and writing on the book, "Jesus The Christ", to which labor I have been devoting for months past all available time. . . .

Jan. 10th, 1915—Sunday. Was engaged in study at the Temple greater part of the day, then attended the prayer circle. . . .

Jan. 12, 1915—Engaged in committee work at the President's office during the early part of the day and in the Temple, as usual, at all spare time. . . .

Jan. 16, 1915—Engaged in President's office during early part of the day and in the Temple the rest of the day. . . .

Feb. 6, 1915—Engaged in committee work as appointed by the Presidency greater part of the day. Succeeded in devoting a few hours to writing.

Feb. 7, 1915—Sunday. Wife and I attended fast meeting in the Temple and during the forenoon and I remained in the Temple engaged in scriptural study during the rest of the day. . . .

Feb. 12, 1915—Lincoln's Birthday. I devoted the day to writing on the book.

Feb. 13, 1915—Engaged in the Temple throughout the day.

Feb. 14, 1915—Sunday. Spent greater part of the day in the Temple. . . .

Feb. 21, 1915—Sunday. Engaged in the Temple during the forenoon. Attended prayer circle during the afternoon; . . .

Feb. 28, 1915—Sunday. Spent greater part of the day in the Temple, as I have spent every day on which I have been free from appointments for months past. Attended prayer circle during the afternoon and was engaged for considerable length of time for administering to the afflicted. . . .

Mar. 28, 1915—Sunday. Engaged in the Temple greater part of the day. Attended prayer circle in the afternoon. . . .

Apr. 19th, 1915—Finished the actual writing on the book, "Jesus The Christ" to which I have devoted every spare hour since settling down to the work of composition on September 14th, last. Had it not been that I was privileged to do this work in the Temple, it would be at present far from completion. I have felt the inspiration of the place and have appreciated the privacy and quietness incident thereto. I hope to proceed with the work of revision without delay. . . .

May 4th, 1915—At meeting of the First Presidency and Twelve in the Temple, I read three chapters of the book. At each of the meetings thus far held for this purpose, all members of the First Presidency and all of the Twelve who are not absent from the city on appointed duties were present. We have now read nine of the 43 chapters. . . .

May 6, 1915—Attended committee meeting at 8:15 a.m. in the Temple. At 9:30 a.m. the Presidency and Twelve sat to hear another reading of the matter prepared for the book. Two chapters were read and passed. Then attended regular council meeting of the First Presidency and the Twelve.

May 7, 1915—Forenoon devoted to reading four chapters of the book to the First Presidency and the Twelve. . . .

May 11, 1915—Forenoon devoted to meeting of First Presidency and Twelve at which three chapters of the book were read. . . .

May 13, 1915—Attended an early morning meeting of the counselors of the First Presidency and Twelve at which three chapters of the book were read. The reading thus far finished includes chapter 21. President Smith was absent, he having left yesterday afternoon for a trip to the Hawaiian Islands. . . .

May 18, 1915—Read three chapters of the book to the Brethren during the forenoon. . . .

May 20, 1915—Attended early meeting of the First Presidency and Twelve and read to the Brethren two chapters of the book. . . .

May 25, 1915—Read two chapters of the book to the First Presidency and Twelve. . . .

May 27, 1915—Attended council meeting of First Presidency and Twelve in the Temple. Before regular services of the council began, I read to the brethren two chapters of the forthcoming book. . . .

June 1, 1915—Attended 12th sitting of the First Presidency and such members of the Twelve as were in town, held for the purpose of hearing read the book "Jesus The Christ". Two chapters were read today. First installment of copy of the book "Jesus The Christ" was delivered to the printer today. Contract provides that the book shall be ready for delivery the first of September. . . .

June 3, 1915—Spent two and one-half hours in reading to the First Presidency and Twelve, then attended regular council meeting of First Presidency and Twelve. . . .

June 8, 1915—Read two chapters of the book to First Presidency and Twelve. . . .

June 15, 1915— . . . then attended a late afternoon meeting of the First Presidency and Twelve at which two more chapters of the book were read. . . .

June 17, 1915—Read one chapter of the book to the First Presidency and Twelve.

June 18, 1915—Immediately after the meeting, President Joseph F. Smith, President Anthon H. Lund, and I met as a committee appointed before President Smith's departure on his recent tour to consider the section in chapter 11 of the book, "Jesus The Christ", relating to the Son of Man. The section was passed in the form in which it had been written. . . .

June 24, 1915—Had an early meeting of the First Presidency and Twelve. I read the last installment of the matter for the book. This was the 18th sitting of the council to hear the reading of the manuscript. Printing is now in progress on the book. . . .

July 4, 1915—Sunday, Fast Day. I was engaged during the day in revising chapters of the book on which the printers are at work during my absence. . . .

July 10, 1915—Engaged during the afternoon in reading proofs of the book that have been sent me and telegraphed specifications of typographical errors.

July 11, 1915—Sunday. Left for home. Engaged in proofreading on the train.

July 12, 1915—Reached Salt Lake City about 9:00 p.m. Spent about 2 hours at the office examining the last proof sheets and then went to the house.

July 14, 1915—Yesterday and today have been engaged in consultation with Church Authorities and in proof reading. . . .

Aug. 7, 1915—Practically every spare moment of my time since my return from San Francisco has been given up to the revision of copy and reading of proofs for the book "Jesus The Christ", the printing is now well advanced. . . .

Aug. 12, 1915—Attended council meeting of First Presidency and Twelve. Since returning from the coast I have devoted every spare hour to the work of revising copy and reading proofs in connection with the book "Jesus The Christ." . . .

Aug. 19, 1915—The attached official notice issued by the First Presidency first appeared in the Deseret Evening News of August 14th, and has been reprinted at intervals since. The purpose of giving this early notice is to advise Church school authorities and officers and other Church organizations concerning the publication of the book so that they may plan to include it in their courses.

This announcement is printed in the news on the 14th signed by Joseph F. Smith, Anthon Lund and Charles Penrose.

OFFICIAL ANNOUNCEMENT

Within the month of September, 1915, there will be issued from The Deseret News press a book entitled Jesus the Christ, written by Elder James E. Talmage, of the Council of the Twelve. This important work has been prepared by appointment, and is to be published by the Church. The field of treatment is indicated on the title-page as "A study of the Messiah and his mission, according to Holy Scriptures both ancient and modern."

The book is more than a "Life of Christ" in the ordinary acceptation of that title, as it not only treats at length the narrative of our Lord's life and ministry in the flesh, together with his death, resurrection, and ascension, but deals also with his antemortal existence and Godship, and with his ministry in the resurrected state, both of old and in the current dispensation. The sacred subject of our Savior's life and mission is presented as it is accepted and proclaimed by the Church that bears his Holy Name.

We desire that the work, "Jesus the Christ" to be read and studied by the Latter-day Saints, in their families, and in the organizations that are devoted wholly or in part to theological study. We commend it especially for use in our Church schools, as also for the advanced theological classes in Sunday schools and priesthood quorums, for the instruction of our missionaries, and for general reading.

JOSEPH F. SMITH,
ANTHON H. LUND,
CHARLES W. PENROSE,

First Presidency of the Church of Jesus Christ of Latter- day Saints. Salt Lake City, Utah, Aug. 13, 1915. . . .

Aug. 29, 1915—Sunday. Attended morning and afternoon sessions of the quarterly conference of the Granit[e] Stake. In accordance with request of the Stake Presidency, I was appointed to this duty with the special provision that I speak on the subject of "Jesus The Christ". . . .

Sept. 3, 1915—Returning to the printers the final proof sheets of the last forms of the book, "*Jesus The Christ*". . . .

Sept. 5, 1915—In the evening I attended by appointment the meeting in the 12th-13th Ward and in accordance with prior requests, spoke on the subject, "Jesus The Christ." . . .

Sept. 7, 1915—Attended regular weekly meeting of the General Board of the Sunday School Union. During the pressing labor in connection with bringing out of the new book, I have been excused from attendance at meetings of auxiliary boards for many months past. Today the First Presidency renewed an appointment originally made about 5 years ago and suspended because of press of work—that I prepare as soon as possible a work dealing with the restoration of the gospel. The book to be in the nature of a companion volume to "The Great Apostasy". . . .

Sept. 9, 1915—Today I had the great pleasure of presenting to the First Presidency the first three copies of the book "Jesus The Christ" to leave the bindery. . . .

Sept. 11, 1915—The first newspaper review and advertisement of the book, "Jesus The Christ", appeared in this evenings Deseret News. Clippings attached. . . .

Oct. 13, 1915—At a conference today attended by the First Presidency, Brother Horrace G. Whitney, Business manager of the Deseret News, and myself. Brother Whitney explained the need of an early beginning on the second edition of the book, "Jesus The Christ". This day marks the end of the first month since the book was placed on sale, and according to Brother Whitney's written report, over half the edition has already been sold. As the book is to be used in the Advanced Theology classes in the Sunday Schools beginning January next, and as it also has been adopted in the Quorum classes of the Melchizedek Priesthood, it appears that a second edition must be issued before the beginning of the coming year. The decision was reached today that plans for the second edition be proceeded with immediately. . . .

Oct. 26, 1915—Was occupied in committee work with President Lyman and in consultation with the First Presidency during the greater part of the day. Definite action was taken by the First Presidency authorizing the Deseret News to proceed with the preparation of a second edition of the book "Jesus The Christ", the issue not to succeed 10,100 copies. Owing to lack of capacity in the Deseret News plant, it is probable that both printing and binding will be done in New York. . . .

Nov. 10, 1915—Engaged with the First Presidency during greater part of the forenoon. Left by evening train for the East. My course of travel lies by a Oregon short line Union Pacific Chicago Northwestern to Chicago. The prime purpose of my going is that of being on the ground in New York during the electrotyping of the book "Jesus The Christ", the type-setting of which is now nearing completion according to telegraphic reports. Proof sheets will be ready for me on the 15th. Our train was delayed at Ogden about three hours waiting for the train from the West. . . .

Nov. 13, 1915—Engaged during greater part of the day in close reading. A stop of 2 hours at Buffalo, 4-6 p.m. gave me an opportunity for much-appreciated exercise. I spent greater part of the two hours in brisk walking. Then went by a Delaware Lackawanna and Western Railway. Read late into the night. Had been able to read critically about 3/4ths of the book while traveling. [14-30 November 1915 were spent proof-reading the second edition of *Jesus The Christ* in New York City; Talmage then returned to Salt Lake City.] . . .

Nov. 23, 1922—Thurs. Attended council meeting of the First Presidency and Twelve, which lasted longer than usual. This is the 76th birthday of our faithful brother, George S. Gibbs, who has been secretary in the office of the First Presidency through many administrations. It is also the 42nd birthday of Brother Richard R. Lyman of the Council of the Twelve.

Today I received a copy of the book "Jesus the Christ," sixth edition, including the 30th thousand. This edition has been printed at the Deseret News establishment from the electroplates used in earlier issues, with some corrections of typographical errors and other minor changes. Both in printing and in binding the new book presents a very attractive appearance. The work has been "out of print" for months past.

A new edition of the combined Doctrine and Covenants and Pearl of Great Price has been finished, and today I examined the first copy. This issue comprises 1500 copies, printed by the W.B. Conkey Company of Hammond, Indiana, and bound in divinity circuit style by James Pott and Company of New York City. This edition is printed on thin paper and forms a companion volume to the India paper Book of Mormon, divinity circuit binding. . . .

{25}

"A Marvelous Work and a Wonder," An Address Delivered on 9 April 1916

(from *Eighty-sixth Annual Conference of the Church of Jesus Christ of Latter-day Saints* [Salt Lake City: Published by the Deseret News, 1916], pp. 124-31)

The presence of these multitudes at each recurring conference of the Church, and particularly the spirit of earnestness and devotion which the people manifest, appeal to me as striking evidences of the marvelous work and the wonder which the God of Israel has accomplished and is accomplishing in these, the last days. That great work, of which the prophets in the ages past have predicted to be characteristic of the day toward which they looked with anxious and eager anticipation, is the establishment of the Church and the development and growth thereof in the dispensation of fulness.

The kingdom of God has been set up upon the earth. In ancient writ, scriptural and otherwise, the expressions "Kingdom of God" and "Kingdom of Heaven" were often used interchangeably; or at least our modern translation of those writings present to us interchangeable usages of these names and titles of the great institutions; but in this, as in many other instances, we find the light of modern revelation illuming and making plain what may otherwise be dark and in part unintelligible. Through the revelations given in this day and age, we recognize the fact that there is a distinction between the kingdom of God and the kingdom of Heaven. The Church established in the present age, embodying the restored Gospel, is the Kingdom of God, it is the Church of Jesus Christ.

The members of that Church are often spoken of as "Mormons", and the Church has come to be known more generally as the "Mormon Church" than by its proper name and distinguishing title, the Church of Jesus Christ of Latter-day Saints. We as a people do not maintain any strong protest against the application of the term "Mormon" and its several derivatives; though we deplore the fact that misunderstanding may arise in the minds of inquirers and investigators respecting the significance of that name, which originally was used as a nickname in its application to the Church. You may call us Mormons if you will; remember, however, as you must—must, if you will have respect unto the truth—that this is not the church of Mormon. Mormon was a man, a very worthy man and a very great man in his day when he lived in the flesh, and a very great personage since that time; but he was a man among men, and while his name is very properly applied to the abridgement of certain early records, which abridgements he made and supplemented by many writings of his own, now published under the name of the Book of Mormon, the Church is not his church, nor is it the church of Peter or James or John, nor is it the church of Joseph Smith, nor of Brigham Young, nor of Joseph F. Smith, nor the church of the present authorities of the body. It is the Church of Jesus Christ and it is the only Church upon the face of the earth affirming divine authorization for the use of the name of the Savior of mankind as part of its distinctive designation.

It is very proper that we inquire as to what particular message the Church thus distinguished has to give to the world respecting its Master, its divine Head, the Son of the living God, in vindication of its claims to so honorable a title as that which it bears. In the first place, it reiterates all the truth that has been given in former ages and earlier dispensations regarding Jesus Christ and His ministry, and it sets forth in plainness, together with other matters of the greatest worth, knowledge beyond all price, which has been given unto the Church as new revelation in the day and age in which we live. Among the distinguishing features of the Church concerning the Savior and Redeemer of the race are these:

First, the Church affirms the unity and continuity of the mission of the Christ in all ages. This, of necessity, involves the actuality, the verity, of His pre-existence and pre-ordination or foreordination in the spirit state.

Second, the fact of His antemortal Godship.

Third, the actuality of His birth in the flesh as the natural issue of divine and mortal parentage.

Fourth, the reality of His death and physical resurrection, as a result of which the power of death over mankind shall be eventually overcome.

Fifth, the literalness of the atonement wrought by Him, and the absolute requirement of individual compliance with the laws and requirements of His Gospel as the only means by which salvation may be attained.

Sixth, the restoration of His Priesthood and the re-establishment of His Church in the current age, which is verily the dispensation of the fulness of times.

Seventh, the certainty of His return to earth in the near future with power and great glory to reign in person and in bodily presence as Lord and King.

In the interest of conciseness I have read these several specifications as they have been summarized and will appear in the forthcoming edition of a work now published by the Church to its members and to the world respecting the life and mission of Jesus the Christ. I invite your attention to the last of these specified points, the certainty of the return of Jesus Christ to earth in the near future, to reign upon the earth in person by bodily presence as the rightful King of earth. You have read, I am sure, of the wondrous incidents connected with the association of the resurrected Christ with the apostles and others between the time of His resurrection and that of His ascension from Mount Olivet, and when, on that eventful day, He led the Eleven who were still faithful to Him, and whom He had ordained to the holy apostleship, out toward Bethany. As He was conversing with them and giving them final instruction and doubtless encouragement, He rose from their midst and they saw Him ascend until He was hidden from their sight. In worshipful wonder they became aware of the presence of personages other than themselves—white-robed messengers from heaven who, remarking their wonder and astonishment, addressed them in these words: "Ye men of Galilee, why stand ye gazing up into heaven? This same Jesus, which is taken up from you into heaven, shall so come in like manner as ye have seen him go into heaven." [Acts 1:11] From that day the apostles preached the return of the Christ to earth, even as prophets before their time had predicted the great event. By the second advent of Christ we do not mean His manifestation to chosen prophets, to individuals or to a few such as His ministrations to Saul of Tarsus or His appearance to Joseph Smith in 1820 and again in the Kirtland temple after the organization of the Church, but a return in glory of which all the world shall know. His coming shall be like unto the lightning that flashes from the east to the west, to be seen of all men.

This Church proclaims the doctrine of the impending return of the Christ to earth in literal simplicity, without mental or other

173

reservation in our interpretation of the scriptural predictions. He will come with the body of flesh and bones in which His Spirit was tabernacled when He ascended from Mount Olivet. One of the characteristic features of the Church concerning that great, and in the language of the scripture, both glorious and terrible event, is its nearness. It is close at hand. The mission of the Church is to prepare the earth for the coming of its Lord. Biblical prophecies are numerous; the Book of Mormon prophecies are abundant, respecting the return of the Christ. His own words, both before and after His crucifixion and resurrection are unambiguous, definite, convincing and convicting unto those who do not close their ears wilfully against the truth. Referring to Himself the Savior said: "For the Son of man shall come in the glory of his Father with his angels; and then shall he reward every man according to his works." Read the context in the 16th chapter of Matthew. The prophets who lived before the meridian of time said comparatively little, though their testimony is abundant and all sufficient, concerning the return of the Christ; for they were devoted to the teaching of the doctrine of His first coming in the flesh, to live among men, to suffer and to die and to be resurrected from the dead. But after His resurrection and ascension the words of inspired teachers were definite in fore-telling the certainty of His return; and in this day and age of the world He has spoken with His own voice unto His prophets, impressing upon them the fact that the time of His coming in judgment is near at hand. Thus, within a few months after the Church was organized, in the year 1830, as recorded in the 29th section of the Doctrine and Covenants, the Lord Jesus Christ said unto His Prophet Joseph Smith:

"For the hour is nigh and the day soon at hand when the earth is ripe; and all the proud and they that do wickedly shall be as stubble, and I will burn them up, saith the Lord of hosts, that wickedness shall not be upon the earth;

"For the hour is nigh, and that which was spoken by mine apostles must be fulfilled; for as they spoke so shall it come to pass;

"For I will reveal myself from heaven with power and great glory, with all the hosts thereof and dwell in righteousness with men on earth a thousand years, and the wicked shall not stand." [D&C 29:9-11]

A month later, or at least in the month following, He spake again admonishing His servants to diligence:

"Wherefore," said He, "be faithful, praying always, having your lamps trimmed and burning, and oil with you, that you may be ready at the coming of the Bridegroom; for behold, verily, verily, I say unto you, that I come quickly. Even so. Amen." [D&C 33:17]

Referring to the teachings of the apostles of old, and particularly to His own instructions unto them, and employing the same figure by which He had made plain unto them that men may know of the imminence of His coming, by the signs which He specified, He said in March, 1831, again speaking through His Prophet Joseph:

"Ye look and behold the fig trees and ye see them with your eyes and ye say that when they begin to shoot forth and their leaves are yet tender that summer is now nigh at hand.

"Even so it shall be in that day when they shall see all these things, then shall they know that the hour is nigh.

"And it shall come to pass that he that feareth me shall be looking forth for the great day of the Lord to come, even for the signs of the coming of the Son of man:

"And they shall see signs and wonders, for they shall be shown forth in the heavens above, and in the earth beneath;

"And they shall behold blood, and fire, and vapors of smoke;

"And before the day of the Lord shall come, the sun shall be darkened, and the moon be turned into blood, and stars fall from heaven;

"And the remnant shall be gathered unto this place,

"And then they shall look for me, and, behold, I will come; and they shall see me in the clouds of heaven, clothed with power and great glory, with all the holy angels; and he that watches not for me shall be cut off." [D&C 45:37-44]

Still further impressing upon the Church in the early days of its history the fact that there was no time to be lost in preparation, for the time was all too short. He made plain the fact that His coming was so near that the intervening time is properly to be spoken of as today. "Behold, now it is called today", said He, "until the coming of the Son of man; and verily it is a day of sacrifice and a day for the tithing of my people; for he that is tithed shall not be burned at his coming, for after today cometh the burning. This is speaking after the manner of the Lord; for verily I say, tomorrow all the proud and they that do wickedly shall be as stubble; and I will burn them up, for I am the Lord of hosts; and I will not spare any that remain in Babylon. Wherefore, if ye believe me, ye will labor while it is called today." [D&C 64:23-25]

The scriptures abound in declarations and reiterations, in repeated and solemn affirmations of the great fact that the day of the Lord's coming will be a day of glory and a day of terror—of glory and recompense unto those who are living righteously, and a day of terror unto the proud and unto all who do wickedly. Now, many have asked, do we interpret that scripture as meaning that in the day of the Lord's coming, all who are not members of the Church shall be burned, or otherwise destroyed, and only this little body of men and women, very small compared with the uncounted hosts of men now living, shall be spared the burning and shall escape destruction? I think not so. I do not think we are justified in putting that interpretation upon the Lord's word, for He recognizes every man according to the integrity of his heart, and men who have not been able to understand the Gospel or who have not had opportunity of learning it and knowing of it will not be counted as the wilfully sinful who are fit only to be burned as stubble; but the proud, who lift themselves in the pride of their hearts and rise above the word of God and become a law unto themselves and who wilfully and with knowledge deny the saving virtues of the atonement of Christ, and who are seeking to lead others away from the truth will be dealt with by Him according to both justice and mercy.

A word concerning the distinction between the Kingdom and the Church. As already stated, the expression "Kingdom of God" is used synonomously with the term "Church of Christ"; but the Lord had made plain that He sometimes used the term "Kingdom of Heaven" in a distinctive sense. In 1832 He called attention to that in these words, addressing Himself to the elders of the Church:

"Hearken, and lo, a voice as of one from on high, who is mighty and powerful, whose going forth is unto the ends of the earth, yea whose voice is unto men—Prepare ye the way of the Lord, make his paths straight.

"The keys of the kingdom of God are committed unto man on the earth, and from thence shall the Gospel roll forth unto the ends of the earth, as the stone which is cut out of the mountain without hands shall roll forth until it has filled the whole earth;

"Yea, a voice crying—Prepare ye the way of the Lord, prepare ye the supper of the Lamb, make ready for the bridegroom;

"Pray unto the Lord, call upon his holy name, make known his wonderful works among the people;

"Call upon the Lord, that his kingdom may go forth upon the

earth, that the inhabitants thereof may receive it, and be prepared for the days to come, in the which the Son of man shall come down in heaven, clothed in the brightness of his glory, to meet the kingdom of God which is set up on the earth:

"Wherefore may the kingdom of God go forth, that the kingdom of heaven may come, that Thou, O God, mayest be glorified in heaven, so on earth, that thy enemies may be subdued, for Thine is the honor, power and glory, forever and ever. Amen." [D&C 65]

Such was the prayer, such is the prayer, prescribed for this people to pray, not to utter in words only, not to say only, but to pray—that the Kingdom of God may roll forth in the earth to prepare the earth for the coming of the Kingdom of Heaven. That provision in the Lord's prayer, "Thy kingdom come, thy will be done on earth as it is in heaven" has not been abrogated. We are praying for the Kingdom of Heaven to come, and are endeavoring to prepare the earth for its coming. The Kingdom of God, already set up upon the earth, does not aspire to temporal domination among the nations. It seeks not to overthrow any existing forms of government; it does not profess to exercise control in matters that pertain to the governments of the earth, except by teaching correct principles and trying to get men to live according to the principles of true government, before the Kingdom of Heaven shall come and be established upon the earth with a King at the head. But when He comes, He shall rule and reign, for it is His right.

Many of us are prone to think that the day of His coming, the day of the setting up of the Kingdom of Heaven in its power and glory is yet far distant. I take it that that assumption is based, perhaps, upon our wish, none the less real, because we hesitate to frame it in words. How would you feel if authoritative proclamation were made here today that on the literal morrow, when the sun shall rise again in the east, the Lord would appear in His glory to take vengeance upon the wicked, and to establish His Kingdom upon the earth? Who amongst you would rejoice? The pure in heart would, the righteous in soul would, but many of us would wish to have the event put off. We are very much in the frame of mind, or we may allow ourselves to fall in the frame of mind of the rule bound Pharisees and the casuistical Sadducees in the days of the Christ in the flesh. They were intent upon keeping the people's interest alive in a future Messiah, in a Christ who was to come, but not one who was amongst them. We are very loath to accept and believe that which we do not want to believe, and the world today does not wish to believe that the coming of the Christ is near at hand, and consequently all kinds of subterfuges are invented for explaining away the plain words of scripture. We rejoice in simplicity. The Gospel of Jesus Christ is wonderfully simple. We as a people value, I believe, scholastic attainments at their full worth. While we foster and encourage the training and development of the mind, I was about to say to the full limit, certainly almost to the limit, of our material ability, as witness the unceasing effort and continuous expenditure of vast funds in the maintenance of church schools, and the willingness with which the Latter-day Saints as members of the community impose upon themselves, in common with their fellow citizens, taxes for the support of schools under state control and direction, we nevertheless hold that scholastic attainments are not essential to a full understanding of the Gospel of Jesus Christ. We do not believe that a diploma from a theological seminary is an essential part of the credentials of a teacher or preacher of the word of God. Nevertheless we endeavor to encourage and aid in a material way the training of the mind and the development of all the faculties that shall be conducive to educational advancement in the truest sense of the term, but we hold the Gospel is simple that all may understand it who will. It is the proud and they who do wickedly who close their eyes and their ears and their hearts to the signs of the times, to the word of the Gospel and to the testimony of Christ. It has long been a favorite excuse of men who were not ready for the advent of the Lord, to say, "The Lord delayeth His coming." Don't attach too much importance to the fact that He has thus far delayed His coming, for He has repeatedly told us that the day of His coming is very, very near, even at our doors. There is a tendency among men to explain away what they don't wish to understand in literal simplicity, and we, as Latter-day Saints are not entirely free from the taint of that tendency. Prophecies that have not yet been fulfilled are by many of us made the subjects of hypothesis and theory and strained interpretation. We read that one of the characteristic signs to precede the second advent of Christ shall be the bringing forth of the tribes that have been lost to history, led away where men have not yet found them, and we are told that they shall be brought forth with a strong hand by the power of God and shall come unto Zion and receive their blessings at the hands of Ephraim. But some people say that prediction is to be explained in this way: A gathering is in progress, and has been in progress from the early days of this Church; and thus the "Lost Tribes" are now being gathered; but that we are not to look for the return of any body of people now unknown as to their whereabouts. True, the gathering is in progress, this is a gathering dispensation; but the prophecy stands that the tribes shall be brought forth from their hiding place bringing their sciptures with them, which scriptures shall become one with the scriptures of the Jews, the Holy Bible, and with the scriptures of the Nephites, the Book of Mormon, and with the scriptures of the Latter-day Saints as embodied in the volumes of modern revelation.

The Lord has said it. I am just simple minded enough, my brethren and sisters, to stand upon the rock of assurance that not one jot or tittle of the word of the Lord shall fail. Do not allow yourselves to think that the coming of the Christ means merely the spread of different or more advanced ideas among men, or simply the progress and advancement of society as an institution. These shall be but incidents of the great consummation, the consummation of this particular stage or epoch of the Lord's work. The Lord Jesus Christ shall come in the clouds of heaven, accompanied by the heavenly hosts, and His advent shall be marked by a great extension of the resurrection of the just, which has been in progress since that resurrection Sunday on which He came forth from the tomb and took up the wounded, pierced body which He had laid down; and those who are not able to bear the glory of His coming because of their wickedness, their foulness, and wilful state of sin, shall by natural means, perish. A strong current of electricity passes safely through a pure conductor, but where resistance is encountered it becomes a destructive power. It was necessary that the work for the dead be undertaken by the living, that temples be reared and this vicarious labor be performed, that the hearts of the departed fathers might be turned toward their yet mortal descendants, and the hearts of mortal children be turned to their dead ancestors, lest the earth be smitten with a curse at the time of the Lord's coming.

The Bible is very simple to those who read it with earnest and honest intent, as are all the scriptures, but it is very puzzling to the theologians, very puzzling, sometimes to Biblical scholars and interpreters who seek to apply to it only those tests that are common among men. I rejoice in the testimony of the Savior that He is verily the Christ and we proclaim Him as such. Great interest is manifest at this time in the work and ministry of Jesus Christ, not only among the Latter-day Saints but in the world in general; and He has been analyzed and measured and written about from many points of view, and as viewed from many different angles. There are volumes of recent publications dealing with the Christ of literature, the Christ of history, the Christ of reason, the Christ of experience. Never lived a man of whom more has been said or sung; and there is none to whom is devoted a greater share of the world's literature. But the tendency is to view Him from this angle or that and not to look with direct vision. I am thankful that the Church to which I belong preaches Christ and Him crucified, and resurrected, the Christ that ascended into heaven, the Christ that shall come again, the Christ that was the offspring in the flesh, as well as in the spirit, of the very Eternal Father, the Christ who is the Savior and Redeemer of mankind, beside whom there is none, beside whose name there is no name under heaven, whereby mankind may be saved. May His Spirit be ever with us, and may we be prepared for His coming, I humbly ask, in His name. Amen.

{26}

"A Fulfilment of Prophecy,"
An Address Delivered on 8 October 1916

(from *Eighty-seventh Semi-Annual Conference*
of the Church of Jesus Christ of Latter-day Saints
[Salt Lake City: Published by the Deseret News, 1916],
pp. 73-76)

I know that I have been in accord with the feelings of the vast multitudes that have assembled at the several sessions of this conference, in appreciation of the words of instruction and encouragement to which we have listened. The people have been fed upon substantial fare. They have heard the truths of the gospel declared in no uncertain terms. Your presiding servants have called your attention to matters that require your present attention. They have not confined themselves to words of praise unmixed with words of warning, but have adapted their testimonies, their admonitions, and their instructions to the needs of the hour.

In the gatherings of the Saints at this time, as on other conference occasions, I find fulfilment of prophecy, and see a working out of the purposes and plans of the Eternal One, a vindication of the prophets of God who have spoken in days past, and of the words of the living prophets who minister amongst the people in the authority of their holy office. In this respect, I feel that the Latter-day Saints cannot be too careful lest they be led to doubt the strict and literal fulfilment of the Lord's word as it has been made known to them. There are men in the world who have set themselves up against the God of Israel, men who have undertaken to measure arms with the Almighty, and to pit their wisdom against the eternal wisdom of God, men who have undertaken to construe, or rather to misconstrue the holy Scriptures, and to declare to the people that these writings do not mean what they say. Beware of them, Latter-day Saints. Stand we firm and steadfast by the revealed word of God and on the words of instruction that are given us from time to time by those whom we sustain before the Lord as his representatives in our midst; and should there come a question of issue between the opinions of men and the word of revelation, I say, *as said* the apostle, Paul, of old, in his written address to the Saints of Rome: "Yea, let God be true, but every man a liar." [Rom. 3:4] Men have made themselves liars before God because they have undertaken to question and even to deny his word.

Do you lack or do you want illustrations? The restoration of the gospel furnishes one. The words of Christ himself, the words of the apostles who followed him in the ministry on earth, the words of prophets who preceded his coming, were to the effect that in the last days the gospel should be restored, for the reason that it would not be found upon the earth; and yet there were those who said that it had always been upon the earth. But the angel whom the apostle-prophet saw coming in the midst of heaven in the last days, has come, bringing the everlasting gospel to the inhabitants of earth: and God is true though men be made out liars by the fulfilment of that sure word. Again, after the restoration, when the words of the prophet declared that the people who had embraced the restored gospel, a mere handful in comparison with those who belonged to each of the many so-called churches in the world, would come to the West and would establish themselves in the midst of the Rocky Mountains where they would become a great and a powerful people, the possibility of such was denied by the nation's wise and great ones, by specialists and leaders. Surely, no people could prosper and become a great and mighty commonwealth without ample means of subsistence. It was declared by statesmen that this vast domain in the West was a worthless area, incapable of supporting human life on a great scale. One of the greatest explorers and pioneers in that period of American history declared that not a bushel of grain could be raised in this valley. Yet the people came, and the prophet-leader pointed to the valley from the Wasatch barrier and declared it to be the appointed place of gathering. Again God had spoken and again men were proved to be liars. If the word be a harsh one, remember I speak it within quotation marks; I take it from the scriptural record.

Would you have other instances? Scientists, psychologists, students of the human mind, have undertaken to analyze and dissect this strange organism "Mormonism," and they have said it arose from delusion; that it has sprung from the seed of deception; that it is the offspring of bigotry and fanaticism; and the man whom we call a prophet of the last days, through whom we say the gospel has been restored and the Church re-established, was an epileptic: and consequently, according to the laws of heredity, which they have diagrammed and set forth in orderly array, the delusion could not persist beyond the third generation, for such would be contrary to formulated law. The world took comfort in that assurance, for it was given by those in whom the people had confidence; but what see we? Under this vast dome here today, are hundreds of the fourth and many of the fifth generation. Yea, let God be true, though every man be a liar.

Only a few months before the outbreak of the terrible world conflict, to which frequent reference has been made in this session and in earlier sessions of this conference, there stood here in this pulpit, where I now stand, one of the nation's great men, who set forth the results of his study and his investigations regarding certain problems; and who declared, as a result, that the conditions of the nations were today such as to make a great international war impossible. There would possibly be, said he, little uprisings, such as then had already begun in Mexico, but a war between the great powers could not take place. He emphasized by reiteration. The financial affairs of the world, he averred, were such as to link and weld the nations together; and should emperors, czars, or kings declare war, the bankers would veto their decision. I spoke with the gentleman here in this stand, at the conclusion of his address, in substance to this effect: "I wish I could believe you, Doctor." "You don't?" "I do not." "What is wrong with my deductions?" "They may be logically drawn, but your premises are wrong. You have failed to take into account certain essential factors; you have discarded and ignored the predictions' [sic] of the prophets; and on such a question as this I shall accept the word of the prophet rather than the conclusion of the academician, even though he be as distinguished as yourself, sir." I could not discuss the matter at length, but such I said. Within a short span of months after that time, several of the most powerful nations of the world were locked in the death-grapple, which has been tightening with the passage of the years. So, as I read the words of the prophet that war should be poured out upon all nations, and that in this day and dispensation, in which we live, this the land of Zion should be the only land wherein safety might be found, I said to myself again: Yea, let God be true, though all the world's wise ones be liars.

With such examples before us, can we doubt as to the future? How think you the Lord looks upon these "plans of mice and men" that "gang aft agley"? I take it that the contemplation of such developments is his humor; for, mark you, the God of heaven is a great humorist. I read that "He that sitteth in the heavens shall laugh; the Lord shall have them in derision." [Ps. 2:4] I read in the further word of the psalmist that as the Lord looketh upon the wicked and seeth him in his temporary, seeming prosperity, spreading himself like a green bay tree, "The Lord shall laugh at him, for he seeth that his day is coming." [Ps. 37:13] When I see how often the theories and conceptions of men have gone astray, have fallen short of the truth, yea, have even contradicted the truth directly, I am thankful in my heart that we have an iron rod to which we can cling—the rod of certainty, the rod of revealed truth. The Church of Jesus Christ of Latter-day Saints welcomes all truth, but it distinguishes most carefully between fact and fancy, between truth and theory, between premises and deductions; and it is willing to leave some questions in abeyance until the Lord in his wisdom shall see fit to speak more plainly.

As the result of the combined labors of wise men I learn that man is but the developed offspring of the beast; and yet I read that God created man in his own image, after his likeness; and again, I stand on the word of God, though it be in contradiction to the theories of men. This spirit of misconstruction, this attempt to explain away the sure word of prophecy, the indisputable word of revelation, is manifest even amongst our own people. There are those who would juggle with the predictions of the Lord's prophets. I read that in the last days one of the conditions preceding the return of the Christ to earth shall be the gathering of the Jews at their ancient capital, and in the land round about; and that another sign shall be the gathering of the people who have been scattered among the nations; and yet another shall be the bringing forth of the Lost Tribes from their hiding place, which is known to God, but unknown to man. Nevertheless, I have found elders in Israel who would tell me that the predictions relating to the Lost Tribes are to be explained in this figurative manner—that the gathering of those tribes is already well advanced and that there is no hiding place whereto God has led them, from which they shall come forth, led by their prophets to receive their blessings here at the hands of gathered Ephraim, the gathered portions that have been scattered among the nations. Yea, let God be true, and doubt we not his word, though it makes the opinions of men appear to be lies. The tribes shall come; they are not lost unto the Lord; they shall be brought forth as hath been predicted; and I say unto you there are those now living—

aye, some here present—who shall live to read the records of the Lost Tribes of Israel, which shall be made one with the record of the Jews, or the Holy Bible, and the record of the Nephites, or the Book of Mormon, even as the Lord hath predicted; and those records, which the tribes lost to man but yet to be found again shall bring, shall tell of the visit of the resurrected Christ to them, after He had manifested Himself, to the Nephites upon this continent. For, as not one jot or tittle of the Law has been permitted to fail, so surely no jot or tittle of the Gospel shall go unfulfilled.

I have heard it said that the predictions relative to the coming of the Christ are to be explained in a figurative way, that he is to dwell in the hearts of men and that is the second advent. Verily, the Christ shall come in person and shall be seen of the righteous and shall stand upon the earth and reign as rightful King and Lord, and shall send forth the law for the government of the world.

May we be kept in tune with the word of the Lord, as it hath been declared, is being declared, and yet shall be declared by his servants, the prophets, I ask in the Master's name. Amen.

{27}

"The Kingdom of God and the Kingdom of Heaven," An Address Delivered on 8 April 1917

(from *Eighty-seventh Annual Conference
of the Church of Jesus Christ of Latter-day Saints*
[Salt Lake City: Published by the Deseret News, 1917],
pp. 65-69)

"Our Father, which art in heaven, hallowed be thy name. Thy kingdom come. Thy will be done in earth as it is in heaven." [Matt. 6:9-10]

Thus did our Lord and Master teach the Saints in olden times to pray. The pattern which He gave for prayer has never been superseded nor abrogated. Thus does the Christian world profess to pray today. "Thy kingdom come. Thy will be done in earth as it is in heaven." If ever there were rational and imperative need for such prayer as this, today witnesses that need. Who will dare affirm that we need no longer pray that the kingdom of heaven may come, or that the will of God is being wrought upon the earth as it is in heaven?

Do you believe that the kingdom of heaven has already been set up upon the earth? I do not. I know that the kingdom of God has been established upon the earth, but the kingdom of God is a preparation for the kingdom of heaven, which is yet to come. The expressions "Kingdom of God" and "Kingdom of Heaven" are oft-times used synonymously and interchangeably in our imperfect English translation of the Holy Bible, particularly in the Gospel according to Matthew, where the expression "Kingdom of Heaven" is most commonly used. But in these instances, as in so many others, the light of modern revelation clears up the darkness of ancient passages; and the Lord has in this day and age made plain the fact, beyond all question, that there is a distinction between the kingdom of God and the kingdom of heaven. The kingdom of God is the Church of Christ; the kingdom of heaven is that system of government and administration which is operative in heaven, and which we pray may some day prevail on earth. The kingdom of heaven will be established when the King shall come, as come He shall, in power and might and glory, to take dominion in and over and throughout the earth.

Thus spake the Lord in the year 1831, calling attention to the imminent duty of the Church and the Saints:

"Hearken, and lo, a voice as of one from on high, who is mighty and powerful, whose going forth is unto the ends of the earth, yea, whose voice is unto men. Prepare ye the way of the Lord, make his paths straight.

"The keys of the kingdom of God are committed unto man on the earth, and from thence shall the gospel roll forth unto the ends of the earth, as the stone which is cut out of the mountain without hands shall roll forth, until it has filled the whole earth;

"Yea, a voice crying,—Prepare ye the way of the Lord, prepare ye the supper of the Lamb, make ready for the Bridegroom;

"Pray unto the Lord, call upon his holy name, make known his wonderful works among the people;

"Call upon the Lord, that his kingdom may go forth upon the earth, that the inhabitants thereof may receive it, and be prepared for the days to come, in the which the Son of Man shall come down in heaven, clothed in the brightness of his glory, to meet the kingdom of God which is set up on the earth;

"Wherefore may the kingdom of God go forth, that the kingdom of heaven may come, that thou, O God, mayest be glorified in heaven so on earth, that thy enemies may be subdued; for thine is the honor, power and glory, for ever and ever. Amen."

Thus reads the revelation known to us as Section 65 of the Doctrine and Covenants. The kingdom of heaven shall come, and then shall justice rule in the earth. No longer shall men rise in unrighteous dominion over their fellows. No longer shall men exalt themselves on thrones, nor adorn themselves with crowns and scepters. The best form of government possible unto man is a monarchy with the right kind of a monarch, who will do only justice, full justice, and with due regard to the claims of mercy, give unto every man his right. Such a government will be democracy and monarchy combined, and such is the government of the kingdom of heaven.

The work of the Church of Jesus Christ of Latter-day Saints may be summed up as the preparation of the earth for the coming of its Lord and King. As in the meridian of time the voice of the Baptist was heard in the wilderness, "Repent ye, for the kingdom of heaven is at hand," so has the voice of that same John the Baptist been heard in this day, restoring the authority of the Priesthood requisite to the administration of the ordinance of baptism, whereby remission of sins may be obtained; and the proclamation is made now, "The kingdom of heaven is at hand." That proclamation is authoritatively sounded throughout the world; and the work of the Church, which is veritably the kingdom of God, is to prepare the earth for the coming of the King of earth and heaven, and for the establishment of the kingdom of heaven upon the earth.

We Latter-day Saints are peculiarly literal in our acceptance of plain scripture. We believe that the Scriptures are very simple to understand, if we can only get the theologians to leave them alone and not confuse us with explanations. The Spirit of the Lord will enlighten the mind of the earnest reader, and will interpret the Scriptures, for that is the Spirit in which the Scriptures were written. When we read in prophecy, ancient and modern, and find in all predictions bearing upon this subject a strict unanimity, without any shadow of contradiction or inconsistency, we hold it to be a fact beyond question that the Christ, Jesus of Nazareth, who lived in the flesh, who was actually crucified, and who did take up that same body of flesh and bones that had lain in the tomb of Joseph of Arimathea, shall come in that same body and stand upon the earth and mingle with His people, and rule and reign.

Forty days after the day in commemoration of which this Easter Sunday is celebrated throughout Christendom, Christ led out His faithful servants, those who had been commissioned to administer in the authority of the holy Priesthood after He would leave, led them out to the historic little mount, Olivet; and there after communing with them and giving them final instructions, answering some of their eager questions, and putting others aside with but partial answer because the brethren were unprepared to fully comprehend, He ascended from their midst. They saw Him ascend; there was no shedding of body or robe; and as they watched Him disappearing in the upper deep they became aware of the presence of two white-robed angels, who addressed them saying: "Ye men of Galilee, why stand ye gazing up into heaven? This same Jesus, which is taken up from you into heaven, shall so come in like manner as ye have seen him go into heaven." [Acts 1 :11]

I admit that we Latter-day Saints are behind the times in many respects. We are still simple-minded enough to believe what the Scriptures say, which is the truth, and which cannot be gainsaid. Time forbids me citing even the most important and most striking of ancient prophecies relating to the coming of the Son of God in the dispensation of fulness, which is known as the day of vengeance. It was shown unto the prophets, however, even in the most ancient of times. Adam learned of it. Enoch, the seventh from Adam, prophesied of it, declaring that in the last days Jesus the Christ would come with ten thousand of His saints to rule in person upon the earth for a thousand years. I find nothing ambiguous in that, nothing requiring an interpreter. If I understand English at all, if I am more than a child in understanding, I can comprehend what that declaration means; and I believe it in its impressive literalness and in all its grand and glorious simplicity.

In preparing the world for the coming of the Lord there is a duty laid upon the Church as an organization, and upon every member of the Church individually; and that duty or obligation is to carry the word to our neighbors, to all with whom we may come in contact. Remember the mission of the Church is not wholly and solely to convert men to the acceptance of its principles and to bring them into membership. The duty laid upon us is also that of warning the world of the judgments that are to come. Can you doubt that the present dread scenes of conflict and slaughter on land and sea, in the air and beneath the water, are insignificant as signs of the times?

In that solemn interview which Christ had with His apostles just after their departure from the temple for the last time, in the course of the evening walk back to Bethany, He rested on the slopes of Olivet, and the apostles came to Him privately to ask certain questions regarding the time of His coming, which He had in part explained to them. Read for yourselves the twenty-fourth chapter of Matthew and the twenty-first chapter of Luke. The burden of the Lord's instruction was this: *Watch, for ye know not the day nor the hour.* He went so far as to tell them that not even the angels in heaven, nor at that time did the Son himself know the time appointed for His return in glory to exercise dominion on the earth. That knowledge He said, rested with the Father only. So in our assurance that the Lord shall come, and that His coming is very near, let us beware of those who undertake to set dates, to designate months and years; for the Lord hath positively declared that that shall not be given to man to know, nor even to the angels who stand in the presence of God. But certain signs are specified, and those signs are today ripening like the fruit in autumntide, when the fulness of summer is past. Who can doubt the imminence of this event, which shall be known as the consummation of the ages?

We do well to bear in mind the fact that the coming of the Christ is not the event spoken of in the Scriptures by the figurative phrase "the end of the world". That is not to be the occasion of the final judgment. Yet when Christ comes He shall execute judgment; and the wilfully hopeless, the unregenerate wicked shall be destroyed. Then there shall be a general resurrection of the righteous dead, and a change from mortality to immortality in the case of many who are living in the flesh at the time of His coming. But following the millennium, a thousand years of peace, shall be the final resurrection, in which men shall stand in their bodies of flesh and bones before the judgment seat of God.

I ask your attentive consideration of one of the many utterances of the Lord concerning His coming, given to us in these modern days, as recorded in the 88th Section of the Doctrine and Covenants. In 1832, the Lord said unto His elders and the Church generally, through the mouth of the Prophet Joseph:

"And I give unto you a commandment, that you shall teach one another the doctrine of the kingdom;

"Teach ye diligently and my grace shall attend you, that you may be instructed more perfectly in theory, in principle, in doctrine, in the law of the gospel, in all things that pertain unto the kingdom of God, that are expedient for you to understand;

★ ★ ★

"Behold I sent you out to testify and warn the people, and it becometh every man who hath been warned, to warn his neighbor.

"Therefore, they are left without excuse, and their sins are upon their own heads.

"He that seeketh me early shall find me, and shall not be forsaken.

★ ★ ★

"Abide ye in the liberty wherewith ye are made free; entangle not yourselves in sin, but let your hands be clean, until the Lord come;

"For not many days hence and the earth shall tremble and reel to and fro as a drunken man, and the sun shall hide his face; and shall refuse to give light, and the moon shall be bathed in blood, and the stars shall become exceeding angry, and shall cast themselves down as a fig that falleth from off a fig tree.

"And after your testimony cometh wrath and indignation upon the people; the testimony of earthquakes, that shall cause groanings in the midst of her, and men shall fall upon the ground, and shall not be able to stand.

"And also cometh the testimony of the voice of thunderings, and the voice of lightnings, and the voice of tempests, and the voice of the waves of the sea heaving themselves beyond their bounds.

"And all things shall be in commotion; and surely, men's hearts shall fail them; for fear shall come upon all people;

"And angels shall fly through the midst of heaven, crying with a loud voice, sounding the trump of God, saying, Prepare ye, prepare ye, O inhabitants of the earth; for the judgment of our God is come; behold, and lo! the Bridegroom cometh, go ye out to meet him.

★ ★ ★

"And the saints that are upon the earth, who are alive, shall be quickened, and be caught up to meet him.

"And they who have slept in their graves shall come forth; for they shall be caught up to meet him in the midst of the pillar of heaven." [vv. 77-78, 81-83, 86-92, and 96-97]

I believe it all without question or mental reservation. And now, as I know that I may be criticized by some, who pride themselves on scholarship, for the child-like simplicity of my acceptance and for my belief in the literalness of these events, I say to you in paraphrase of the utterance of Paul: Brethren, I come not to you with excellency of speech or of wisdom, declaring unto you the testimony of God. For I am determined not to know anything amongst you save Jesus Christ and him crucified, the Christ who is to come. And I am with you in weakness and in fear and in much trembling. And my speech and my preaching unto you is not with the enticing words of man's wisdom, but in demonstration of the Spirit and of power. That our faith may not stand in the wisdom of men, but in the power of God. So be it, in the name of Christ. Amen.

{28}

"There Are Four States, Conditions, or Stages in the Advancement of the Individual Soul"

(from *Liahona—The Elder's Journal* 16 [16 July 1918]: 867-68)

There are four states, conditions, or stages in the advancement of the individual soul, specified in Sacred Writ. These are the (1) the unembodied, (2) the embodied, (3) the disembodied, (4) the resurrected state.

In other words, (1) every one of us lived in an antemortal existence as an individual spirit; (2) we are now in the advanced or mortal stage of progress; (3) we shall live in a disembodied state after death, which is but a separation of spirit and body; (4) and in due time each of us, whether righteous or sinful, shall be resurrected from the dead with the spirit and body reunited and never again to be separated.

As to the certainty of the antemortal state, commonly spoken of as preexistence, the Scriptures are explicit. Our lord repeatedly averred that He had lived before He was born in flesh (see John 6:62; 8:58; 16:28; 17:5); and as with Him so with the spirits of all who have become or yet shall become mortal.

We were severally brought into being, as spirits, in that preexistent condition, literally the children of the Supreme Being whom Jesus Christ worshiped and addressed as the Father. Do we not read that the Eternal Father is "the god of the spirits of all flesh" (Numb. 16:22; 27:16), and more specifically that He is "the Father of spirits" (Heb. 12:9). In the light of these Scriptures it is plainly true that the spirits of mankind were there begotten and born into what we call the preexistent or antemortal condition.

The primeval spirit birth is expressively described by Abraham, to whom the facts were revealed, as a progress of organization, and the spirits so advanced are designated as intelligences: "Now the Lord had shown unto me, Abraham, the intelligences that were organized before the world was; and among all these there were many of the noble and great ones." (Pearl of Great Price, Abraham 3:22).

The human mind finds difficulty in apprehending the actuality of infinite or eternal process, either from the present onward to and beyond what we call in a relative sense perfection, on, on, without end; or backward through receding stages that had no beginning. But who will affirm that things beyond human comprehension cannot be?

In the antemortal eternities we developed with individual differences and varied capacities. So far as we can peer into the past by the aid of revealed light we see that there was always gradation of intelligence, and consequently of ability, among the spirits, precisely as such differences exist among us while we are mortal.

"That all men are created equal" is true in the sense in which that telling epigram was written into the scriptures of this Nation as a self-evident truth; for such laws as men enact in righteousness provide for the protection of individual rights on a basis of equality, and recognize no discriminating respect of persons. But if applied as meaning that all men are born with equal capacities, or even inherent abilities in like measure for each, the aphorism becomes absurd and manifestly false.

Every spirit born in the flesh is an individual character, and brings to the body prepared for its tenancy a nature all its own. The tendencies, likes and dislikes, in short the whole disposition of the spirit may be intensified or changed by the course of mortal life, and the spirit may advance or retrograde while allied with its mortal tabernacle. Students of the so-called science with a newly coined name, Eugenics, are prone to emphasize the facts of heredity to the exclusion of preexistent traits and attributes of the individual spirit as factors in the determination of character.

The spirit lived as an organized intelligence before it became the embodied child of human parents; and its preexistent individualism will be of effect in its period of earth-life. Even though the manifestations of primeval personality be largely smothered under tendencies due to bodily and prenatal influence, it is there, and makes its mark. This is in analogy with the recognized laws of physical operation—every force acting upon a body produces its definite effect whether it acts alone or with other and even opposing forces.

The genesis of every soul lies back in the eternity past, beyond the horizon of our full comprehension, and what we call a beginning is as truly a consummation and an ending, just as mortal birth is at once the inauguration of earth life and the termination of the stage of antemortal existence.

The facts are thus set forth in the revealed word of God:

"If there be two spirits, and one shall be more intelligent than the other, yet these two spirits, notwithstanding one is more intelligent than the other, have no beginning; they existed before, they shall have no end, they shall exist after, for they are gnolaum, or eternal." (Abraham 3:18).

To every stage of development, as to every human life, there is beginning and end; but each stage is a definite fraction of eternal process, which is without beginning or end. Man is of eternal nature and divine lineage.

{29}

"'Mormonism' and the War"

(from the *Improvement Era* 21 [October 1918]: 1,029-31)

The prompt and liberal response of "Mormon" communities to the Nation's call for concerted and determined effort in the current world crisis is very generally known, thanks to the generous liberality of the press and the commendable freedom fostered by the potent spirit of the times.

Liberty Bond quotas, Red Cross apportionments, War Savings allotments, all have been largely over-subscribed in every "Mormon" city, town and hamlet. In addition to the generous contributions of its members as individuals, the Church as a body has devoted half a million dollars to Liberty Bond purchases, and this was done on unanimous vote of its membership in general conference assembled.

But beyond all contributions measured in terms of money is the un-hesitating response of men, who have leaped to their places in the ranks by the thousands for the hundreds asked, offering their lives in pledge of patriotic devotion. In this ready and whole-souled cooperation the "Mormon" people claim neither preeminence nor special credit. They have tried to do their part in common with the mighty citizenry of our land. All classes in Utah and adjacent states are working shoulder to shoulder, without distinction as to former nationality or creed.

In addition to the imperative demands of citizenship, to which Latter-day Saints are responding with unsurpassed devotion and zeal, our people consider duty in the present crisis as a requirement of their religious profession. We have particular concern in the outcome of the great conflict, for we solemnly proclaim that to this Church has been given the divine appointment to preach, the restored Gospel of Jesus Christ in all the world; and the discharge of this high commission is possible in its entirety only as free speech, liberty of conscience, and a free press are insured among the nations.

The frightful war forced upon liberty-loving peoples is a belated attempt on the part of Lucifer to try anew the issue on which he was defeated in the primeval world, as the Scriptures attest. His plan of compulsion, by which every soul would be bereft of agency, was rejected in the council of the heavens, and the plan of liberty and individual freedom was adopted, with Jesus Christ as the fore-ordained Redeemer of the race.

The decision brought war, and Lucifer and his hordes were cast out upon the earth. In these last days that same Lucifer, or Satan, as he is now known, is operating through those who are ready to do his bidding, to rivet the shackles of monarchial despotism upon mankind.

Autocracy is the form of government that prevails in hell; and individual freedom is the basal principle of the gospel of Jesus Christ. Any man who seeks to enforce unrighteous dominion upon his fellows is the devil's own agent.

Citizenship in the kingdom of God is offered to all men on equal terms, for truly God is no respecter of persons. The Church proclaims this fundamental tenet in her Article of Faith:

"We believe that through the atonement of Christ, all mankind may be saved, by obedience to the laws and ordinances of the gospel."

Obedience to righteous law is an essential of true liberty. That liberty, falsely so called, which regards not the rights of others, is but evil license for selfish dominion with all its attendant abominations.

Our missionary elders have time and again been imprisoned in Germany, and others have been forcibly banished from the empire of boasted kultur, because they bore the message of freedom and individual agency. Formerly they went into that land with only the Scriptures and their own testimony of the truth as weapons in the conflict with sin. Now many of those selfsame men are on their way back wearing the uniform of the Nation, and with Browning guns as their instruments of persuasion.

The world is preparing for the consummation of the ages, which is the second coming of Christ. It is wise to be on guard against spurious prognostications as to the precise time of the great event, for, as the Scriptures affirm, this shall not be revealed even to the angels in heaven. Nevertheless, every day witnesses the ripening of the specified signs into actualities. The conditions set forth by Christ and His apostles as characteristic of the day of His coming are being realized with the exactness of detailed fulfilment.

The world war, with all its frightful atrocities incident to autocracy's determination to subvert the God-given birthright of agency and national freedom, is one of the most significant of the portentous signs of the times.

Heaven offers her bounties to man; his title thereto must be established by effort.

"Mormonism" holds that right shall yet triumph, tyranny be overthrown, and the liberties of mankind be established and made to endure.

{30}

"Judiciary System of the Church of Jesus Christ of Latter-day Saints"

(from the *Improvement Era* 21 [April 1919]: 498-99)

The essential purpose of the Gospel of Jesus Christ is to save mankind from sin, and to enable the sinner to retrieve his character through contrite repentance and by further compliance with the laws and ordinances based on the Atonement wrought by the Savior of the race.

The Church of Jesus Christ, which as a corporate entity is the organized body of which the Gospel is the vital spirit, must of necessity provide a system of order and discipline for the guidance and government of its members.

In accordance with the revealed law of the Church, a complete judiciary organization is maintained in the Church of Jesus Christ of Latter-day Saints; and its operation has been strikingly effective from the beginning.

On the basis of territorial classification, the smallest fully organized unit is the Ward, which is presided over by a Bishop, with whom are associated two other High Priests as Counselors, the three constituting the Ward Bishopric. As assistants to the Bishopric, there are deacons, teachers and priests.

Wards are aggregated in broader territorial units, known as Stakes, each Stake comprising such Wards as are conveniently situated, without numerical limitation except as the requirements of efficiency make necessary. The presiding body within a Stake is the Stake Presidency, consisting of the President and two Counselors, each of the three being a High Priest. Assisting the Stake Presidency is a High Council, composed of twelve High Priests.

The General Authorities have jurisdiction over the entire Church, according to their respective callings. At the head stands the President with two other High Priests as Counselors, the three constituting the First Presidency of the Church. Next in authority is a body of twelve High Priests, specially ordained as Apostles, and these form the Council of the Twelve Apostles.

The usual order of reformatory and discipline ministry is in general as follows. Should knowledge of any case of wrongdoing, or lack of harmony between or among members, come to the attention of the Bishopric of a Ward, it is their duty to delegate two or more priests or teachers to visit the parties concerned, and to try by brotherly mediation to bring about a reconciliation, or if there be evidence of actual sin, to report the facts to the Bishopric and make formal accusation. If the case so warrants, the Bishopric sit as a court, before whom the accused person appears after due notice and summons. If he denies the allegations of misconduct, he is given trial, in which his rights are scrupulously protected. Should he be found guilty, the Bishop's court requires the offender to effect restitution if such be practicable, or to make amends so far as the nature of the case allows; or, in cases of grave offense, formally withdraws fellowship from the guilty one, or excommunicates him. The penalties never involve fines, deprivation of liberty, or levies on property; and the extreme judgment that can be rendered is that of excommunication from the Church, or, for lesser offenses, disfellowshipment.

An appeal may be taken from the Bishop's court to the Stake Presidency and High Council, which tribunal possesses both appellate and original jurisdiction. Appeals from the action of a High Council may be made to the First Presidency only, whose decision is final. The Council of the Twelve Apostles is designated as the Traveling Presiding High Council of the Church, and they may officiate as a trial court anywhere within the Church; though this they do only in cases of very serious concern, or wherein Church members of different local units are involved, or as the First Presidency directs them to assume jurisdiction.

The purpose and basal plan of operation of the ecclesiastical courts was thus set forth by Joseph Smith, and the affirmation is authoritative through formal acceptance by the Church:

"We believe that all religious societies have a right to deal with their members for disorderly conduct according to the rules and regulations of such societies, provided that such dealings be for fellowship and good standing; but we do not believe that any religious society has authority to try men on the right of property or life, to take from them this world's goods, or to put them in jeopardy of either life or limb, neither to inflict any physical punishment upon them; they can only excommunicate them from their society, and withdraw from them their fellowship." (Doctrine and Covenants 134:10).

That the courts of the Church in no sense assume to oppose or supersede the secular law is shown in a revelation given as early as

1831, wherein it is expressly required that if members of the Church commit crime, if they kill, or rob, or lie, they *"shall be delivered up unto the law of the land."* See Doctrine and Covenants 42.

We hold that in matters of difference between brethren, in which no specific infraction of the secular law is involved, and in offenses called "civil" as distinguished from "criminal", it is as truly unworthy of members of the Church today as it was in Paul's time that "brother goeth to law with brother" and that it stands to our shame if righteous judgment cannot be rendered among ourselves. See 1 Cor. 6:5-7.

{31}

The Lord's Tenth

(Salt Lake City: Office of the Presiding Bishop of the Church of Jesus Christ of Latter-day Saints, 1923)

"The earth is the Lord's and the fulness thereof." [Ps. 24:1]

In acknowledgment of the supreme possessorship so declared, the great Landlord required of His tenants a rental of their time and substance. In acknowledgment of our relation as tenants, to Him as Owner, we are commanded to devote specifically oneseventh of our time, one day in seven, to His exclusive service. Of our substance and the increase thereof, the Lord calls for a tenth. This is the tithe.

Abraham a Tithe-Payer

Payment of tithes was so prominent a feature of the Mosaic Law that the yet earlier practice may be easily lost sight of. Tithing is older than Israel. Thus we read in connection with the account of Abraham's return from his victorious pursuit of the marauding and murderous enemies of his people:

"And Melchizedek king of Salem brought forth bread and wine: and he was the priest of the most high God.

"And he blessed him, and said, Blessed be Abram of the most high God, possessor of heaven and earth:

"And blessed be the most high God, which hath delivered thine enemies into thy hand. And he gave him tithes of all." (Genesis 14:18-20.)

In this connection it is interesting to consider the New Testament comments relating to the same incident and extolling the greatness of Melchizedek, the high priest, in that even the patriarch, Abraham, paid tithes to him:

"For this Melchisedec, king of Salem, priest of the most high God, who met Abraham returning from the slaughter of the kings, and blessed him;

"To whom also Abraham gave a tenth part of all; first being by interpretation King of righteousness, and after that also King of Salem, which is, King of peace; ★★★

"Now consider how great this man was, unto whom even the

patriarch Abraham gave the tenth of the spoils.

"And verily they that are of the sons of Levi, who receive the office of the priesthood, have a commandment to take tithes of the people according to the law, that is, of their brethren, though they come out of the loins of Abraham:

"But he whose descent is not counted from them received tithes of Abraham, and blessed him that had the promises." And without all contradiction the less is blessed of the better.

"And here men that die receive tithes; but there he receiveth them, of whom it is witnessed that he liveth." (Hebrews 7:1, 2, 4-8.)

Jacob's Vow

The law of the tithe in ancient Israel was well understood. We find it especially enjoined, and plainly it had been recognized before the exodus. Call to mind the incident of Jacob in distress, seeking his way back to his father's house, and how he covenanted with the Lord. This is the scriptural record:

"And Jacob vowed a vow, saying If God will be with me, and will keep me in this way that I go, and will give me bread to eat, and raiment to put on,

"So that I come again to my father's house in peace; then shall the Lord be my God:

"And this stone, which I have set for a pillar, shall be God's house: and of all that thou shalt give me I will surely give the tenth unto thee." (Genesis 28:20-22.)

Tithing in the Mosaic Code

If the sanctity of the tithe as a tenth part had not been fully understood in that day, one may well inquire as to why Jacob specified the tenth rather than some other fraction, such as the fifth or the seventh or the twelfth. But he vowed to give unto the Lord the tenth of all that he would receive, and this was in accordance with the proportion paid by Abraham before that time, and with the precise specification of the tenth part in the law given later under the administration of Moses. Let us remember that the very word "tithe" means a tenth, no more, no less. This was the requirement made of the people of Israel after they had been brought out from Egypt:

"And all the tithe of the land, whether of the seed of the land, or of the fruit of the tree, is the Lord's: it is holy unto the Lord.

"And if a man will at all redeem ought of his tithe, he shall add thereto the fifth part thereof.

"And concerning the tithe of the herd, or of the flock, even of whatsoever passeth under the rod, the tenth shall be holy unto the Lord.

"He shall not search whether it be good or bad, neither shall he change it: and if he change it at all, then both it and the change thereof shall be holy, it shall not be redeemed." (Leviticus 27:30-33.)

Following the development of the children of Israel into a theocratic nation, the practice of paying tithes in kind became one of the features by which they, the worshipers of Jehovah, were distinguished from all other people.

As long as the Israelites faithfully complied with the law of the tithe they prospered; and when they failed the land was no longer sanctified to their good.

Holy prophets admonished, rebuked, and reproved with sharpness as the people time and again fell into transgression, forgot the Lord, and neglected to give of their substance as required by the law which they professed to observe.

Hezekiah (see 2 Chronicles 31:5-10) and Nehemiah (see Nehemiah 13:10-13) were particularly forceful in their efforts to arouse the people to the jeopardy that threatened as a consequence of their neglect of the law of the tithe; and, later, Malachi, voiced the word of Jehovah in stern rebuke, forceful admonition, and encouraging promise relative to the payment of the Lord's tenth.

In the Meridian of Time

At the time of our Lord's personal ministry in the flesh, the law of the tithe had been supplemented by innumerable rules, comprising unauthorized exaction often based upon mere trivialities. Christ approved the tithe, but made plain the fact that other duties were none the less imperative. See Matthew 23:23.

The law of the tithe was still professedly observed during the apostolic period of old, and for a considerable time thereafter, more or less completely. Gradually, however, the practice of the tithe was robbed of its sacred character and it was made to serve as a means of state and secular taxation.

Under Secular Law

Early in the ninth century Charlamagne undertook to collect the tithe by force and made it a part of the state revenue; and thus was the sanctity of the tithe further obscured. In England the tithe was imposed by authority of the civil law. Of land rental and all the produce a tenth was collected, whether willingly paid or otherwise; for the tithe was held to belong to the established church. Under the act regulating the tithe-rent charge it is made possible to pay the rental in money; though until comparatively recent years the tithes were to be paid in kind. The "great tithes" were those levied upon corn, wood and certain other produce of the fields and forest, and the "lesser tithes" came from specified secondary earnings. By a strange construction it was argued that that which is in the earth is not to be considered as produce, and, therefore, coal and the precious metals were not to be tithed for there was no increase therein. Turf, which does grow visibly, is exempted also, while wood that is cut with the ax is to be tithed. Such strange inconsistencies arose through man's attempt to tamper with the law of God and to administer the same without divine authority.

Admonition and Promise

As already pointed out the observance of the law of tithe was periodically neglected or ignored by the Israelites of old, of whom it was especially required, and prophets raised their voices in proclamation of the Lord's displeasure. Consider the severe reproof and the encouraging promise voiced by the Lord through the mouth of Malachi:

"Even from the days of your fathers ye are gone away from mine ordinances, and have not kept them. Return unto me, and I will return unto you, saith the Lord of hosts. But ye said, Wherein shall we return?

"Will a man rob God? Yet ye have robbed me. But ye say: Wherein have we robbed thee? In tithes and offerings.

"Ye are cursed with a curse: for ye have robbed me, even this whole nation.

"Bring ye all the tithes into the storehouse, that there may be meat in mine house, and prove me now herewith, saith the Lord of hosts, if I will not open you the windows of heaven, and pour you out a blessing, that there shall not be room enough to receive it.

"And I will rebuke the devourer for your sakes, and he shall not destroy the fruits of your ground; neither shall your vine cast her fruit before the time in the field, saith the Lord of hosts.

"And all nations shall call you blessed: for ye shall be a delightsome land, saith the Lord of hosts." (Malachi 3:7-12.)

Law of the Tithe Today

The Latter-day Saints profess to be observers of the law of the tithe. The requirement thus made of them is not directly based upon the fact that tithe-paying was part of the Mosaic code, but because the law has been re-established in the Church in this dispensation of restoration and fulness.

Concerning the duties of the people relating to the tithe in this day the Lord has definitely spoken.

In a revelation given to Joseph Smith the Prophet at Far West, Missouri, July 8, 1838, in answer to the supplication: "Oh, Lord, show unto thy servants how much thou requirest of the properties of thy people for a tithing," we read:

"Verily, thus saith the Lord, I require all their surplus property to be put into the hands of the bishop of my church in Zion,

"For the building of mine house, and for the laying of the foundation of Zion and for the priesthood, and for the debts of the Presidency of my Church.

"And this shall be the beginning of the tithing of my people.

"And after that, those who have thus been tithed shall pay one-tenth of all their interest annually; and this shall be a standing law unto them forever, for my holy priesthood, saith the Lord.

"Verily I say unto you, it shall come to pass that all those who gather unto the land of Zion shall be tithed of their surplus properties, and shall observe this law, or they shall not be found worthy to abide among you.

"And I say unto you, if my people observe not this law, to keep it holy, and by this law sanctify the land of Zion unto me, that my statutes and my judgments may be kept thereon, that it may be most holy, behold, verily I say unto you, it shall not be a land of Zion unto you.

"And this shall be an ensample unto all the stakes of Zion. Even so. Amen. (Doctrine and Covenants, Sec. 119.)

Authority to Administer the Tithes

As of old, so in this day, the tithe is the Lord's and therefore is holy. Tithing funds or properties of any kind paid as tithes are not to be administered by unappointed hands. The priests of ancient Israel were charged with this sacred duty; and in the present dispensation the same order prevails. Responsibility for the handling of the tithes is placed upon the bishops today, and they, thus officiating, act in their capacity as presiding officers of the Aaronic Priesthood. Again, as of old, so now, the tithes are to be paid at the places appointed and to the duly ordained and commissioned receivers. Today the Bishop of the Church, who is known as the Presiding

Bishop, is assisted by many ward bishops, and to these as representatives of and assistants to the Presiding Bishop, the tithing is to be paid and is to be by them forwarded to the office of the Presiding Bishop. The order of the Church as at present constituted provides that the several bishops may convert into cash the produce paid as tithing in kind, and deliver the proceeds to the Presiding Bishop.

It is an interesting fact that during recent years, particularly during the two decades last past, attempts have been made by many sects and denominations to revive the ancient practice of the tithe. Churches are organizing from among their members societies or clubs of "tithers," who voluntarily pledge themselves to pay to their respective churches a tenth of their individual incomes. Among some of these societies the tithers are permitted to indicate the purpose to which their contributions shall be applied. The great difficulty which our sectarian friends find in re-establishing the practice of the tithe amongst their numerous sects is—and they realize it in part—that they have no priests nor Levites amongst them authorized to receive the tithe and administer it strictly in accordance with divine command. The authority of the Holy Priesthood is essential to the regulation of the tithing system of the Lord. Tithing is the Lord's revenue system, and He requires it of the people, not because He is lacking in gold or silver, but because they need to pay it.

Voluntary Yet Required

Tithe-paying must be a voluntary, free-will sacrifice, not to be exacted by secular power, nor enforced by infliction of fine or other material penalties. While in one sense the obligation is self-assumed, it is nevertheless one to be observed with full purpose of heart by the earner who claims standing in the Church and who professes to abide by the revealed word given for the spiritual development of its members.

It is essential that men learn to give. Without provision for this training the curriculum in the school of mortality would be seriously defective. Human wisdom has failed to devise a more equitable means of individual contribution for community needs than the simple plan of the tithe. Every one is to give in the amount proportionate to his income, and to so give regularly and systematically. The spirit of giving makes the tithe holy; and it is by means thus sanctified that the material activities of the Church are carried on. Blessings, specific and choice, are placed within the reach of all. In the Lord's work, the widow's penny is as acceptable as the gold piece of the millionaire.

The Latter-day Saints believe that the tithing system has been divinely appointed for their observance; and they esteem themselves blessed with thus being permitted to have part in the furtherance of God's purposes. Under this system the people have prospered severally and as an organized body. It is the simple and effective revenue law of the Church; and its operation has been a success from the time of its establishment. Amongst us it obviates the necessity of taking up collections in religious assemblies, and makes possible the promulgation of the Church's message through the printed and spoken word, the building and maintenance of Temples for the benefit of both the living and the dead, and phases of service to mankind too numerous to mention.

There is an important distinction between tithes and other offerings. While the observance of the tithing law must be willing and voluntary, tithe-paying is nevertheless required, demanded in fact, by the Lord of those who, by their own free will, have become His covenant children by baptism.

A great and all too common mistake is that we consider the paying of tithes as the giving of a gift unto the Lord. This does not express the whole truth. Provision is made for freewill offerings as any man may choose to make; and if he offers with pure purpose of heart and is himself an approved giver, his gift shall be accepted and be counted unto him for righteousness; but such is not the tithe; the tithe is rather a debt than a gift.

The Tithe as a Rental

As the matter presents itself to my mind, it is as though there had been a contract made between myself and the Lord, and that in effect He had said to me: "You have need of many things in this world—food, clothing, and shelter for your family and yourself, the common comforts of life, and the things that shall be conducive to refinement, to development, to righteous enjoyment. You desire material possessions to use for the assistance of others, and thereby gain greater blessings for yourself and yours. Now, you shall have the means of acquiring these things; but remember they are mine, and I require of you the payment of a rental upon that which I give into your hands. However, your life will not be one of uniform increase in substance and possessions; you will have your loses, as well as your gains; you will have your periods of trouble as well as your times of peace. Some years will be plenty unto you, and others will be years of scarcity. And, now, instead of doing as mortal landlords do—require you to contract with them to pay in advance, whatever your fortunes or your prospects may be—you shall pay me not in advance, but when you have received; and you shall pay me in accordance with what you receive. If it so be that in one year your income is abundant, then you can afford to pay me a little more; and if it be so that the next year is one of distress and your income is not what it was, then you shall pay me less; and should it be that you are reduced to the utmost penury so that you have nothing coming in, you will pay me nothing."

Have you ever found a landlord of earth who was willing to make that kind of a contract with you? When I consider the liberality of it all, and the consideration that my Lord has had for me, I feel in my heart that I could scarcely raise my countenance to His Heaven above if I tried to defraud Him out of that just rental.

A Privilege to All Alike

Consider further how therein and thereby He has provided that even the humblest may receive abundantly of the blessings of His house. The wealth of heaven is not reserved for the rich people of earth; even the poorest may be a stockholder in the great corporation of our God, organized for the carrying on of His purposes, in spreading the Gospel, in the building of Temples and other houses of worship to His name, and in doing good to all mankind.

Let it not be forgotten that the present is a day of sacrifice, and a day for the tithing of all who profess to be members of the Church of Jesus Christ, to whom the promise is given that they shall be preserved in the day of burning incident to the second advent of the Christ. See Doctrine and Covenants 64:23; compare Malachi chapter 4.

After all, the prime or great purpose behind the establishment of the law of the tithe is the development of the soul of the tithe payer, rather than the providing of revenue. The latter is an all-important purpose, for so far as money is needed for the carrying on of the work of the Church the Lord requires money that is sanctified by the faith of the giver; but blessings beyond estimate, as gauged by the coin of the realm, are assured unto him who strictly conforms to the law of the tithe because the Lord hath so commanded.

{32}

"The Purpose in the Creation of the World," An Address Delivered on 6 October 1923

(from *Ninety-fourth Semi-Annual Conference of the Church of Jesus Christ of Latter-day Saints* [Salt Lake City: Published by the Church of Jesus Christ of Latter-day Saints, 1923], pp. 48-55)

Wherever I go among the Latter-day Saints, as my duty calls me, meeting them in the various wards and stakes and in the missions, I find them imbued with a spirit of deep earnestness, hopefulness, confidence, trust and faith, mingled with concern and serious thought. They are happy; nevertheless, their happiness is more than levity, for in their rejoicing there is thoughtfulness and deep interest as to their present and future.

We rejoice that the work of God is progressing, that through the ages "one unceasing purpose runs"; that all that is past has been in preparation for that that now is, and is for that which is to come; that there was a beginning, even as there shall be an end, to this particular phase of the Lord's purposes concerning his children.

THE PURPOSE IN THE CREATION OF THE WORLD

The earth was created primarily for the carrying out of the divine purposes concerning man. The astronomer regards it as one of the stellar units; the geologist looks upon it as the field for his investigation; but beyond such conceptions we regard it as one of the many spheres created with definite purpose, in which the destiny of the human race is the chief element and was the principle concern of the Creator, in bringing it into existence. We read, as the Lord revealed unto his friend and servant, Abraham, that before the earth was framed the Creator and those immediately associated with him looked out into space and said: We will take of these materials, and we will make an earth whereon these unembodied spirits may dwell; and we will prove them herewith, to see if they will do whatsoever the Lord their God shall command them.

Now, that being the purpose for which this world was created, we can readily understand that there is a very close relationship between earth and man. We read that when the transgression in Eden was passed upon by the voice of judgment the Lord said unto Adam: "Cursed is the ground for thy sake; ★★★ Thorns also and thistles shall it bring forth to thee; ★★★ In the sweat of thy face shalt thou eat bread." This seemingly dire pronouncement would be nothing but fiction did it not mean that a great change came upon the earth itself under the curse; and the Scriptures reveal a very significant relationship between the development of earth processes and that of mankind. Indeed the earth has been personified. Righteous Enoch, we are told, regarded it as being conscious and sentient, for we read:

"And it came to pass that Enoch looked upon the earth; and he heard a voice from the bowels thereof, saying: Wo, wo is me, the mother of men; I am pained, I am weary, because of the wickedness of my children. When shall I rest, and be cleansed from the filthiness which is gone forth out of me? When will my Creator sanctify me that I may rest, and righteousness for a season abide upon my face?" (Moses 7:48).

Following further revelation unto this prophet and seer, concerning the then future development of the human race and the purposes of God concerning such, he cried out in anguish to the Lord: "When shall the earth rest?" It was then shown unto him that the resurrected Christ would return to the earth in a dispensation to be known as the last, the dispensation of fulness and restitution; and that he, the Lord, would inaugurate the millennial reign of peace. "And the day shall come that the earth shall rest, but before that day the heavens shall be darkened, and a veil of darkness shall cover the earth: and the heavens shall shake, and also the earth: and great tribulations shall be among the children of men, but my people will I preserve. " [Moses 7:61.]

Has it not been made known unto us that we may sanctify the earth or defile it according to our acts? There is a close connection between the righteousness or sinfulness of mankind and the occurrence of natural phenomena, benign or malignant as we regard them, good or bad, preserving or destroying as the case may be. Now the gross materialist may say there is no relationship between the righteousness of man and earthquakes, or between man's probity and floods. But there is!

Touching this matter, I read to you my words, including scriptural citations, spoken on an earlier occasion: We learn from Scripture that Adam's transgression brought about a fallen condition, not of mankind alone, but likewise of the earth itself. In this and in numerous other epochal events, wherein the direct interposition of Divine action is affirmed, nature is seen to be in intimate relation with man.

Thus the sins of mankind may produce calamity in the form of destructive phenomena, which we may properly call natural because deserved; and human righteousness may invoke peaceful and beneficent cooperation of those elements.

"Cursed is the ground for thy sake" was the Divine fiat to the first man. In contrast, note the assurance given to Israel that by faithfulness the seasons should be made propitious, that nurturing rains should come, bringing such harvests that the people would lack room to store their products. (See Mal. 3:8-12).

Abject apostasy from the laws of God in Noah's time brought about the Deluge, in which were all the fountains of the great deep broken up, and the windows (more properly flood-gates) of heaven were opened.

Enoch, who lived before Noah, was sent to proclaim repentance to the degenerate race, and so great was the power and authority vested in him that "he spake the word of the Lord, and the earth trembled, and the mountains fled, even according to his command; and the rivers of water were turned out of their course." He foresaw the coming of the Noachian flood, and the events of history, including the Savior's ministry, down to the days of the Lord's second advent, when "the heavens shall be darkened, and a veil of darkness shall cover the earth; and the heavens shall shake, and also the earth." (Moses 7:13; 61).

As a fit setting for the tragedy on Calvary, a pall of darkness fell about the place, and, when the Crucified Lord expired, "the earth did quake, and rocks rent." (Matt. 27:51).

DISRUPTION SIGNALIZED THE SAVIOR'S DEATH

On the Western Continent, widespread disruption signalized the Savior's death; and destruction befell the wicked who had flouted prophetic warnings and inspired admonitions to repentance. Many of the Nephites had forgotten the signs and wonders by which the fact of the Lord's birth had been made known, and had fallen into abominable wickedness. Then, at the time of the crucifixion, great and terrible tempests broke over the land, with thunderings, lightnings, and both elevations and depressions of the earth's crust, so that mountains were sundered, and many cities destroyed by earthquake, fire, and the inrush of the sea. For three hours the unprecedented holocaust continued; and then thick darkness fell, in which it was found impossible to kindle a fire. The awful gloom was like unto the darkness of Egypt in that its clammy vapors could be felt. This condition lasted until the third day, so that a night a day and a night were as one unbroken night; and the impenetrable blackness was rendered the more terrible by the wailing of the people, whose heartrending refrain was everywhere the same: "O that we had repented before this great and terrible day!" Then, piercing the darkness, a Voice was heard, proclaiming that destruction had befallen the people because of wickedness, and that those who had lived to hear were the more righteous of the inhabitants, to whom hope was offered on condition of, more thorough repentance and reformation. (3 Nephi, Chap. 8).

MODERN PROPHECY ON THE SUBJECT

As was foreseen, aye, and foretold, by the Christ himself and by his prophets who lived before his mortal birth and by those who lived after, in the earlier ages, and by the prophets of the present dispensation, great destruction has come and shall come upon the earth because of the sins of the human race. In section 88 of the Doctrine and Covenants, that section known unto us as the "Olive Leaf" as named by the prophet who received the word from the Lord and gave it unto the people in 1832, December 27, it is thus declared:

"For not many days hence and the earth shall tremble and reel to and fro as a drunken man; and the sun shall hide his face, and shall refuse to give light; and the moon shall be bathed in blood; and the stars shall become exceedingly angry, and shall cast themselves down as a fig that falleth from off a fig-tree.

"And after your testimony cometh wrath and indignation upon the people.

"For after your testimony cometh the testimony of earthquakes, that shall cause groanings in the midst of her, and men shall fall upon the ground and shall not be able to stand.

"And also cometh the testimony of the voice of thunderings, and the voice of lightnings, and the voice of tempests, and the voice of the waves of the sea heaving themselves beyond their bounds.

"And all things shall be in commotion; and surely, men's hearts shall fail them; for fear shall come upon all people." [D&C 88:87-91]

THE RECENT CALAMITY IN JAPAN

What has been called the greatest calamity in history is fresh in our minds. Hundreds of thousands of human beings have lost their lives in the great seismic disturbances in Japan. I have only to say that the occurrence of such earthquakes is in accordance with predictions. The Lord forbid that I should assume to pass judgment upon those who are immediately affected, upon those who have lost their lives through such catastrophies. It is beyond the wisdom of men to correctly deduce results by applying general laws or causes to individual cases; and whenever the judgments of the Lord are permitted to fall upon the earth and upon its inhabitants, there are many of the innocent who suffer with the guilty. Many go down who are not personally culpable and who are not directly responsible for that which has come.

RIGHTEOUS AND CULPABLE SUFFER TOGETHER

We know the Lord does permit these calamities to come upon those who, according to our means of judgment and powers of analysis, may not have deserved the fate, but death, remember, is not finality. It is that which follows death with which we should have concern. Many are allowed to die in tempest and earthquake, whose death is but a passage into the blessed realms, because they are deserving of blessings; while unto others death does come as a judgment; and the Lord knows who fall because of their sins and who are permitted to fall because of their righteousness.

We have an instance in point concerning the connection of affliction and distress with individual culpability. You remember the Lord and his apostles once came to a blind beggar upon the street near the temple gates; "And his disciples asked him, saying, Master, who did sin, this man, or his parents, that he was born blind?"

Incidentally let us note that those who asked that question had an understanding of premortal existence, for surely the man could not have sinned in the flesh and brought upon him blindness at birth as a result. But the explanation given by the Lord is the important point for us to consider: "Jesus answered, Neither hath this man sinned, nor his parents; but that the works of God should be made manifest in him." The Lord's purposes were worked out in the case, for the man was healed, and the instance stands as a testimony for or against those who have become acquainted with the circumstance.

Incident to a period of cruel intolerance in religious matters among the aboriginal people of this continent, we read that evil-hearted persecutors put to death many women and children by burning, thinking that by this means they could terrify the rest into a denial of their faith. The Prophets Alma and Amulek were forced to witness the awful scenes. Though themselves in bonds they were brought there to witness the agony of the victims; and Amulek with zeal and righteous indignation desired to invoke the power of God to save those innocent sufferers: "But Alma said unto him: The Spirit constraineth me that I must not stretch forth mine hand: for behold the Lord receiveth them up unto himself, in glory; and he doth suffer that they may do this thing, or that the people may do this thing unto them, according to the hardness of their hearts, that the judgments which he shall exercise upon them in his wrath may be just; and the blood of the innocent shall stand as a witness against them, yea, and cry mightily against them at the last day." (Alma 14:11).

NATIONS AS WELL AS INDIVIDUALS HELD TO ACCOUNT

The Lord deals with individuals; and salvation is an individual affair; but, nevertheless, he deals also with nations, for he is the God of nations, which are set up or put down, are preserved or destroyed, according to their fitness; and all this is done in the Lord's due time and way. "Blessed is the nation whose God is the Lord," sang the psalmist. "Righteousness exalteth a nation; but sin is a reproach to any people," declared the author of the book of Proverbs.

It has been pointed out that a distinguishing feature of the last days and of the imminence of the second coming of Christ would be the proclaiming of the gospel amongst all nations. "And this gospel of the kingdom shall be preached in all the world for a witness unto all nations; and then shall the end come," said the Lord himself in the flesh on the very eve of his great sacrifice. So also in these latter-days the Lord has made plain the fact that nations shall be held to account. In a commandment to the elders of his Church, given in February, 1831, and recorded in section 43, he said:

"Lift up your voices and spare not. Call upon the nations to repent, both old and young, both bond and free, saying: Prepare yourselves for the great day of the Lord;

"For if I, who am a man, do lift up my voice and call upon you to repent, and ye hate me, what will ye say when the day cometh when the thunders shall utter their voices from the ends of the earth, speaking to the ears of all that live, saying Repent, and prepare for the great day of the Lord?

214

"Yea, and again, when the lightnings shall streak forth from the east unto the west, and shall utter forth their voices unto all that live, and make the ears of all tingle that hear, saying these words—Repent ye, for the great day of the Lord is come?

"And again, the Lord shall utter his voice out of heaven, saying: Hearken, O ye nations of the earth, and hear the words of that God who made you.

"O, ye nations of the earth, how often would I have gathered you together as a hen gathereth her chickens under her wings, but ye would not!

"How oft have I called upon you by the mouth of my servants, and by the ministering of angels, and by mine own voice, and by the voice of thunderings, and by the voice of lightnings, and by the voice of tempests, and by the voice of earthquakes, and great hailstorms, and by the voice of famines and pestilences of every kind, and by the great sound of a trump, and by the voice of judgment, and by the voice of mercy all the day long, and by the voice of glory and honor and the riches of eternal life, and would have saved you with an everlasting salvation, but ye would not!"

In another revelation, section 84, we read:

"For I, the Almighty, have laid my hands upon the nations to scourge them for their wickedness.

"And plagues shall go forth, and they shall not be taken from the earth until I have completed my work, which shall be cut short in righteousness—

"Until all shall know me, who remain, even from the least unto the greatest, and shall be filled with knowledge of the Lord."

Yet further:

"And thus, with the sword and by bloodshed the inhabitants of the earth shall mourn, and with famine and plague and earthquake and the thunder of heaven, and the fierce and vivid lightning also, shall the inhabitants of the earth be made to feel the wrath, and indignation, and chastening hand of an Almighty God, until the consumption decreed hath made the full end of all nations." (87:6).

Now, I do not believe in trying to explain away the words of God that predict calamity, but are nevertheless full of assurance unto the righteous, be it a righteous man or a righteous nation. We should awaken to their dread import. The Lord is dealing with the nations of the earth, and his Spirit has departed in large measure from nations that have defied him and his commandments, and as a result, they, being left largely to themselves, war with one another, and seek all means by which they can destroy one another most expeditiously. Now, the Lord is not the author of these evil things; the nations are bringing these inflictions upon themselves, and there shall be a consummation brought about as the Lord hath decreed, which shall mean an end of all nations as such, if they will not observe the law and the commandments of the Lord their God.

THE WAY OF ESCAPE

Is there any way of escape? Yes, there is. The Lord sent word by his prophets unto the wicked city of Ninevah, and the cry was raised in her streets: "Yet forty days, and Ninevah shall be overthrown." Then from the king upon his throne, down to the beggar in the streets, the people wailed because of their wickedness, and opened their hearts to the warning voice. They fasted and prayed, and confessed their sins before the Lord, and Jonah, the prophet who had been sent unto them, looked on to witness the destruction of the city, and seemed indeed to be disappointed because he was denied a view of the spectacle he awaited. But the Lord reasoned with the prophet in this wise: The people have turned to me, and have repented of their sins. Shall I destroy them when they have turned unto me?

Even now, if the nations will turn unto the Lord it shall be unto them as it was unto Ninevah—they shall be spared; but if they will not, then the Lord will permit the predicted judgments to come upon them until they are brought to a realization of the fact that they do depend upon the Lord God of heaven and of earth. The forces of nature are co-operating and are permitted to wreak destruction and the end is not yet. Latter-day Saints, remember the admonition of the Lord: "Stand ye in holy places," and we cannot do that unless we are holy. "Stand ye in holy places, and be not moved," but await the working out of the Lord's purposes, the while living lives of righteousness and crying repentance unto the people of the world.

THE TIME OF CHRIST'S ADVENT IS NEAR

This is the day of consummation, and the coming of the Lord is nearer than we are willing to admit. Let us not seek to set times or dates, for such we are told shall never be made known until the day of the Lord's coming; not even the angels in heaven are to know beforetime. Therefore, away with all attempts to fix times for the Lord.

216

But he has told us that the time of his advent is near; and it is over a hundred years nearer than it was when he spake first to his prophet in this dispensation. I pray that we be prepared, and that we be found ready for the consummation of the ages, the coming of the Lord in his might and majesty to rule and reign. I ask this in his name, Amen.

{33}

"The Book of Mormon and the Book of Isaiah," An Address Delivered on 6 April 1929

(from *Ninety-ninth Annual Conference
of the Church of Jesus Christ of Latter-day Saints*
[Salt Lake City: Published by the Church of Jesus Christ
of Latter-day Saints, 1929], pp. 44-49)

Speaking of the Book of Mormon, concerning which we heard very valuable instruction yesterday, I venture to emphasize the thought that we apply very diligently in our lives the principles and precepts set forth in that volume of scripture. The Book of Mormon is more than a book in the ordinary sense. It is the best of all the literature written in this Church for missionary work. For many years I have urged, as have my brethren likewise, that our missionaries strive to get the Book of Mormon into the hands of the people, both members and nonmembers of the Church. I am happy in the realization that while a few years ago we sold copies of the Book of Mormon in lots of tens and scores, sending them out to the missions, we now send them by thousands. The statistics regarding the sale and distribution of that work, particularly as reported by the mission presidents, furnish a testimony beyond all question of the pouring out of the Spirit of the Lord upon the people of the world.

AS TO BOOK OF MORMON LANDS

I sometimes think we pay a little undue attention to technicalities, and to questions that cannot be fully answered with respect to the Book of Mormon. It matters not to me just where this city or that camp was located. I have met a few of our Book of Mormon students who claim to be able to put a finger upon the map and indicate every land and city mentioned in the Book of Mormon. The fact is, the Book of Mormon does not give us precise and definite information whereby we can locate those places with certainty. I encourage and recommend all possible investigation, comparison and research in this matter. The more thinkers, investigators, workers we have in the field the better; but our brethren who devote themselves to that kind of research should remember that they must speak with caution and not declare as demonstrated truths points that are not really proved. There is enough truth in the Book of Mormon to occupy you and me for the rest of our lives, without our giving too much time and attention to these debatable matters.

HOW TO KNOW FOR ONE'S SELF

I speak specifically of the testimony that has come to the Latter-day Saints, and that will come to any members of the Church or other earnest investigator who will read the book rightly as to its genuineness. The divinely-inspired promise written by Moroni has found literal fulfilment in scores of thousands of cases. I refer to his last word respecting the record which he was about to hide up unto the Lord. It is recorded in the tenth chapter of Moroni: "And when ye shall receive these things, I would exhort you that ye would ask God, the Eternal Father, in the name of Christ, if these things are not true; and if ye shall ask with a sincere heart, with intent, having faith in Christ, he will manifest the truth of it unto you, by the power of the Holy Ghost." Then he very pertinently adds: "And by the power of the Holy Ghost ye may know the truth of all things."

Many of us have received that testimony; but of those who have so received there are some who do not stand by it as they should. I think it well that we speak plainly to one another at times. There are those who forget what the Lord has said through the Book of Mormon, and who are led away into the jungle of error, much of which belongs to the marshy and uncertain ground preempted in the name of higher criticism. Permit me to give you an example; one may suffice.

THE BOOK OF ISAIAH AND THE BOOK OF MORMON

It has been declared and proclaimed by a certain school of Bible students, commentators and scholars, that the Book of Isaiah was written not entirely by Isaiah the Prophet, the son of Amoz—in many respects the greatest of the prophets of that age—but that the book is the work of at least two men, and perhaps of many, part of it written by Isaiah himself, and the other part by another man, without local habitation or name, who lived somewhere, near the end of the period of the Babylonian captivity or exile, fully a century after the death of Isaiah the Prophet. That idea concerning the duality of the Book of Isaiah has been exploited, and there are learned readers of the Bible, who, with superior air, point out certain chapters of the Book of Isaiah which they say were not written by Isaiah the Prophet, but by this "deutero" or second Isaiah. So he is called in view of even the scholars' ignorance as to his true name or place of abode. The claim is made that the chapters of Isaiah from the second to the thirty-ninth inclusive, were really written by Isaiah, and that thence on to the end of the sixty-sixth chapter, the last in the book, the subject matter is not the writing of Isaiah at all, but that of another man, who falsely ascribed the authorship to the Prophet.

Such is the speculation concerning the duality of authorship in that book; but, once started, these learned investigators have undertaken to dissect Isaiah and to spread before the gaze of the people both his gross and minute anatomy, to the extent of denying his authorship of other parts of chapters, and of certain verses, singling them out from the rest, and they have left to the credit of the Prophet Isaiah only twenty-four and a half chapters of his book.

BOOK OF ISAIAH COMPLETED BEFORE 600 B.C.

I well remember when the positive and emphatic denial of the unity of the Book of Isaiah was put forth by the German school of theologians. So too I remember the many questions that arose among our people regarding it, not a few of such questions coming to me personally. To some of the inquirers I said: "Why trouble yourselves about the matter? I know that the claim is false." "Well, have you looked into it?" I was asked. "Sufficiently so," I replied, "for I have received the testimony promised by the Lord through the Prophet Moroni concerning the integrity and genuineness of the Book of Mormon."

In the Second Book of Nephi, I find transcriptions of several chapters of Isaiah, that is to say, chapters as the material is now divided and designated in our Bible—twelve chapters at least, taken from the brass plates of Laban, which plates were brought from Jerusalem to Lehi in the wilderness, as you know, 600 years before the birth of Christ. Laban was a rich man. He could afford to have books made of metal sheets, while others perhaps were content with poorer and less enduring material—just as some people can now afford to have de luxe editions and others are willing to accept poorer paper and bindings. But on those plates of brass, brought from Jerusalem in the year 600 B.C., you will find the writings of Isaiah, not only the early chapters allowed to Isaiah by modern scholars, but the later chapters as well, which are ascribed by the critics to the second or false Isaiah. Let us remember that we have in the Book of Mormon transcriptions from the brass plates of Laban, comprising the record of Isaiah, ofttimes word for word the same as the translation appearing in the Bible, chapter after chapter. The entire Book of Isaiah must have been in existence at that time.

Abinidi, a Book of Mormon prophet, quoted from what is now called the fifty-third chapter of Isaiah to the priests of Noah; and the fifty-third chapter comes in that portion which is ascribed to the false Isaiah; but the Nephites had it, Lehi had it, Laban had it six hundred years before Christ; and my testimony as to the genuineness of the Book of Mormon is sufficient to set at rights with me any question as to the authorship of the Book of Isaiah.

INTEGRITY OF ISAIAH AFFIRMED BY THE RESURRECTED LORD

Would you have higher authority than that of mortal prophets of Book of Mormon record? Then take the words of the Lord Jesus Christ himself when he appeared a resurrected being amongst the Nephites. In preaching to them he quoted one entire chapter of Isaiah—as we find recorded in the twenty-second chapter of Third Nephi. That quotation by our Lord is practically identical with the fifty-fourth chapter of Isaiah. I speak of the chapters as we now have them. I repeat, Jesus Christ quoted to the Nephites almost word for word what Isaiah had written in what we now know as the fifty-fourth chapter of his book. Then the Lord said: "And now, behold, I say unto you, that ye ought to search these things. Yea, a commandment I give unto you that ye search these things diligently; for great are the words of Isaiah."

This is the testimony of the Lord Jesus Christ. In other places, before his death, he had cited Isaiah. While in the flesh he quoted from that prophet, and from the latter chapters of the book, which modern critics say are not the words of Isaiah. By way of further illustration read John 12:38, wherein we find citation from the fifty-third chapter of Isaiah, which modern critics affirm was not written by Isaiah the Prophet; and in the fortieth verse of the same chapter appears a citation from the sixth chapter of Isaiah, which part the critics do ascribe to Isaiah himself.

But be it remembered that the critics who thus seek to rend, mutilate and generally discredit the Book of Isaiah are not the only ones whose voice should be heard in so important a matter. They have no monopoly of the truth, and when they die wisdom will not perish with them. A great institution of wide influence, The Philosophical Society of Great Britain, otherwise known as the Victoria Institute, has taken up the matter of the unity of Isaiah, and has pointed out the errors of the critics with respect to the claim of duality, thus registering its decision that the Book of Isaiah is a unit, written by the son of Amoz, the prophet whom the Lord verily loved.

STUDENTS AND TEACHERS, BE
CONSISTENT AND TRUE TO YOUR TESTIMONY

Regretfully I find that in some of our theological classes, and in our seminaries, not only pupils but teachers are following after that false lead and are segregating the words of the Book of Isaiah, part as being his and other portions as the works of another. Could there be a grosser inconsistency than that of proclaiming a belief in the divine inconsistency than that of proclaiming a belief in the divine authenticity of the Book of Mormon while teaching or believing that the Book of Isaiah is other than what it purports to be—the writings of Isaiah the son of Amoz throughout?

I cannot feel those in our Church schools and seminaries who put the theories of men above the revelations of God have any rightful place among the teachers in our theological institutions, whether quorum classes, seminaries, or Church school of any name or grade.

DIFFERENCES IN STYLE OF WRITING

On what, you may ask, do these critics base this segregation of chapters and verses, as to authorship, in the Book of Isaiah? On two points: First comes the difference in style of composition. The only part of the Book of Isaiah, which is admitted to have been written by the prophet, is worded generally in a spirit of sadness; the tone or color is that of depression, dark presage, as befits the subject. The author is telling of the calamities that will come upon Israel unless they repent and turn from their wicked ways. The picture is painted in dark colors. The latter part of the book, from the fortieth chapter on, is more joyous, much more cheerful. The author is speaking of the triumph that shall eventually come to God's people. The critics say that Isaiah could not have written in these strikingly different styles. Do you find any modern writer telling a sorrowful tale in happy and exultant words? Is it so that one writer cannot inscribe a story of grief and at another time a story of surpassing joy? Our literature contradicts the thought! Think of the two splendid poems by Milton, his twin pictures, "L'Allegro" and "Il Penseroso," known to most of our students of literature. One is a picture of pessimism, pensiveness, and gloom; the other a scene of optimism, joy and gaiety. There could not be greater contrast. Milton could adapt his style to his theme and did so splendidly; but Isaiah, preaching and speaking under the inspiration of the living God, could not do it, according to the critics who have assailed his work.

BE TRUE TO YOUR TESTIMONY!

To my younger brothers and sisters, to my student friends, I say stand by your testimony. When you have received it from the Lord, let it be your guide. It will be no handicap to you in your researches, your studies, your explorations and investigations. It will not detract from your reputation for learning, if you deserve any such reputation, provided you stand by the truth. As you know, in the Book of Mormon we have that wonderful story of the iron rod seen by Lehi. To those of you who want to explore I say, in all earnestness, tie fast your guide rope to the rod of iron, which is defined as the Word of God. Hold to it firmly, and you may venture out into the region of the unexplored in search of truth if you will; but do not loosen your hold on the rope; and remember that there is very little safety in holding to a rope that is loose at both ends.

By following this course I have had many satisfying explanations of questions that troubled me. Let me illustrate. It has been the general conception that certain animals known to have existed on the eastern hemisphere were not to be found on the western hemisphere in Nephite times: but in the Book of Mormon I find record, positive and simple, that certain of these animals were found by Lehi and his colony. Now, the testimony that the Lord had given me as to the integrity of the Book of Mormon did not furnish me with all details by which I could confront the evidence that was being gathered, which was all of a negative character, relating to the alleged nonexistence of the horse and other animals upon the western continent at the time indicated. Some of you may say that as you do not find, ordinarily at least, the bones of buffaloes in this section, that buffaloes never lived here. But go search in the gravels of City Creek, and you may be lucky enough to find, as I have found, the bones and horns of buffaloes. One shred of positive evidence will nullify a volume of negative assumption; and the declarations made in the Book of Mormon, if not already verified, will surely be verified every whit.

The Book of Mormon is not to be judged according to the canons of criticism applicable to any book professing to be the product of a modern brain, any more than is the Holy Bible to be so judged. Each of these is a volume of scripture, profusedly giving the revealed word of God.

The second objection made by the critics as to accepting Isaiah as a unit is based on the prophet's mention of King Cyrus, the Persian, a century and a half before Cyrus was born. As King Cyrus is named, the record containing the account of him, says the critics, could not have been written until after his birth, reign, and accomplishment of the divinely-appointed work ascribed to him by the prophet; in short, they say, that account must have been written by somebody who lived after Cyrus, the Persian king. Is there no prophecy? Are there no prophets? And, by the way, is Cyrus, the Persian, the only one whose name was given before birth? What of Ishmael, of Isaac, of John the Baptist? What of the Lord Christ himself? Their names were all prescribed and recorded long before their respective births.

Josephus, the Jewish historian, knew nothing of the alleged duality of the Book of Isaiah; for he tells us that Isaiah's prophecy was presented to King Cyrus, named therein, and "that the fact of his own name being in the text greatly encouraged him to carry out the prediction."

Some of us are very apt to be led away by a statement because we find it in a book bearing the name of some man assumed to be great. Let us read in a more discriminating way, and seek for the guidance of the Lord as we read.

I bear you witness, as witness has been borne before, and I speak it to you with all the assurance that the Three Witnesses and the Eight Witnesses put their testimony on record—that the Book of Mormon is just what it claims to be, as set forth by the ancient historian and prophet, the translation of whose words appears on the title page of the current work. There is nothing in the Book of Mormon to be explained away. The Book teaches, explains, and expounds; it will settle many of your problems, it will guide you in the path of truth. I know of what I speak for I have found it to be a reliable guide. Brethren and sisters, hold fast to the iron rod. May God help us so to do, I pray in the name of the Lord Jesus Christ. Amen.

{34}

"Idolatry and Adultery,"
An Address Delivered on 4 October 1930

(from *One Hundred and First Semi-Annual Conference*
of the Church of Jesus Christ of Latter-day Saints
[Salt Lake City: Published by the Church of Jesus Christ
of Latter-day Saints, 1930], pp. 70-75)

"For behold, my soul delighteth in plainness unto my people, that they may learn." [2 Ne. 25:4]

These are the words of an ancient Hebrew prophet, addressed to the people whose leader he was, commissioned and appointed of God.

The spirit of plainness has characterized the addresses of this conference so far, and if I speak plainly unto you at this time I trust you will understand that I speak under the same spirit that impelled Nephi in the utterance cited.

WHAT IS THE MATTER WITH THE WORLD?

We do not believe in treating ourselves with gratulation to the extent that we feel because we are the covenant people of God—and we boldly proclaim this fact—that all is well with us and that we are right in the sight of God to the extent he would have us be. Gentle but firm admonishment has been given in earlier addresses. Well deserved commendations have been made of the good that our people have accomplished and are accomplishing, and the question of what is the matter with the world, which occasionally we see in bold headlines in newspapers and magazines, has been touched upon.

The great trouble with the world today as I understand it is that it has become idolatrous. We read of idolatry and think of it as a practice or series of practices in the past. This is an idolatrous generation, defying the commandments written by the finger of God—"Thou shalt have no other gods before me," and an idolatrous generation is an adulterous generation.

IDOLATRY AND ADULTERY

Have you never pondered over that remark of the Savior to those who came seeking a sign at his hand, when there were signs all about them? They had seen the sick healed, the lame made to walk, the deaf made to hear, the blind made to see, the dead raised to life, and still they came asking for a sign: and he answered them as befitted their hypocrisy:

"An evil and adulterous generation seeketh after a sign." [Matt. 12:39]

I ask, have you ever considered the connection between the awful sin of adultery and that godlessness that made those curiosity-seekers come asking for a sign? The word "adultery" and the word "idolatry" were originally one, that is, they sprang from the same root, and mean essentially the condition of being false to a solemn covenant.

The Lord compared himself—though in terms of rebuke—to the Israelites of old, as their husband. "I am married to you," he said; and further, in effect: "O recreant Judah, backsliding Israel. I am married unto you. I love you as a husband loves his wife, and yet you go after strange gods and desert me, with whom you have made covenant."

LIVING SCRIPTURES

That was adultery and idolatry, and such is characteristic of the world today. How far does it affect the Latter-day Saints? Let us consider later. But first I cite you to a bit of ancient scriptural history, and as introductory to such citation, I take the opportunity of saying that every dispensation of the Lord's dealings with mankind, from the Adamic down, has been characterized by living scriptures. The accumulated scriptures of earlier dispensations were quite essential to the people lest they would dwindle in unbelief. These ancient records are the world's treasure; but ancient scripture is not enough. In every dispensation there have been oracles of God empowered to speak the will and the word of the Lord, and what they spoke became scripture, technically after it was written; and these scriptures are preserved for our guidance.

A BIT OF ANCIENT HISTORY

Here is the historic instance I would cite to you. Call to mind the history of King Nebuchadnezzar, whom the Lord used as a scourge unto the covenant people because they had gone astray. Aye, because they had deserted him, their husband, and had fallen into the ways of idolatry and adultery, he sent Nebuchadnezzar to scourge them. The pagan king led Israel captive. He went so far as to take from the temple in Jerusalem the sacred vessels of gold and silver that has been used in the ceremonies and ordinances of the holy house. Eventually

Nebuchadnezzar was brought to see the power of God and rendered praise unto him.

His successor, Belshazzar, referred to by historians as the son or the grandson of Nebuchadnezzar, was lifted up in the pride of his heart, and on the occasion of a great feast he called for the vessels that had been brought from the temple that he might display before his people his power and proclaim anew the captivity of Judah.

You know the story. As he and his lords with their wives and concubines there in the court were drinking from those vessels, a mystic hand appeared, writing upon the wall. None of the king's sooth-sayers or wise men could interpret the writing. Belshazzar was greatly frightened. Then Daniel was called, he who had interpreted the dream of Nebuchadnezzar, and he spoke plainly, for his soul delighted in plainness. He recited the troubles that had come upon Nebuchadnezzar, and then added:

"And thou his son, O Belshazzar, hast not humbled thine heart, though thou knewest all this;

"But hast lifted up thyself against the Lord of heaven; and they have brought the vessels of his house before thee, and thou, and thy lords, thy wives, and thy concubines, have drunk wine in them; and thou hast praised the gods of silver, and gold, of brass, iron, wood, and stone, which see not, nor hear, nor know: and the God in whose hand thy breath is, and whose are all thy ways, hast thou not glorified." [Dan. 5:22-23]

Then did he interpret the divinely cryptic writing, part of which interpretation made clear to Belshazzar that he had been weighed in the balance and found wanting, and his kingdom was to be taken from him.

PRESENT DAY APPLICATION

Ancient history, you say, yes but is it not applicable to conditions in the world today? Men are praising the gods of silver and of gold and of all the other valuable commodities that make up wealth, and the God in whose hand their breath is and whose are all their ways they will not recognize. Do you wonder that wickedness and crime have increased to terrifying proportions under those conditions? The prophets of old foresaw it. They spoke of the days of wickedness and vengeance immediately precedent to the second coming of the Lord, which I reiterate, for it has been spoken before, is near at hand.

Now, O Israel, ye Latter-day Saints, how far do these conditions exist among us as a people, laying claim even to higher title than that of which Israel of old were so proud? There were certain signs by which that ancient people were known among their pagan contemporaries. I mention three, as many as time will permit.

The Israelites were distinguished in the first place as worshipers of a living God, a personal God, in whose image they had been created and made. No other nation on the face of the earth recognized the living God. That was a sign by which the covenant people, descendants of Abraham, through Isaac and Jacob, were known. Another sign was this, they observed every seventh day as the Sabbath of the Lord their God; and the Lord had said: This shall be a sign between thee and the nations: They shall know that ye are my people, because ye observe my Sabbaths. And the third sign I mention is that they were tithed of all they possessed. Those were set forth prominently as the banners of Israel, by which all nations should know that they were the covenant people of God.

Now I repeat, in every dispensation living scriptures are given. The history of the past is of value, but the great principles are restated, the fundamental laws are reenacted. Christ came to fulfil and supersede the law of Moses, and yet with his own lips in the flesh he restated every commandment in the Decalog, giving it to the new dispensation. He cited prophecies of the past, connecting up the earlier dispensations with that in which he lived and at the head of which he stood in a particular sense, not only as the head of all dispensations, but in the sense of his being there in mortality.

Where do we stand with respect to those signs? Are we worshiping the true and living God, or are we going idolatrously after the gods of gold and silver, of iron and wood, and brass, diamonds and other idols of wealth? Are we worshiping our farms, our cattle and sheep? Who is our God? To whom are we yielding homage, allegiance and worship? Not worship by means of words only, in ritualistic form, but worship in action, devotion, and sacrificial service?

COMMENDATION AND ADMONITION

I feel it is the duty of those who stand as your presiding servants and your leaders to call attention to the defects of the people as well as to praise their good deeds: and I say that we are not fully living up to those signs characteristic of the Lord's covenant people. Where are you spending your Sabbaths? Are you tithed? No other people on the face of the earth is making such a record, and I believe no other people in past ages have made such a record as the Latter-day Saints are making, in the matter of the payment of tithes. But collectively we are about a fifty percent tithe-paying people. Are we in the habit of leaving our tithing settlement until the end of the year and then making some donation or gift, calling it tithing, trifling with the word of God and his law? I doubt if there be one man in fifty, perhaps not one in a hundred, who leaves the payment of his tithing until the end of the year who pays a tithe. Unless he keeps his books with all the care that a bookkeeper in a great business corporation could give he does not know what he has to tithe. But the Lord would have you tithed as his people of old were tithed, paying when they received.

I know that this people are the people of the Lord, that they are acceptable unto him, but we are not reaching fully the requirements that the Lord has made upon us: and too many Latter-day Saints are going after strange gods, setting their hearts on their hay and their corn, their bonds and their stocks, their automobiles and the luxuries of the world, to the neglect of their duties in the Church. Though I would be no prophet of evil, of disaster, or of calamity, I feel to say that if the Latter-day Saints do not obey the law that God has given with respect to the tithes, they will have less and less to tithe, this in the Lord's own time.

EXHORTATION TO GREATER EFFORT

Let us lift the banners of Zion, the banner of the true worship of the living God, the banner of Sabbath observance, make it a holy day for the service of the Lord, not a day of idle rest and sleep and inactivity, but a day of activity in the Lord's important service. This he has required of us, and he never has modified the requirement by the slightest amendment. Keep flying the banner of the sacred tithe for the Lord. He would have his people tithed that the land may be sanctified unto them. It is for our good that the law of the tithe has been given. We cannot advance in the knowledge of God and the things pertaining to exaltation in the kingdom of God unless we have that training.

I can join with full heart and soul with my brethren and sisters in that joyous hymn, "Zion prospers, all is well." But I remember also the words of the Lord given unto the Nephites of old: "Therefore, wo be unto him that is at ease in Zion! Wo be unto him that crieth: All is well!" It depends upon how we say it and how we sing it. Zion is prospering and will continue to prosper in spite of you, my brother, you forty per cent Latter-day Saint; in spite of myself, whatever my rating may be, and I am trying to attain the one hundred per cent standard. Zion will prosper in spite of me, if I am not faithful. But wo unto him who sits down in idle complacency, neglecting the commandments of God.

I pray that we may be what we profess to be, in the name of Jesus Christ, Amen.

{35}

"Beware of Deception,"
An Address Delivered on 4 April 1931

(from *One Hundred and First Annual Conference
of the Church of Jesus Christ of Latter-day Saints*
[Salt Lake City: Published by the Church of Jesus Christ
of Latter-day Saints, 1931], pp. 26-31)

About 420, probably 421 of our present era, as we reckon the years, Moroni, an ancient Nephite prophet, the last of a long line, closed the record of his people, and left the seal of his testimony upon all that had been inscribed upon the metallic plates which were made to receive the account of the Lord's dealings with that people, from the time they had been led from Jerusalem, across the deep, to this American continent. I pray you heed these words of his.

"And again, I exhort you, my brethren, that ye deny not the gifts of God, for they are many; and they come from the same God. And there are different ways that these gifts are administered; but it is the same God who worketh all in all; and they are given by the manifestations of the Spirit of God unto men, to profit them.

"For behold, to one is given by the Spirit of God, that he may teach the word of wisdom;

"And to another, that he may teach the word of knowledge by the same Spirit;

"And to another, exceeding great faith; and to another, the gifts of healing by the same spirit;

"And again, to another, that he might work mighty miracles;

"And again, to another, that he may prophesy concerning all things;

"And again, to another, the beholding of angels and ministering spirits;

"And again, to another, all kinds of tongues;

"And again, to another, the interpretation of languages and of divers kinds of tongues.

"And all these gifts come by the Spirit of Christ; and they come unto every man severally, according as he will.

"And I would exhort you, my beloved brethren, that ye remember that every good gift cometh of Christ.

"And I would exhort you, my beloved brethren, that ye remember that he is the same yesterday, today, and forever, and that all these gifts of which I have spoken, which are spiritual, never will be done away, even as long as the world shall stand, only according to the unbelief of the children of men." [Moroni 10:8-19]

THE EVIL GIFT

And now I pass over several paragraphs of comment upon what has gone before, and read you another admonition from this ancient revelator:

"And again I would exhort you that ye would come unto Christ, *and lay hold upon every good gift, and touch not the evil gift, nor the unclean thing.*" (Moroni 10:30.)

A very strong contrast is here drawn. The principal gifts of the Spirit are listed in other scriptures, in the Bible, in the volume of latter-day revelation, the Doctrine and Covenants; but the enumeration I have read to you is perhaps as comprehensive as any. The prophet plainly proclaims the fact that these are characteristic of the Church of Christ. Miracles, as the manifestations of such gifts are sometimes called, will not be done away as long as men are receptive to the operations of the Spirit of the Lord, as long as men are willing to receive and to heed.

But the admonishment is: "Touch not the evil gift, nor the unclean thing." What is meant by that? Satan from the first has been a great imitator; he is an experienced strategist. Never has the Lord set his hand to do a specific thing for the good of his people upon the earth, of outstanding feature, but that Satan has attempted to imitate it in some degree.

FROM GOD OR FROM SATAN?

The Lord manifested himself to Moses, and talked to the man face to face. Moses records the fact, and adds that he could not have looked upon the Lord with his physical eyes, but that the glory of the Lord was upon him, and he was able to see with his spiritual eyes.

Then came Satan, the audacious, the father of lies, and represented himself as being the son of God in the distinctive sense. Moses was able to discern and perceive.

"And it came to pass that Moses looked upon Satan and said: Who art thou? For behold, I am a son of God, in the similitude of his Only

Begotten; and where is thy glory, that I should worship thee?

"For behold, I could not look upon God, except his glory should come upon me, and I were strengthened before him. But I can look upon thee in the natural man. Is it not so surely?" [Moses 1:13, 14]

Oh, that we all had such power of discernment. That is a gift of the Spirit, to which we are entitled and we will have it as we live for it. With that gift we shall be free, to a great extent, from the deception that otherwise might lead us astray.

As the Lord gives revelations, so does Satan, each in his way. As the Lord has revelators upon the earth, so has Satan, and he is operating upon those men by his power, and they are receiving revelations, manifestations, that are just as truly of the devil as was his manifestation to Moses, to which I have referred.

BEWARE OF DECEPTION

We need the power of discernment. We need the inspiration of the Lord, that we may know the spirits with whom we have to deal, and recognize those who are speaking and acting under the influence of heaven, and those who are the emissaries of hell. Many have been led away in this Church. Go back to 1830. In September of that year, a few months only after the Church had been organized, Satan was at work, and men were receiving revelations which were put forth to offset those that were given to the Church through the Lord's chosen revelator, the Prophet Joseph Smith. He had been instrumental in translating the ancient records, and he had been given the aid of the Urim and Thummim. Hiram Page found a peculiar stone, and used that, as the devil seems to have influenced him, until the Lord had to speak and declare that that which Hiram Page had given unto the people was not of him, and that when he had revelations to give to the Church he would give them through the man who was sustained as the revelator at the head of the Church, and not through somebody else. Read Doctrine and Covenants, section 28.

Nevertheless the Lord makes plain in the scriptures of these days that his wondrous gifts, the gifts of the Spirit, can be possessed by those who live for them and they will be given severally, according as the Lord will, and he wills to give them unto those who will use them rightly, and not unto those who would dishonor them.

FALSE PROPHECIES

The Lord does not work miracles to satisfy idle curiosity or to

233

gratify the lust of the evil-doer. When you hear, if hear you should, of men who are receiving revelations concerning the conduct of this Church, and those men are not such as you have sustained by the uplifted hand before the Lord as your representatives with the Lord, and as his prophets and revelators unto you, you may know that those men are not speaking by the power of God.

Now do not be deceived. If men come to you and tell you that they have received manifestations and revelations telling of great developments that are to come, beware! So live that you may have the power of discernment. When they tell you that it has been made known to them that great wealth is to be taken out of the hills, under their direction; that they are to bring it forth with the prime purpose of using that wealth for the building up of the Church, for the erection of a great temple, toward which eventuality the eyes of the Latter-day Saints are turned, you may know that they are not of God. No temple will ever be built as the result of the gifts of a rich man, or of a few rich men. In building temples the Lord requires a specific kind of money. It must be sanctified money. It must be the money of sacrifice, and he needs the pennies of the faithful poor as much as the gold pieces of the rich.

We may all have part in building the great temple to which reference is often made, as we have all had the privilege of taking part in building the temples that have already been erected.

SPURIOUS IMITATIONS

Satan has tried to appear as an angel of light in earlier dispensations. He is doing so today. John the Revelator warned the people of this very day in which we live. He wrote for our warning of what would take place. He saw evil powers, and he calls them the spirits of devils, working miracles and deceiving the people. It was so in olden time. While the Lord was speaking through Isaiah and the other great prophets of pre-meridian time, Satan was at work with his witches and wizards, with his soothsayers, giving spurious messages and trying to lead the people astray.

When the Christ came in person manifesting his inherent power over men and evil spirits, when he cast out unclean spirits that were afflicting men, there arose many who undertook to exorcise the demons, and to imitate the work of Christ so far as was possible. And when the Gospel was again brought to earth, and the Priesthood restored in this, the last dispensation, there was a great revival and increase in the manifestations called spiritualistic phenomena, in the

234

effort to put something forth that looked like the original and the genuine, and so lead people astray.

Oh, ye Latter-day Saints, ye mighty men of testimony, ye women of wondrous assurance, shall you, shall we, forget what the Lord has given us by way of certain knowledge, and be led away by false lights, by those who are receiving spurious revelations, as they call them, for guidance?

SATAN A LIVING PERSONAGE

Now, I know that it is not quite in accord with the advanced thought of the day, according to certain cults, to believe that Nephi realized fully the claims that would be set up in the last days, these days. Read what goes before in the twenty-eighth chapter of Second Nephi, before that which I shall read to you, and you will see that the prophet is referring to the time in which we live. He tells us that it will be necessary in this day that the kingdom of the devil shall shake, and he foretells that the devil will "rage in the hearts of the children of men, and stir them up to anger against that which is good."

"And others will he pacify, and lull them away into carnal security, that they will say: All is well in Zion; yea, Zion prospereth, all is well—and thus the devil, cheateth their souls, and leadeth them away carefully down to hell.

"And behold, others he flattereth away, and telleth them there is no hell; *and he saith unto them: I am no devil, for there is none*—and thus he whispereth in their ears, until he grasps them with his awful chains, from whence there is no deliverance."

LATTER-DAY WARNING

In the present dispensation the Lord has warned his people against the doctrines of devils voiced by men in the service of Satan. Read Doctrine and Covenants, section 46, especially verses 7 to 9.

I trust that we may have the power of discrimination, the gift of discernment, that we may know the spirits with whom we have to deal, that we may not forget the voice of the Shepherd but that we may know him, and follow him, and be true to our profession, looking to those whom we sustain as being our representatives before the Lord, for through them will come whatever is necessary that this people, as a people, that this Church, as his Church, shall receive. I hope that none of us shall be defiled through dallying with the evil gift, the devil's gift, the unclean thing, which is abominable in the sight of the Lord. I so pray, in the name of Jesus Christ. Amen.

{36}

The Evolution Controversy

(Entries from the Journal of James E. Talmage, 1929-33,
Archives and Manuscripts, Harold B. Lee Library,
Brigham Young University, Provo, Utah)

Oct. 3, 1929—I attended a meeting of the Council of the Twelve, beginning at 9:00 o'clock, and then the regular weekly meeting of the First Presidency and the Twelve beginning at 10 o'clock. The members of the First Council of the Seventy sat with us for special inquiry into the probable effect of a recent address delivered in the Tabernacle by Elder B. H. Roberts. . . .

Jan. 2, 1931 Fri.—Attended a 9:30 a.m. meeting of the Council of the Twelve, held in President Rudger Clawson's office. The purpose of this gathering was to consider a protest made by Elder Brigham H. Roberts, senior president of the First Council of the Seventy, against a discourse delivered by Elder Joseph Fielding Smith of the Council of the Twelve at a genealogical conference held in April last. The main point at issue is the affirmation by Elder Smith that prior to the Fall there was no death of either plants or animals upon the earth. At today's meeting Elder Roberts responded to an invitation and made an oral and extemporaneous address, supporting his protest. It should be said that what is herein called a "protest" was simply a letter addressed to the First Presidency, later referred by them to the Twelve, asking whether the utterances of Elder Smith were to be considered as expressions of personal opinion or as authoritative statements sustained by the First Presidency and Twelve. By common consent and agreement Brother Roberts is to present his views in writing. . . .

Jan. 7, 1931, Wed.—Attended a meeting of the Council of the Twelve, beginning at 9:30 a.m. Elder B. H. Roberts read a carefully prepared and lengthy paper on the subject of the Antiquity of man, summarizing much geological evidence, and arguing for the existence of pre-Adamites. The paper, covering fifty typewritten pages, was taken under advisement by the Council. . . .

Jan. 14, 1931 Wed.— . . . Had a somewhat extended conference with Presidents Heber J. Grant and Anthony W. Ivins on the question of the Antiquity of Man, these brethren having invited me to give my opinion on certain points. . . .

Jan. 21, 1931 Wed.—Sat with the Council of the Twelve, which convened at 1:30 p.m., and listened with interest and profit to a lengthy paper read by Elder Joseph Fielding Smith, in reply to the paper presented by Elder B. H. Roberts, regarding the Antiquity of Man, and, as Elder Smith affirmed, the utter absence of death in any form upon the earth before the time of Adam's fall. Like the paper of Elder Roberts, this was taken under advisement. . . .

Apr. 7, 1931 Tues.—Attended a called meeting of the General Authorities of the Church, all present, beginning at 9 a.m. and lasting until nearly 1 p.m. The principal subject was the consideration of a subject brought to the front by Elder B. H. Roberts, who addressed a letter to the First Presidency asking whether certain utterances by Elder Joseph Fielding Smith, made at a meeting under Genealogical Society auspices last October, were to be accepted as an expression of personal opinion or as an authoritative pronouncement. Involved in this question is that of the beginning of life upon the earth, and as to whether there was death either of animal or plant before the fall of Adam, on which proposition Elder Smith was very pronounced in denial and Elder Roberts equally forceful in the affirmative. As to whether pre-Adamite races existed upon the earth there has been much discussion among some of our people of late. The decision reached by the First Presidency and announced to this morning's assembly . . . is a wise one on the premises. This is one of the many things upon which we cannot speak with assurance and dogmatic assertions on either side are likely to do harm rather than good. . . .

Aug. 9, 1931 Sun.—I was the speaker at the afternoon services in the Tabernacle taking the subject "The Earth and Man." . . .

Nov. 5, 1931, Thurs.—I attended Council meetings as usual. President Heber J. Grant was absent in California. At both the 9 o'clock meeting of the Council of the Twelve and the 10 o'clock meeting of the combined Councils the subject of my address delivered on August 9 was again considered, the question being as to whether it is wise to publish that address. As there is a difference of opinion among brethren of the Twelve, President A.W. Ivins took the matter back into the hands of the Presidency today. . . .

Nov. 16, 1931, Mon.—I was called into brief consultation by the

First Presidency on the subject of my Tabernacle address on August 9.

Nov. 17, 1931, Tues.—According to appointment made yesterday the First Presidency gave special attention to the matter of my Tabernacle address before referred to, going over it with considerable care, though it was apparent to me that the brethren had before considered it among themselves and had reached their decision. This they announced to me by way of instruction to send back the copy which I had recalled from the printer, and to have the address published in the *Deseret News* of the next Saturday evening, and further to have it printed in pamphlet form. I shall make further comment when the address is actually in print. . . .

Nov. 21, 1931, Sat.—The address of August 9 appears in the Church section of this day's *Deseret News*, and the delivery of the pamphlets carrying the address was made to us today. The cause of the long delay in publishing this address, and some incidental points of interest, should perhaps be noted here. The subject is "THE EARTH AND MAN." A copy of the complete pamphlet will be bound in with this Journal. See entry herein for Tuesday, April 7, 1931.

On Apr. 5, 1930, Elder Joseph Fielding Smith of the Council of the Twelve made an address at the Genealogical Conference, which was published in "The Utah Genealogical and Historical magazine" of October, 1930. This address was entitled "Faith Leads to a Fulness of Truth and Righteousness."

The following is taken from page 148 of the magazine referred to:

"No Death on the Earth Before Adam"

"As I have read, the Lord pronounced the earth *good* when it was finished. Everything upon its face was called good. *There was no death in the earth before the fall of Adam.* I do not care what the scientists say in regard to dinosaurs and other creatures upon the earth millions of years ago that lived and died and fought and struggled for existence. When the earth was created and was declared *good* peace was upon its face among all its creatures. Strife and wickedness were not found here, neither was there any corruption. I do not know how long the earth was in course of preparation. I do not care. That has nothing to do with the plan of salvation. It is sufficient for me to know that after some lengthy period of time, or times, called days, the earth was finished and pronounced good by its Creator. *All life in the sea, the air, on the earth, was without death. Animals were not dying. Things were not changing as we find them changing in this* mortal *existence, for mortality had not come.* Today we are living in a world of change because we are living under very different conditions from those which prevailed in the beginning and before the fall of man."

Elder B. H. Roberts, Senior President of the First Council of the Seventy, inquired by letter addressed to the First Presidency as to whether these utterances of Elder Smith were to be construed as an expression of his personal opinion or as a doctrine of the Church. The Twelve considered the matter in several sessions and reported to the First Presidency, whose action is noted herein under date of April 7 last. Many of our students have inferred from Elder Smith's address that the Church refuses to recognize the findings of science if there be a word of scriptural record in our interpretation of which we find even a seeming conflict with scientific discoveries or deductions, and that therefore the "policy" of the Church is in effect opposed to scientific research.

In speaking at the Tabernacle on August 9 last I had not forgotten that in the pronouncement of the First Presidency mentioned under date of April 7 last it was advised and really required that the General Authorities of the Church refrain from discussing in public, that is preaching, the debatable subject of the existence of human kind upon the earth prior to the beginning of Adamic history as recorded in scripture; but, I had been present at a consultation in the course of which the First Presidency had commented somewhat favorably upon the suggestion that sometime, somewhere, something should be said by one or more of us to make plain that the Church does not refuse to recognize the discoveries and demonstrations of science, especially in relation to the subject at issue. President Anthony W. Ivins, of the First Presidency, presided at the Tabernacle meeting, and three members of the Council of the Twelve were present—Elders George F. Richards, Joseph Fielding Smith and Richard R. Lyman. Of course, Elder Smith, and in fact all of us, recognize that my address was in some important respects opposed to his published remarks, but the other brethren named, including President Ivins, expressed their tentative approval of what I had said.

I am very grateful that my address has come under a very thorough consideration, and I may say investigation, by the First Presidency and the Council of the Twelve. The discussions throughout as relating to the matter have been forceful but in every respect friendly, and the majority of the Twelve have been in favor of the publication of the address from the time they first took it under consideration. I have hoped and fervently prayed that the brethren would be rightly guided in reaching a decision, and, as the Lord knows my heart, I have had no personal desire for triumph or victory in the matter, but have hoped that the address would be published or suppressed as would be for the best. The issue is now closed; the address is in print. . . .

Jan. 31, 1933—Announcement is made today of the discovery of "microscopic living organisms in the fragments of meteorites." If this alleged discovery is confirmed it will be regarded as one of great importance. . . .

{37}

"The Earth and Man,"
An Address Delivered on 9 August 1931

(from the *Deseret News,* 21 November 1931, pp. 7, 8)

"In the beginning, God created the heaven and the earth.

"And the earth was without form, and void; and darkness was upon the face of the deep. And the Spirit of God moved up on the face of the waters." (Gen. 1:1, 2.)

Any question as to when that beginning was is largely futile, because unanswerable. In the first place we have no time unit by which to measure back through the ages to the time at which, so far as the earth is concerned, time began.

Years are as inadequate in any attempted survey of the stages of earth development as are miles to the astronomer who would span the distances of interstellar space. He speaks in terms of light–years, such unit being the distance traversed by a ray of light speeding on at the rate of approximately 186,000 miles per second throughout a year.

Secondly, we are without information as to what stage of earth development is indicated by "the beginning." And what is a beginning in nature? At best it is but a new start in advance of what had passed up to that point of time; and every beginning is an ending of what went immediately before, even as every consummation is a commencement of something greater, higher, and therefore superior to the past.

The Earth Older Than Man.

To the thoughtful mind there can be no confusion of the beginning spoken of in the opening verse of Genesis with the advent of man upon the changing earth; for by the scriptural record itself we learn of stage after stage, age after age of earth processes by which eventually this planet became capable of supporting life—vegetable, animal and human in due course.

Whether or not scientists have been able to see, however, dimly, the way by which the earth as an orb in space was formed, matters little except as a subject of academic interest. For many years it was very generally believed that the earth, once formless and void, passed through stages of cooling of superheated gas to liquid, thence to the solid state, as the Nebular Theory assumed; but this conception has given way to the later thought that the earth as a solid spheroid has resulted from the bringing together of solid particles once diffused in space—this being the basis of the Planetesimal hypothesis.

But this we know, for both revealed and discovered truth, that is to say both scripture and science, so affirm—that plant life antedated animal existence and that animals preceded man as tenants of earth.

Life and Death Before Man's Advent.

According to the conceptions of geologists the earth passed through ages of preparation, to us unmeasured and immeasurable, during which countless generations of plants and animals existed in great variety and profusion, and gave in part the every [sic] substance of their bodies to help form certain strata which are still existent as such.

The oldest, that is to say the earliest, rocks thus far identified in land masses reveal the fossilized remains of once living organisms, plant and animal. The coal strata, upon which the world of industry so largely depends, are essentially but highly compressed and chemically changed vegetable substance. The whole series of chalk deposits, and many of our deep-sea limestones contain the skeletal remains of animals. These lived and died, age after age, while the earth was yet unfit for human habitation.

From the Simple to The Complex.

From the fossil remains of plants and animals found in the rocks, the scientist points to a very definite order in the sequence of life embodiment, for the older rocks, the earlier formations, reveal to us organisms of simplest structure only, whether of plants or animals. These primitive species were aquatic; land forms were of later development. Some of these simpler forms of life have persisted until the present time, though with great variations as the result of changing environment.

Geologists say that these very simple forms of plant and animal bodies were succeeded by others more complicated; and in the indestructible record of the rocks they read the story of advancing life from the simple to the more complex, from the single-celled protozoan to the highest animals, from the marine algae to the advanced types of flowering plant—to the apple tree, the rose, and the oak.

What a fascinating story is inscribed upon the stony pages of the earth's crust! The geologist, who through long and patient effort has learned at least a little of the language in which these truths are written, finds the pages illustrated with pictures, which for fidelity of detail excel the best efforts of our modern engravers, lithographers and half-tone artists. The pictures in the rocks are the originals, the rest at best but copies.

In due course came the crowning work of this creative sequence, the advent of man! Concerning this all-important event we are told that scientists and theologians are at hopeless and irreconcilable variance. I regard the assumption or claim, whichever it be, as an exaggeration. Discrepancies that trouble us now, will diminish as our knowledge of pertinent facts is extended. The Creator has made record in the rocks for man to decipher; but he has also spoken directly regarding the main stages of progress by which the earth has been brought to be what it is. The accounts cannot be fundamentally opposed; one cannot contradict the other; though man's interpretation of either may be seriously at fault.

Adam a Historic Personage.

So far as the history of man on the earth is concerned the scriptures begin with the account of Adam. True, the geologist does not know Adam by name; but he knows and speaks of man as an early, continuing and present form of earth-life, above and beyond all other living things past or present.

We believe that Adam was a real personage, who stands at the head of his race chronologically. To my mind Adam is a historic personage, not a prehistoric being, unidentified and uncertain.

If the Usher [James Ussher, 1581-1656] chronology be correct, or even approximately so then the beginning of Adamic history as recorded in scripture dates back about 4,000 years before the birth of Christ. We as a Church believe that the current reckoning of time from the birth of Christ to the present is correct, namely 1931 years—not from last New Year's day, January 1, but from the month that came to be known among the Hebrews as Nisan or Ahib, corresponding with our late March and early April. So we believe that we are now living in the 1931st year since the birth of Christ, and therefore 5931 years since the beginning of the Adamic record.

This record of Adam and his posterity is the only scriptural account we have of the appearance of man upon the earth. But we have also a vast and ever-increasing volume of knowledge concerning man, his early habits and customs, his industries and works of art, his tools and implements, about which such scriptures as we have thus far received are entirely silent. Let us not try to wrest the scriptures in an attempt to explain away what we cannot explain. The opening chapters of Genesis, and scriptures related thereto, were never intended as a text-book of geology, archeology, earth-science or man-science. Holy Scripture will endure, while the conceptions of men change with new discoveries. We do not show reverence for the scriptures when we misapply them through faulty interpretation.

Primary and Secondary Causes.

There has been much discussion over the alleged conflict between the teachings of science and the doctrines of the revealed word concerning the origin of man. Let it be remembered that the term origin is almost invariably used in a relative sense. The mind of man is unable to grasp the fundamental thought of an absolute or primary origin. Every occurrence man has witnessed is the result of some previously acting cause or purpose; and that cause in turn was the effect or result of causes yet more remote. Perhaps we have never been able to trace an effect to its primary or original cause. Man may say that he understands the origin of an oak in the acorn from which it sprang; but is not the acorn the fruit of a yet earlier oak, and so in reality rather a continuation than a beginning? Yet there is something fascinating in the thought of a beginning; the persistence of a process once started is far less mysterious than its inception.

It is not enough to refer effects to the "First Great Cause;" it is unsatisfying and not always reverent to answer questions as to how things came to be what they are by the easy statement that God made them so. With such an answer the scientific man has little patience. The fact that all created things are the works of God and that all processes of nature are due to him as the administrator of law and order is to the scientific mind an axiom requiring neither argument nor demonstration. The botanist knows that God makes the plant grow; but he, weak mortal, is devoting time and energy of body, mind and spirit, to a study of the way in which God works such a marvelous miracle. The geologist knows that God created the earth; but the best effort of his life is put forth in the hope of finding out in some degree, however small, the method by which the Creator wrought this wondrous world. The astronomer gazing into the starry depths sees in their orderly procession the Lord Eternal walking in his majesty and might; and in humility the student of the heavenly bodies spends days and nights striving to learn a little of the way in which God worked out the marvel of the universe.

In proportion as any one of these may learn of the ways of God he becomes wise. To be able to think as God thinks, to comprehend in any degree his purposes and methods, is to become in that measure like unto him, and to that extent to be prepared for eventual companionship in his presence. The scientist is busily engaged in the study of secondary causes—the ways and means by which God works and through which he accomplishes his miracle, ever beginning, never ending—and in his search for the truth the student of science scarcely dares lift his eyes to look toward the First Great Cause, the Eternal Power that stands and operates behind and above all the secondary causes, or what we call the processes of nature.

The Origin of Man.

The question involved in the origin of man therefore, is not raised as a challenge to the belief and declaration that he came to earth through divine direction, but is in the nature of an inquiry as to the conditions under which he came. There are many who claim that man's advent upon the earth was effected through processes of evolution from lower forms, processes that had been operative for ages, processes by which man is made kin to the brute and a development from the lowest type of organism. Others affirm that he differs from all mortal creatures of lower rank not only in degree but in kind; in short, that he is not one with the animal creation and that therefore his coming was in no sense a natural and necessary result of earlier animal life. Discussion on this question has developed intense animus, and too often the quest for truth has been lost sight of in the strife for triumph.

In speaking of the origin of man we generally have reference to the creation of man's body; and, of all the mistakes that man has made concerning himself, one of the greatest and the gravest is that of mistaking the body for the man. The body is no more truly the whole man than is the coat the body. The man, as an individual intelligence, existed before his earthly body was framed and shall exist after that body has suffered dissolution. Let it not be assumed that belief in the existence of man's spirit is a conception founded upon scriptural authority only; on the contrary, let it be known that it is in accordance with the best and most advanced scientific thought and philosophic belief of the day to hold that man consists of spirit and body; and divine revelation makes plain that these together constitute the soul.

We have difficulty in comprehending processes for which we find no analogy in things familiar. Even were it possible for us to know in detail the way in which the body of man was formed and then endowed with the power of procreation, insuring the perpetuity of the race, it would throw but little light upon the subject of the ultimate origin of man. We know but little of things beyond the sphere upon which we live except as information has been revealed by a power superior to that of earth, and by an intelligence above that of man. Notwithstanding the assumption that man is the culmination of an evolutionary development from a lower order of beings, we know that the body of man today is in the very form and fashion of his spirit, except indeed for disfigurements and deformities. The perfect body is the counterpart of the perfect spirit and the two are the constituent entities of the soul.

By What Standard?

Much depends upon the standard by which we judge as to whether any particular organism shall be pronounced of high or lower rank. By the standards of powers of flight, in which the bird excels, man is a very inferior being; if judged by fleetness of foot, he is far below the deer; by gauge of strength he is inferior to the horse and the elephant; and yet man holds dominion over these and all other living things of earth. In certain important points of body structure man stands low in the scale if he be graded strictly in accordance with the accepted standard of mammalian anatomy.

In the course of creative events the earth came to a condition fitted for the abiding place of the sons and daughters of God; and then Adam came forth upon the earth. But the beginning of man's mortal existence upon the earth was not the beginning of man; he had lived before, even as he shall live after the earth has passed away and its place taken by a new earth and a new heaven.

Man and the Ape.

It has been stated by certain extremists that evolution affirms that man is in the line of posterity from the ape. But scientists today discredit this view. The most that even radical evolutionists assert is that the similarity of structure between man and certain apes indicates

246

the possibility of a common ancestor of the two; but between man and the ape there are more essential differences than resemblances.

True, man does not excel in strength of limb, agility, or speed, but in the God-given powers of mind and in the possession of superior ambition and effort. Hear the words of one who, until his death was regarded as among the foremost of American geologists, James D. Dana:

"Man's origin has thus far no sufficient explanation from science. His close relations in structure to the man-apes are unquestionable. They have the same number of bones with two exceptions, and the bones are the same in kind and structure. The muscles are mostly the same. Both carry their young in their arms. The affiliations strongly suggest community of descent. But the divergencies . . . especially the cases of degeneracy in man's structure, exhibited in his palmigrade feet and the primitive character of his teeth, allying him in these respects to the Lower Eocene forms, are admitted proof that he has not descended from any existing type of ape. In addition, man's erect posture makes the gap a very broad one. The brute, the ape included, has powerful muscles in the back of the neck to carry the head in its horizontal position, while man has no such muscles, as any one of the species can prove by crawling for a while on 'all fours'. Beyond this, the great size of the brain, his eminent intellectual and moral qualities, his voice and speech, give him sole title to the position at the head of the kingdoms of life. In this high position, he is able to use Nature as his work-mate, his companion, and his educator, and to find perpetual delight in her harmonies and her revelations . . .

"Whatever the results of further search, we may feel assured, in accord with Wallace, who shares with Darwin in the authorship of the theory of Natural Selection, that the intervention of a Power above nature was at the basis of man's development. Believing that nature exists through the will and ever-acting power of the Divine Being, and that all its great truths, its beauties, its harmonies, are manifestations of his wisdom and power, or, in the words nearly of Wallace, that the whole universe is not merely dependent on, but actually is, the will of one Supreme Intelligence, nature, with man as its culminant species, is no longer a mystery." —James D. Dana, Manual of Geology, 4th edition, page 1036.

These lines were written shortly before the death of the writer—and constitute his last testament and testimony as to the origin of the species to which he himself belonged.

Man's Place in Nature.

In the work already cited, the same author wrote:

"Man stands in the successional line of the quadrumana, at the head of the animal kingdom, But he is not a primate among primates. The quadrumana are, as Cuvier called them, quadrumana from the first to the last. They are brute mammals, as is manifested in their carnivore-like canines and their powerful jaws; in their powerful muscular development: in their walking on all fours and the adaption thereto exhibited in the vetebrae, producing the convexity of the back; and also in other parts of the skeleton. Man, on the contrary, is not quadrumanous. . . .

"Man was the first being, in the geological succession, capable of an intelligent survey of Nature and a comprehension of her laws; the first capable of augmenting his strength by bending Nature to his service, rendering thereby a weak body stronger than all possible animal force; the first capable of deriving happiness from truth and goodness; of apprehending eternal right; of reaching toward a knowledge of self and God; the first, therefore, capable of conscious obedience or disobedience of a moral law, and the first subject to debasement of his moral nature through his appetites.

"There is in man, therefore, a spiritual element in which the brute has no share. His power of indefinite progress, his thoughts and desires that look onward even beyond time, his recognition of spiritual existence and of a Divinity above, all evince a nature that partakes of the infinite and divine. Man is linked to the past through the system of life, of which he is the last, the completing, creation. But, unlike other species of that closing system of the past, he, through his spiritual nature, is more intimately connected with the opening future." James D. Dana, Manual of Geology, 4th edition, pp. 1017–18.

A Later Authority.

Let me cite a later authority than Dana. Among the living no anthropologist has been more pronounced in upholding the theories of Darwin and Lamarck than Dr. Henry Fairfield Osborn.

By the theories mentioned man was said to have risen from tree-climbing ape-like ancestors. In his address as retiring president of the American Association for the Advancement of Science, December, 1929, Dr. Osborn affirms the untenability of the views he had so long and aggressively advocated. He regards the human bones unearthed at Piltdown, Sussex, England, as typical of the "Dawn Man" who was in every distinguishing characteristic, a man not part man and part ape, but as to brain capacity and other evidences of mentality equal to some races now living. Yet Osborn holds to a communal origin of man and anthropoids related in structure, away back in the late Tertiary age of geologic history.

Thus theories come, endure for a season and go, like the fungi of the night; nevertheless they serve their purpose as temporary aids in human thought and endeavor.

The Time Element.

The outstanding point of difference between those who take the opening chapters of Genesis and cognate scriptures as the whole and only reliable record of the creation of earth and man, and the students of earth-science who fail to find an adequate record in scripture, is the point of time during which man in some state has lived on this planet.

Geologists and anthropologists say that if the beginning of Adamic history dates back but 6000 years or less, there must have been races of human sort upon earth long before that time—without denying, however, that Adamic history may be correct, if it be regarded solely as the history of the Adamic race.

This view postulates, by application of Dana's affirmation already quoted: "that the intervention of a power above Nature" brought about the placing of, let me say, Adam upon earth.

It is but fair to say that no reconciliation of these opposing conceptions has been effected to the satisfaction of both parties. We have not yet learned how to correlate geologic time-periods with terms of years, except as estimates, for which no absolute dependable foundation may be found.

Nobility of Adam's Race.

I do not regard Adam as related to—certainly not as descended from—the Neanderthal, the Cro-Magnon, the Peking or the Piltdown man. Adam came as divinely directed, created and empowered, and stands as the patriarchal head of his posterity—a posterity, who, if true to the laws of God are heirs to the Priesthood and to the glories of eternal lives.

Were it true that man is a product of evolution from lower forms, it is but reasonable to believe that he will yet develop into something higher. While it is a fact that eternal progression is a characteristic of man's divine birthright, as yet we have learned nothing to indicate that man shall develop physically into any other form than that which he now appears.

Many attempts have been made by those who regard man as an animal to frame some definition by which he may be distinctively described among his fellow animals: but of such attempts none have been satisfactorily successful. The difficulty lies in the fact already stated, that man differs from the animal creation not only in degree but in kind; he is the only being who has any conception of a pre-existent state or an existence beyond the grave; the only being whose thoughts turn toward God and who feels in his soul the inspiring impulses of kinship to Deity. Believe not those who would make man but little above the brutes, when in truth he is but little below the angels, and if faithful shall pass by the angels and take his place among the exalted sons of God. The spirit of man is the offspring of the Eternal Father, and his body, if unmarred, is in the very form and fashion of that spirit.

The Ante-Mortal State.

We have been told that Jesus Christ is in very truth our Elder Brother, and as to his pre-existence in the spirit state there is little room for question. That his spirit was in the form of the earthly body which he afterward took, and which body was slain, buried, and resurrected, and with which body he ascended into heaven, is attested by scripture. Going back to the time immediately following the dispersion from Babel, we read of a prophet to whom the unembodied Lord revealed himself, saying: "Behold, this body, which ye now behold, is the body of my spirit; and man have I created after the body of my spirit; even as I appear unto thee to be in the spirit will I appear unto my people in the flesh." (Book of Mormon, Ether 3:16.)

It is evident from this scripture that in his pre-existent state, that is to say in the state in which he existed prior to his earthly birth, Jesus Christ had the same form and stature that he afterward presented in the flesh. By natural processes his spirit shaped for itself a body from the material of earth, which body underwent a course of graded development until it reached maturity; in which state that body was the counterpart of the spirit whose material tabernacle it was. As with Jesus so with all the sons and daughters of God; each had a spiritual existence before he entered upon this stage of mortal existence, and in each case the body is formed and fashioned by the power of the immortal spirit.

In this process of body shaping, the spirit may be hindered, hampered, and interfered with, through influences of heredity, through prenatal defects or through accident and disease.

As to how were formed the bodies of the first human beings to take tabernacles, the revealed word gives no details, while science has practically nothing to offer by way of explanation. As Dana so positively declares in the work already cited, "Man's origin has thus far no sufficient explanation from science."

Man's mortal existence is but temporary to this earth; he came hither from another realm, in which he lived in an unembodied state and to which, in the natural order, he shall return in a disembodied state, following the change known as death. After the body of the first man had been made ready through the direct operation of the creative power, the spirit of man entered that body. Note the sublimity of the scriptural declaration: "And the Lord God formed man of the dust of the ground, and breathed into his nostrils the breath of life; and man became a living soul." (Gen. 2:7).

A Power Above Nature.

In the study of all the created things over which he has dominion, man has found it possible to investigate with some degree of success the secondary causes, or natural processes through which the creative power has operated to bring about the system that we designate as Nature; but in the study of his own eternal self he is brought at once to the contemplation of the First Great Cause as to his origin. The power that lies at the basis of man's development is "a Power above Nature." That is to say, man as a mortal being, exists as the result of a special and particular creation. Through graded stages the earth was brought into a state suited to the support of life. In orderly sequence plants and animals appeared; and when at last the world was prepared for its royal ruler, he came, even as he had been declared:

"And God said, Let us make man in our image, after our likeness; and let them have dominion over the fish of the sea, and over the fowl of the air, and over the cattle, and over all the earth, and over every creeping thing that creepeth upon the earth.

"So God created man in his own image, in the image of God created he him; male and female created he them.

"And God blessed them and God said unto them, Be fruitful, and multiply, and replenish the earth, and subdue it; and have dominion over the fish of the sea, and over the fowl of the air, and over every living thing that moveth upon the earth." (Gen. 1:26-28).

Such is the declaration of scripture regarding Adam's advent upon earth; and such is fair summary of our knowledge upon the subject.

Evolution, True and False.

Evolution is true so far as it means development, and progress, and advancement in all the works of God; but many of the vagaries that have been made to do duty under that name are so vague as to be unacceptable to the scientific mind. At best, the conception of the development of man's body from the lower forms through evolutionary processes has been but a theory, an unproved hypothesis. Theories may be regarded as the scaffolding upon which the builder stands while placing the blocks of truth in position. It is a grave error to mistake the scaffolding for the wall, the flimsy and temporary structure for the stable and permanent. The scaffolding serves but a passing purpose, important though it be, and is removed as soon as the walls of that part of the edifice of knowledge have been constructed. Theories have their purpose and are indispensable, but they must never be mistaken for demonstrated facts. The Holy Scriptures should not be discredited by theories of man; they cannot be discredited by fact and truth. Within the Gospel of Jesus Christ there is room and place for every truth thus far learned by man, or yet to be made known. The Gospel is not behind the times, on the contrary it is up-to-date and ever shall be.

It is natural for the young and immature mind to think that what to it is new must of necessity be new to the world. Comparatively inexperienced students are discovering from time to time apparent discrepancies between the faith of their fathers and the development of modern thought; and these they are apt to magnify and exaggerate, when as a matter of fact, their greatgrandfathers met the same seeming difficulties and yet survived. Believe not those who assert that the gospel of Jesus Christ is in any way opposed to progress or inconsistent with advancement.

In the Lineage of Deity.

Man is the child of God, he is born heir to boundless possibilities, the child of the eternities to come. Among mortal beings, the law holds true that the posterity of each shall be after his kind. The child therefore, may become like unto the parent; and man may yet attain the rank of godship. He is born in the lineage of Deity, not in the posterity of the brute creation.

I cite my words of an earlier day, with a quotation.

Man's Relative Littleness.

The insignificance of man in comparison with the earth on which he dwells, and even with limited topographical features of his world, has ofttimes been dwelt upon. Draw to scale a towering mountain and a man standing at its base or on its summit—what does the man amount to? But then the earth as a planet is small compared with some others of its own system, to say nothing of the relative sizes of earth and sun. In turn, our entire solar system, in the measurement of which miles cease to have meaning—so vast it is—ranks low in dimensions as we gauge it with other families of worlds in the great galaxy of stars to which it belongs and that immeasurable galaxy is but one among many, and not the greatest of them all.

Dream Vision of the Infinite.

This hour is not well suited to the presentation of mathematical data relating to the extent of the universe; though it may permit us to indulge the contemplation of thoughtpictures, bewildering though that indulgence may be. John Paul Richter's "Dream Vision of the Infinite" has been brought to English readers through several renditions; and I ask you to follow or accompany me through one of these, generally worded along the lines of the version given us by Thomas De Quincey:

"God called up from dreams a man into the vestibule of heaven, saying 'Come thou hither and I will show thee the glories of my house.' And to the servants that stood around the throne he said 'Take the man and strip from him his robes of flesh; cleanse his vision and put a new breath into his nostrils; only touch not with any change his human heart—the heart that fears and trembles.'

"It was done; and, with a mighty angel for his guide, the man stood ready for his infinite voyage. Then, from the terraces of heaven, without sound or farewell, they wheeled away into endless space. Sometimes, with solemn flight of angel wings they fled through Zaarrahs of darkness, through wildernesses of death that divided the worlds of life. Sometimes they swept over frontiers that were quickening under prophetic motions from God.

"Then, from a distance that is counted only in heaven, light dawned for a time through a sleepy film. By unutterable pace the light swept to them, they by unutterable pace to the light. In a moment the rushing of planets was upon them; in a moment the blazing of suns was around them.

"Then came eternities of twilight, that revealed, but were not revealed. To the right hand and the left towered mighty constellations, that by self-repetitions and answers from afar, that by counterpositions, built up triumphal gates, whose architraves, whose archways—horizontal, upright—rested, rose—at altitudes, by spans that seemed ghostly from infinitude. Without measure were the architraves, past number were the archways, beyond memory the gates!

"Within the stairs that scaled the eternities above, that descended to the eternities below: above was below, below was above, to the man stripped of gravitating body. Depth was swallowed up in height insurmountable; height was swallowed up in depth unfathomable. Suddenly, as thus they rode from infinite to infinite, suddenly as thus they tilted over abysmal worlds, a mighty cry arose—that systems more mysterious, that worlds more billowy, other heights and other depths were coming, were nearing, were at hand!

"Then the man sighed and stopped, shuddered and wept. His overladen heart uttered itself in tears; and he said 'Angel, I will go no farther; for the spirit of man aches with this infinity. Insufferable is the glory of God. Let me lie down in the grave and hide myself from the persecutions of the infinite; for end, I see, there is none!'

"And from all the listening stars that shone around issued a choral chant, 'The man speaks truly; end is there none that ever yet we heard of.' 'End is there none?' the angel solemnly demanded. 'Is there, indeed, no end? And is this the sorrow that kills you?' Then the angel threw up his glorious hands to the heaven of heavens, saying 'End is there none to the universe of God! Lo, also, there is no beginning!'"

The Spiritual Grandeur of Man.

What is man in this boundless setting of sublime splendor? I answer you: Potentially now, actually to be, he is greater and grander, more precious according to the arithmetic of God, than all the planets and suns of space. For him were they created; they are the handiwork of God; man is his son! In this world man is given dominion over a few things; it is his privilege to achieve supremacy over many things.

"The heavens declare the glory of God; and the firmament showeth his handiwork." (Psa. 19:1.) Incomprehensibly grand as are the physical creations of the earth and space, they have been brought into existence as means to an end, necessary to the realization of the

254

supreme purpose, which in the words of the Creator is thus declared:

"For behold, this is my work and my glory—to bring to pass the immortality and eternal life of man." (Pearl of Great Price, page 4.) [Moses 1:39]

It is decreed that this earth shall become a celestialized, glorified sphere. Such is the revealed word. Science has nothing to say on the matter; it can neither refute nor prove. But the Lord, even God, hath spoken it—and so shall it be! Amen.

{38}

"The Need for Religion,"
An Address Delivered on 8 October 1932

(from *One Hundred and Third Semi-Annual Conference
of the Church of Jesus Christ of Latter-day Saints*
[Salt Lake City: Published by the Church of Jesus Christ
of Latter-day Saints, 1932], pp. 76-80)

We have heard many strong testimonies, many fervent admonitions, much good advice, quotations of numerous scriptures, every one to the point, in this conference. You will agree with me in the thought that it is good for us to be here and to have been here in earlier sessions. When this conference shall end we are not going away disappointed, but enriched and encouraged, I trust, in the duties that lie immediately before us.

RELIGION A SUPPORT

Of late I have found the thought welling up in my mind, even more forcefully and persistently than usual: Of what use to me is my religion under these times of special stress and test? I take it that even if you had not known before you came here that we are living under times of pressure and strain you would know it by this time, for several speakers have emphasized the fact. If you had not realized that there is something called the depression abroad in the world, you must have found it out by this time, for that also has been mentioned by speaker after speaker.

The word "depression" has become decidedly trite, but I do not know any other word in the English language that exactly expresses the condition we wish to describe. Now, we must recognize that as an existing condition. It is no mere theory, but a solemn fact. It is not merely a local condition, it is not only nation-wide, but world-wide.

PRESENT CONDITION FORETOLD

It may be small comfort to remind you that this thing was definitely foretold. It may perhaps not soften the fact of your financial difficulties to tell you that you have heard of these hard times from the mouths of those whom you sustain as your leaders, utterances made from this stand, and from the pulpits in your several stakes and wards for lo, these many years past. Some of you will know that I, with my brethren, have been very plain in citing to you scriptures, perhaps apologizing in a way for appearing a little pessimistic, yet begging you to understand the predictions as being the nature of optimistic warnings in the way of caution and counsel.

True, this reminder may not be of any more comfort to you than that to a boy who is writing in the after effects of eating green apples to be told that he was warned against green apples.

FAILURE TO UNDERSTAND

Remember that the Lord said to his disciples in the day of his personal ministry: I tell you these things beforehand, that when they come to pass you may see and understand.

He knew very well that not many of them would open their ears and their hearts and understand at the time what he said. He told them of the troubles that were about to befall Jerusalem. He told them of the persecutions that were coming upon them, his chosen ones. He told them of the crucifixion that was awaiting himself, and they could not or would not understand but tried to explain away his words as passing remarks incident to the times. Do you not remember how he tried to make them understand that he was speaking in earnest, and that he wanted them to take his words literally?

On that solemn march of his on the way to Jerusalem and the tomb, traversing the roads slowly, and halting wherever he found people willing to listen to him, he stopped and beckoned his followers to come up, and said to them: Let this thing sink down deep into your ears and hearts—I, the Son of Man, am on my way to Jerusalem to be handed over to wicked men, I am to be crucified and on the third day shall rise again.

Then he passed on, and they talked among themselves wondering—What in the world does he mean by rising again? Even after he had risen from the sepulcher there were many who doubted. When the women came from the tomb with the gladsome news some of the disciples treated the story as but an idle tale based on emotional imagination.

Well, that may be a trait of human nature developed through the centuries, but I trust we can rise above it, and open our eyes and our hearts and come to an understanding of what the Lord has told us, of what he is telling us, for he speaks today in terms that are literal and in the language that we best can understand.

Oh, there are so many tongues spoken among men; the world is a babel; but of the tongues used by the Lord in his communication with men he selects for each occasion the language that they ought to understand. He spoke through the voice of prophecy, year after year, decade after decade, century after century, telling of the wars that would surely come in the last days, warning the people against the conditions that would make those wars certain. But would men hear? On the very eve of the outbreak of the World War there stood in this very pulpit one of the world's greatest thinkers, who declared conditions to be such that there never could be another great war between and among the major powers of the world; that the financial interests of the world were such as to forbid. Then having demonstrated, by the citation of statistics and figures many, that there could not be such a war, he proceeded to demonstrate that if war did break out in spite of all, it could not last more than six weeks; for there was not enough wealth in the world to keep a war going with present-day weapons and under conditions of modern fighting, more than a few weeks.

I heard him speak, and I had occasion afterward to say to him: "Doctor, you have left out some important factors of your problem." He said: "What are they?" "The words of the prophets; for the war will come. It has been predicted conditionally, and the conditions are such as to make its coming certain." And I heard the refrain of ancient prophecy: "Behold, I will proceed to do a marvelous work among this people, even a marvelous work and a wonder: for the wisdom of their wise men shall perish and the understanding of their prudent men shall be hid."

BODY, MIND AND SPIRIT

We recognize that a human being is more than a physical creation. The man who thinks otherwise is behind the times, in the first place, even in the matter of the fads and fashions of changing conjecture. Do you think you are nothing more than a makeup of bones and muscles, of nervous tissue and blood and other anatomical structures of your body? You are more than that! You know it, and the man who says he is nothing more really feels or fears that he is. He feels that he is something more than that, though he may try to persuade himself otherwise. There is something in this human frame of ours that existed before the body was formed. Some people call it soul, spirit, mind, and some by names that are less common among us—gnome or devil; but it is there. It is the immortal spirit that existed in the primeval kingdom, in its period of pristine childhood, before ever it came to take its place in this school of mortality, and to assume the student's garb of flesh.

A man is more than body and mind; he consists of body and mind and spirit, though we may regard the mind as being an attribute of the spirit. We know that our educators have risen above the thought that education should deal only with the mind.

We have had intellectual giants developed among us who were of small practical use, comparatively speaking, and some of them have proved a detriment and hindrance to the progress of the race. We have had physical giants with the strength of huge animals but with minds dwarfed, and spirits shrunken and shriveled.

SPIRITUALITY NEGLECTED

Educators today are recognizing the need of symmetrical training, developing the body and the mind. But that would not be a symmetrical education because aside from the mind, even though the mind be an attribute of the spirit, there is the spirit itself, and the race has not developed spiritually in due proportion. Let the evolutionists show to what extent man has developed spiritually during the last several centuries. And the fact that man has become unsymmetrical in his development is the all-important fact, I take it, lying at the basis of the disturbed conditions in society today.

AN INSTANCE

By the way, only yesterday I noticed an item regarding two great structures in the city of London, not very far apart, St. Paul's Cathedral, a triumph of architecture, a monument to the great architect, Sir Christopher Wren, and the Bank of England, in the same section of the city. It has been discovered that both those buildings are leaning over, their foundations seem to be sinking, with the possibility of their eventual fall, and capable engineers have been called into consultation.

I noted that Professor Miles Walker, who is the president of the engineering section of the British Association for the Advancement of Science, had something to do with the consideration of that problem, and he draws attention to the fact that the cases in point are not the only kinds of displacement to be considered in this world of ours today—the sinking of great buildings. He suggests that some of our social structures, spiritual structures, if you like, are sinking and coming out of plumb, and there is danger of their collapse. He proposes that the British Government organize an experimental colony to be managed by engineers—remember, he is an engineer and the president of the Engineering Section of the great British Association for the Advancement of Science—a colony to be directed by engineers, to demonstrate how far it is possible to maintain, say one hundred thousand people, with all the best of modern facilities of life, in a state of semi-isolation, separating them from conditions that bring about the "restraints and social errors of modern civilization."

It is very interesting to note that the recommendation was overwhelmingly rejected and the great man was given to understand that science, in one sense, has already gone ahead too fast, and that the spiritual part of man has not kept up. One of our American newspapers, a leading one, the *Philadelphia Public Ledger,* makes comment on that in these words:

"An ancient seer, who knew nothing of modern engineering or of the achievements of science laid down the rule that in a successful society men would do justly, love mercy, and walk humbly with their God.

"Every Utopian experiment has failed because it has not stressed the spiritual side of life with its sense of social obligation and the need of unselfishness. They have ignored the weaknesses of human nature.

"If Professor Walker were dealing with machines, his plan might succeed. Man, however, is not a machine. The experiment in Russia to make a machine out of him is slowly but surely breaking down."

SUPPORT UNDER ADVERSITY

"Man, know thyself." Oh, that we may know ourselves and know that we are children of the Eternal One, and that this body is a secondary creation, a later construction, and that it is not the only thing about man, nor the principle thing, for the body will die—though surely it shall be resurrected—but the spirit can not die, and the spirit is really the man.

Now, what is my religion doing for me under these conditions? It should be a support. It should show me that notwithstanding these stresses and seemingly unfavorable forces there is purpose and plan in the experiences through which the human race is passing. It should teach me to be more considerate because of the suffering about me, in which perhaps I share, and to be more willing to help. It should teach me to be more tolerant, to be kind, to be kinder

260

than I have been, and not to fight complainingly against the conditions that befall. You know that winter is coming by and by. Will you grumble and complain because of the ice and snow? It has to come, and the wise man will prepare for it.

LIBERALITY TOWARD OTHERS

My religion ought to teach me to have greater respect for my fellows, and to realize that this is the day of which the prophets have spoken, when all that can be shaken in the institutions of men shall be shaken. Are they not shaking all about us? Have your banks not shaken and fallen? Have your theories of philosophy not been found faulty? Have the conjectures of scientific men not been reversed, changed, and in some instances shaken to pieces? Only that which has been established by a power greater than man shall endure.

My religion ought to teach me to regard my fellow as entitled to his views, as well as I am to mine, in matters political as in all else, I believe in men taking part in politics. We have to do so in order to function in government, even as has been said. But I say to you Latter-day Saints if you, my brother, claim to be a Republican, be a straight, honest one. And if you, my other brother claim to be a Democrat, be a genuine Democrat. I know too many honorable Democrats to believe that all the good is in the Republican party, or the reverse. Some people even say: "Both can not be right." "Oh, is that so? Then if the Republicans are right the Democrats must be wrong." Would the proposition stand analysis? According to that, if the Democrats are good the Republicans are bad, out and out. Well now, I know good people and I know bad people, according to my mode of analysis, in both these parties, and I have been led to say sometimes that I think each is a little worse than—perhaps I should say better than—the other. Do not think because your neighbor does not vote your ticket that he is reprobate and bound for destruction. Do your duty as citizens, as I try to do mine, and do not feel that your neighbor is not entitled to his views. Do not let rancor and hatred find a place in your heart because of political differences.

VALUE OF OPPOSITION

Perhaps no greater truth was ever expressed than that revealed through the prophet Lehi: "It must needs be that there is an opposition in all things." As it is we sometimes have trouble in getting any considerable part of our citizens to the polls, and how many do you think would go if we had only one party and one ticket in the field? There must needs be opposition. Let it be honorable opposition. Let differences of opinion be held in honesty. Oh, let us be men, remembering our divine origin, and conducting ourselves accordingly.

May we go hence encouraged to greater effort, to endure and to meet what comes, in the right spirit, and to serve the Lord our God in our actions, as we profess to do according to the words of our mouths, I humbly pray, in the name of Jesus Christ. Amen.

{39}

"Timeliness,"
An Address Delivered on 9 April 1933

(from *One Hundred and Third Annual Conference
of the Church of Jesus Christ of Latter-day Saints*
[Salt Lake City: Published by the Church of Jesus Christ
of Latter-day Saints, 1933], pp. 107-109)

We are reassembled at the time and place appointed, and if we have come, as I feel that we have, with the spirit of righteous desire and faith in our hearts, we should receive a continuation of the blessings that have been so marked in the earlier sessions of this conference.

TIMELINESS

Time and timeliness are very important in the affairs of men, and no less in the ever unfolding purposes of the Lord our God. He does things in his own due time, and that is always the right time. In the establishment of this nation, of which we have heard much, he chose the time, after due preparation had been made. I believe that had an attempt been made by men to establish a democracy, such as this, a hundred or fifty or twenty years earlier, it would have been a failure.

There is a time for seeding and there is a time for harvest.

Many of us become impatient and desire to reap the harvests of the fields and the orchards even before the harvests of the snows have been garnered in the storage recesses of these everlasting hills.

There was a time for the establishment of this Church.

It was the Lord's time. Great and numerous events had been leading up to it, and at the appointed time it was established, never again to be thrown down.

EXAMPLES OF TIMELINESS

There is a marked timeliness in the advice and counsel and instructions given to the Latter-day Saints from period to period. Many could not understand, or would not understand why, but a few years ago, during the epoch of recognized prosperity, the usual advice and counsel to the people in regard to things temporal was emphasized, perhaps more than ever before. People were told to get out of debt,

263

and to keep out of debt, and not to go into expanding schemes whereby their means would be tied up. They were told of the very conditions that are now upon us. It is true that through all the decades past since the people came to these mountains, advice of this kind had been given; but it was intensified in recent years, and those who had ears to hear listened and acted upon the counsel given. To others it was mere repetition, and they permitted it to pass.

There was a time when our Elders were preaching among the nations of the earth the doctrine of the gathering, and urging upon the people, the members of the Church in those other countries, to make arrangements to come to Zion as soon as they could. That was when immigration into this country was unrestricted, and the Perpetual Emigration Fund was maintained for the assistance of worthy saints who were otherwise prepared to come to this land. They were told at that time I heard the Elders of the Church declare it when I was a boy in my native land—that the day would come when it would not be possible for people to come to Zion, and they should take advantage of the opportunities that they then possessed. And so it is with many other developments.

COUNSEL IN SEASON

Now, at this conference there has been much emphasis laid upon the necessity of attention to personal health and the conditions that tend to conserve and insure health of body and mind. I can imagine that some who are deaf to the finer sounds of the Gospel, as declared by the Lord's representatives, may well say: "We have heard that before. We have heard too many sermons about the Word of Wisdom." There is significant meaning in the emphasis that has been given to this subject at the current conference, and those of you who are receptive—and I trust most of you are—must know there is a deep significance in the emphasis being laid upon that topic just now.

Have you not read of the pestilences, including perhaps strange diseases, that are to sweep the earth? They are among the judgments that were foretold for these days. We had a taste of such back in 1918-1919, when the great influenza carried, according to the established records, over sixteen millions of people to their graves. Now, all other things being equal, it is the healthy and the strong who are more likely to survive under the assault of disease.

Latter-day Saints, look to your bodies, look to your health, as you have been again and again advised to do; and if disease and pestilence

264

come let it not take you because of your blamable condition of ill health.

We have heard of these ills—calamities we call them though they may be blessings to the race in disguise—that are characteristic of these days. They have been predicted, and some people are apt to place responsibility if not blame for all these upon the Lord, and to envision him as a God of vengeance. He is a God of love, and it is necessary that some of these experiences shall come upon mankind, that they may be better prepared for what the Lord has in store for them by way of blessing.

FOREKNOWLEDGE NOT A DETERMINING CAUSE

It is not fair to blame the Lord, even in thought, because he gives us warning of what is to come. It is most irrational and illogical so to do. He, with his omniscience, knows what is to come to individuals and nations, and he gives warnings. Many of us take that warning to be an expression of divine determination to punish and to afflict. Well, others besides the Lord are subjects of ill-directed blame sometimes. I have suffered from it. On one occasion I undertook to warn a merry party of intending picnickers not to set out on their jaunt, because a storm was coming, a violent storm. I had consulted the instruments that told of its coming. But they knew better and they went, and they came back in some fashion. I wish you could have seen them. But the tragical part of it was they blamed it all on me.

Shall it be that because the storm is predicted we should believe that the foreknowledge so used is a determining cause? You know better. Let us be thankful for the warnings that the Lord has given and is giving, and prepare ourselves against the tempest.

Oh, Latter-day Saints, we have to bear the conditions that have been foretold, and that are now being realized. Let us do it with faith and resignation, never faltering, knowing that the Lord will bring out all things well, for his word shall not fail, nor shall his purposes be turned aside.

I am happy to be in harmony with the spirit of this conference, to find myself receptive to the advice that has been given.

May the Lord's peace and support be with us now, henceforth and forever, I humbly pray, in his name. Amen.

{40}

"Priesthood—Decline of the Primitive Church," An Address Delivered on 23 July 1933

(from the *Deseret News*, 29 July 1933, pp. 4, 8)

Under the administration of the apostles of old the Church of Jesus Christ grew to be both big and great. Please note the distinction. Bigness is a matter of size, bulk or numbers; greatness has to do with quality. While our Lord yet lived and labored among men the Church he established was not a big institution; nevertheless it was the greatest religious organization on the face of the earth.

Racial barriers between Jews and Gentiles came to be so far broken down as to bring into the Church people of many nationalities, so that during the lives of the apostles the terms Jew and Gentile carried no distinctive meaning as to membership or non-membership in the Church:

"For by one Spirit we are all baptized into one body, whether we be Jews or Gentiles, whether we be bond or free; and have been all made to drink into one Spirit." (1 Cor. 12:13.)

And again, the same apostle writing to the Gentile members in Galatia, designating them as Greeks, gave them cheer and encouragement in these lines:

"For ye are all the children of God by faith in Christ Jesus. For as many of you as have been baptized into Christ, have put on Christ. There is neither Jew nor Greek, there is neither bond nor free, there is neither male nor female; for ye are all one in Christ Jesus." (Gal. 3:26-28.)

The Disciples Called Christians

We are provided with a very convenient name, however, by which to designate the members of the ancient Church, a name that did not originate among themselves but was fastened upon them by their opponents. We read that Barnabas and Paul—while the latter was yet known as Saul of Tarsus spent a whole year at Antioch "with the church, and taught much people. And the disciples were called Christians first in Antioch." (Acts 11:26.)

Whether or no[t] the name was applied in ridicule or hate it has become so far sanctified that today there is but one higher distinction than to be called a Christian, and that is to be in fact a Christian.

A studious reader of the Acts, the Epistles and the Revelation of John can not fail to be impressed by the fact that the early Christian Church was far from being a homogeneous organization with unified membership, all seeing alike in matters of doctrine, principles and practice. Quite to the contrary, the Church was plagued by internal dissension, schisms, and the elements of disruption almost from the beginning of the apostolic administration. This condition of disruption grew in proportion to the loss of respect and cessation of obedience on the part of the members toward the Holy Priesthood and the men who ministered by its authority.

Beware of False Teachers

That the Church would be troubled by assault from without and by dissension within was plainly foretold by the Lord and later by his apostles. In that affecting interview with the disciples, given as he sat on the Mount of Olives, following his last discourse within the temple walls, Jesus answered some of their questions, saying:

"Take heed that no man deceive you. For many shall come in my name, saying, I am Christ; and shall deceive many . . . And many false prophets shall rise, and shall deceive many. And because iniquity shall abound, the love of many shall wax cold. But he that shall endure unto the end, the same shall be saved." (Matt. 24:4-13).

On the sad occasion of Paul's last meeting with the elders of the church at Ephesus, he told them that one there present would see his face again, as by the spirit he had learned that the day of his martyrdom was near, and continued: "For I know this, that after my departing grievous wolves enter in among you, not sparing the flock. Also of your own selves shall men arise, speaking perverse things, to draw away disciples after them." (Acts 20:28-30) As later events show, the wolves did enter the fold, as false teachers clad in the lamb-like garb of piety, but inwardly none the less ravening wolves.

To the saints in Corinth Paul wrote in pleading words mingled with reproof, warning them against divisions and contention and chiding them for their selfish preferences. Hear his words:

"Now I beseech you, brethren, by the name of our Lord Jesus Christ, that ye all speak the same thing, and that there be no divisions among you; but that ye be perfectly joined together in the same mind and in the same judgment. Now this I say, that every one of you saith,

I am of Paul; and I am of Appollos; and I of Cephas; and I of Christ. Is Christ divided? Was Paul crucified for you? Or were ye crucified for you? Or were ye" (1 Cor. 1:10-13). *[Editor's note: omitted from the original printing is the end phrase of this scripture which reads "baptized in the name of Paul?"]*

To the offending members among the Corinthians he brought accusations o[f] vile offenses such as were not even named among the Gentile outsiders, and by the exercise of his authority delivered such gross sinners over to Satan. See chapter 5.

He reproved the Corinthians for their lack of understanding of what the sacred ordinance which he, and he alone, calls the Lord's Supper. The sacrament of bread and wine had been perverted into a mere matter of eating and drinking, for the satisfying of their appetites rather than in remembrance of him whose body and blood had been sacrified for them and for the world. It is pleasing to know that the sharp discipline thus administered brought about a partial repentance and a measure of reformation at Corinth.

To the Christian church in Galatia, Paul wrote in terms of sorrowful reproach because of defection, due to their following after false teachers, who seemingly had undertaken to supplant the gospel of Jesus Christ by some miscalled gospel more attractive to their sensuous minds:

"I marvel that ye are so soon removed from him that called you into the grace of Christ unto another gospel. Which is not another. But there be some that trouble you, and would pervert the gospel of Christ. But though we, or an angel from heaven, preach any other gospel unto you, than that which we have preached unto you, let him be accursed." (Gal. 1:6-8.)

Falling Away Predicted

In addressing the Thessalonian Christians Paul warned them against the error, strongly advocated by some in that day, that the time of Christ's second advent was then imminent. It appears that deception was being practiced, and that the probability of forged letters being presented as having come from the apostles was apparent; for Paul instructs the people that they be not deceived "by word nor by letter as from us." It is clearly set forth that the false teachings and the inevitable departure from the way of the Lord herein referred to were no local or merely then present dangers, but that on the other hand the evils afflicting the Church would continue with increasing virulence.

The earnestness of Paul's appeal and warning is best expressed in his own words:

"Now we beseech you, brethren, by the coming of our Lord Jesus Christ, and by our gathering together unto him: That ye be not soon shaken in mind, or be troubled, neither by spirit, nor by word, nor by letter as from us, as that the day of Christ is at hand. Let no man deceive you by any means: for that day shall not come, except there come a falling away first, and that man of sin be revealed, the son of perdition; who opposeth and exalteth himself above all that is called God, or that is worshipped, so that he as God sitteth in the temple of God, showing himself; that he is God."

It shall be shown how painfully literal has been the fulfillment of this prophecy in the blasphemous assumptions of the apostate church at a later date. But the evil forces were then active, the deadly germs were spreading like foul contagion from member to member, from church to church:

"For the mystery of iniquity doth already work," declared the apostle, "only he who now letteth will let, until he be taken out of the way. And then shall that wicked be revealed, whom the Lord shall consume with the spirit of his mouth, and shall destroy with the brightness of his coming." (2 Thess. 2:1-8.)

The seemingly obscure expression, "he who now letteth will let," may be more readily understood by remembering that in the olden style of English *let* had the meaning of *restrain* or *hinder*. In the Revised Version of the New Testament the passage reads "For the mystery of lawlessness doth already work, only there is one that restraineth now, until he bet [sic] taken out of the way."

Just who or what is meant as exercising a restraint on the powers of iniquity at that time has given rise to discussion.

Some hold that the presence of the apostles operated in this way, and that after their departure the powers of evil would have greater sway; while other's believe that the restraining power of the Roman government is referred to. It is known that the policy of Rome, then called Mistress of the World, was to discountenance religious contention, and to allow a large measure of liberty in forms of worship so long as the pagan deities were not maligned nor their shrines dishonored.

Mystery of False Doctrine

The expression "mystery of iniquity" as used by Paul is significant. Prominent among the early perverters of the Christian faith were those

269

who assailed its simplicity and lack of exclusiveness. This was so different from the mysteries of Judaism and the mystic rites of heathen idolatry as to be disappointing to many; and the earliest changes in the Christian form of worship, toward the degradation which is eventually reached, were marked by the introduction of spectacular ceremonies.

He admonished the Colossians to distinguish between the teachings of Christ and the philosophies of men:

"Beware lest any man spoil you through philosophy and vain deceit, after the tradition of men, after the rudiments of the world, and not after Christ."

The same apostle warns Timothy of the fast approaching declension, and refers to some of the pernicious teachings that would be impressed upon misguided members of the Church, teachings which he calls "doctrines of devils." He admonishes Timothy to put the brethren in remembrance of these things, as is becoming in a good minister of Christ, "nourished up in the words of faith and of good doctrine."

"Now the Spirit speaketh expressly that in the latter times some shall depart from the faith, giving heed to seducing spirits, and doctrines of devils.

"Speaking lies in hypocrisy; having their conscience seared with a hot iron;

"Forbidding to marry, and commanding to abstain from meats, which God hath created to be received with thanksgiving of them which believe and know the truth." (1 Tim. 4:1-3)

In another epistle to Timothy, while laboring under the premonition that his own death was near Paul urges zeal and energy in the preaching of the Gospel; for the dark shadows of false doctrine were then gathering thickly about the Church. His admonition is pathetic in its earnestness:

"I charge thee, therefore before God, and the Lord Jesus Christ, who shall judge the quick and the dead at his appearing and his kingdom;

"Preach the word; be instant in season, out of season; approve, rebuke, exhort with all long suffering and doctrine.

"For the time will come when they will not endure sound doctrine; but after their own lusts shall they heap to themselves teachers, having itching ears;

"And they shall turn away their ears from the truth, and shall be turned unto fables." —(2 Tim. 4:1-4.)

Heresies Foretold

Peter the Apostle prophesied in language so plain that none may fail to comprehend, concerning the heresies that would be preached as doctrine in the Church; and he reminds the people that as there were false teachers in olden times even so would there be such in their time and in the future.

"But there were false prophets also among the people, even as there shall be false teachers among you, who privily shall bring in damnable heresies, even denying the Lord that bought them, and bring upon themselves swift destruction.

"And many shall follow their pernicious ways; by reason of whom the way of truth shall be evil spoken of.

"And through covetousness shall they with feigned words make merchandise of you; whose judgment now of a long time lingereth not, and their damnation slumbereth not." (2 Pet. 2:1-3).

In his general epistle to the Saints, Judge [sic] reminds them of earlier warnings:

"But, beloved, remember ye the words which were spoken before of the apostles of our Lord Jesus Christ:

"How that they told you there should be mockers in the last time, who should walk after their own ungodly lusts.

"These be they who separate themselves, sensual, having not the Spirit." (Jude 17-19.)

In an earlier part of his epistle Jude encourages the Saints *not* only to hold but to contend for the faith which had once been delivered to them:

"For, there are certain men crept in unawares, who were before of old ordained to this condemnation, ungodly men, turning the grace of our God into lasciviousness, and denying the only Lord God, and our Lord Jesus Christ."

John the apostle was no less definite in his declaration of iniquity within the Church and respecting those who had separated themselves from the Church because of the spirit of wickedness that had taken possession of them:

"Beloved, believe not every spirit, but try the spirits whether they are of God: because many false prophets are gone out into the world." (1 John 5:1.)

As the Revelator, this same John who had spoken of the disruption then manifest in the Church, set forth, as he had seen in vision, to what extent the power of Satan would be permitted to prevail for the time being. Describing the spirit of unrighteousness as a hideous beast, and its instigator, Satan, as the dragon, he says:

"And they worshipped the dragon which gave power unto the beast; and they worshipped the beast, saying, Who is like unto the beast? Who is able to make war with him?

"And he opened his mouth in blasphemy against God, to blaspheme his name, and his tabernacle, and them that dwell in heaven.

"And It was given unto him to make war with the Saints, and to overcome them; and power was given him over all kindreds, and tongues, and nations.

"And all that dwell upon the earth shall worship him whose names are not written in the book of life of the lamb slain from the foundation of the world.

"If any man have an ear, let him hear." (Rev. 13:4, 6-9).

Note another prophecy based on the vision of John the Revelator. Referring to latter-day conditions, but speaking in the past tense of things he had seen in vision, he declares:

"And I saw another angel fly in the midst of heaven having the everlasting gospel to preach unto them that dwell on the earth, and to every nation, and kindred, and tongue, and people, Saying with a loud voice, Fear God, and give glory to him; for the hour of his judgment is come: and worship him that made heaven, and earth, and the sea, and the fountains of water." (Rev. 14:6, 7).

While it is true that the scripture last quoted does not specifically affirm the advancing apostasy, the breaking up of the Church is treated as an event actually accomplished.

The Revelator looked beyond the period of disruption and saw the brighter day of the restoration of the Gospel—a reestablishment of the Church through angelic agency. It is illogical to assume that the Gospel was to be brought to earth by a heavenly messenger if that Gospel was already extant upon the earth. Equally unreasonable is it to say that a restoration or reestablishment of the Church of Christ would be necessary or possible had the Church continued with rightful succession of Priesthood and power. If the Gospel had to be brought again from the heavens, the Gospel must have been taken from the earth. Thus the prophecy of a restoration is proof of an apostasy general and complete.

After the Apostles Left

Dissension in the Primitive Church and declension of the organization proceeded rapidly in the days immediately following the departure of the ancient apostles. Those men of God had labored with might and main to prepare the soil of the minds of men, to implant therein the living seed of the one and only Gospel of Jesus Christ, and to nourish that seed to maturity. At times their hearts were filled with righteous joy over the conversion of souls. Gladly they endured stripes, imprisonment, and all the tortures incident to persecution for the Gospel's sake. But their hearts must have been very heavy and their souls afflicted with sorrow, as they looked upon the gathering clouds of weakening faith and the many withdrawals from the Church, under pressure of persecution from without and dissension among those who professed membership.

One by one the apostles passed, as a procession of martyrs, leaving the Church operative, however, save only for the high authority of the apostleship which was taken from the earth with them. It had been their duty, at once solemn and sorrowful, which duty they had discharged with full fidelity, to predict the coming night when Satanic darkness would enshroud the souls of men.

If the early Christian Church had become weak through internal diseases and enfeebled by vicious and persistent onslaughts of pronounced opponents, even while the apostles were present in person, what was to be expected after these prophetically inspired leaders had departed? In the foreknowledge of God it had been seen that for a season the Church would be driven into the wilderness, and the world of mankind be left in spiritual darkness because of iniquity.

Simplicity Followed by Mystery

As a divine institution the Church soon ceased to exist, the powers of the holy priesthood were literally taken from the earth. In place of the plain, simple requirements and ordinances of the gospel, MYSTERY came to hold sway, typified by a woman of scarlet, seated upon a beast displaying the "names of blasphemy" and holding in her hand a golden cup full of abomination and filthiness, upon whose forehead was written:

"MYSTERY, BABYLON THE GREAT. THE MOTHER OF HARLOTS

273

AND ABOMINATIONS OF THE EARTH. And I saw the woman drunken with blood of the Saints, and with the blood of the martyrs of Jesus." (Rev. 17:5).

A study of the progress of the GREAT APOSTASY will demonstrate how clear had been the vision, how accurate the description given by John, of the institution that boasted so arrogantly of being the lineal successor of the Church established by him who affirmed, "MY KINGDOM IS NOT OF THIS WORLD."

Index

A

"A Peep through a Microscope," talk by J. E. T., 37

Aaronic Priesthood, 160

Abinidi, quotes Isaiah, 221

Abiogenesis, 21

Abraham, 130, 192, 209, 228, paid tithe, 201-202, was a polygamist, 71

Adam, 145, 148, 189, 210, 246; a historic personage, 243; Ancient of Days, 138; not descended from Neanderthal, 249; (and Eve) principle of Word of Wisdom revealed to, 108-11

adultery, and idolatry, 225-27

agency, 145, 195-96

Alma, and Amulek, 214; on repentance, 112-13; on resurrection, 130

An Address: The Church of Jesus Christ of Latter-day Saints to the World, J. E. T. helps prepare, xxv

angel, and Moses, 87-88

antemortal state, *see* preexistence

antiquity of man, 236, 237

ape, and man, 246-47

apostasy, 143, 155-57, 266-74

apostle, J. E. T. called as, xxv-xxvi, 90-93; definition of, 119; duties of, 118, 119-20, 198

apostolos, 119-20

Arnold, Sir Edward, translates "Pearls of the Faith," 87-88

Articles of Faith, asked to publish lectures regarding, 46; controversial matters in, xxiii-xxiv; journal entries regarding, 44-62; letter of appointment on from First Presidency, 46; official announcement, 57-58; selections from first edition, 63-70

Articles of Faith, change in wording of Fourth, xxiii-xxiv, 49-50; J. E. T. present when they are re-adopted by the church, xxi

astrology, xiv; science of, 32; a false science, 34-35; terms and meanings, 31-32

atheism, 5, 8

Atonement, 146; definition of, 149-51

Aveling, "The Student's Darwin," 25

B

baptism, 152; proper form of, 49; of J. E. T., xv, 1-3

Baptist church, 158

Bathsheba, mother of Solomon, 72

Bathybius, 20-21

bee, story of unwise, 86-87

Belshazzar, 227

Bentley, President and Sister Maud, 9

Bible, 101-102, 123-27, 179-80, 232; and records of Ten Tribes, 179; parts of figurative, 123-24

bicycle story, xxii

"Birth and Growth of the Earth," talk by J. E. T., 12-13

"Birth and Growth of Worlds," talk by Prof. R. A. Proctor, 4

Bishop, definition of, 119; duties of, 198

Blair, George, home missionary, 52

"Blasphemy," talk given by J. E. T., 52

bodies, 107-13; temple of the Holy Ghost, 108; body, soul combined, 108

Book of Abraham, 111-12

Book of Mormon, 101; and Book of Isaiah, 218-24; and records of Ten Tribes, 179; J. E. T. revises, xxix

Booth, Merry May, see Merry May Booth Talmage

Brandley, Elsie Talmage, see Talmage, Elsie

Brandley, Harold, husband of Elsie, with J. E. T. at his death, xxxi

brevet rank, none in Church of Christ, 118

Buffon, naturalist, 17-18

C

Calvinist church, 99, 158

Cannabis Indica, see hashish

Cannon, Abraham H., apostle, member of Articles of Faith reading committee, xxii, 48; reads letter from First Presidency thanking J. E. T., 53; replaced by Anthon H. Lund, 55

Cannon, (President) Angus, 47

Cannon, (President) David, 42

Cannon, George Q., comments on ambiguity in church literature regarding the Holy Ghost, xxiii, xxxix n47, 50-51; hears voice of Holy Ghost, 55-56; in audience of theology class 48; on Brigham

Young and rebaptism, 49-50; on price of Articles of Faith, 56

Capel, Monsiegnor, J. E. T. attends lecture on science and religion by, 6

Carpenter, Dr., microscopist, 77-78

Catholic church, 158

Challenger, 20

Charlamagne, 203-204

chastity, law of not broken in Garden of Eden, 110-11

Christians, 267; meaning of Easter to, 99-100; Mormons accused of not being, 99-100

chrysalis, an analogy of resurrection, 95

Church of England, 158

Church of Jesus Christ of Latter-day Saints, church in God's name, 99-100, 136, 160; and scientific research, 239; is a Christian church, 99-100; is abreast of the very best of scientific conception, 126; is up-to-date, 98-99, 252; offices of priesthood, 117-21; progressivism of, 102

Civil War, 105-106

Clark, J. Reuben, assists J. E. T. in typing manuscript for Articles of Faith, xxiv; marriage solemnized by J. E. T., xxiv, xxxviii n43; with J. E. T. at his death, xxxi

Clawson, Rudger, 236; agrees with Reed Smoot on League of Nations, xviii, xxxviii n33

Congregationalist church, 99, 158

Congress, enacts anti-polygamy legislation, 73

Conkey, Henry W., 60

Constitution, 105-106

Creator, made record in rocks, 243

Ivins, Anthony W., 237, 239; agrees with H. J. Grant on League of Nations, xviii; informs J. E. T. of call to the apostleship, xxv, 90

J

Jacob, (Israel), 228; practiced polygamy, 71; vow to pay tithe, 202

Japan, 213

Jehovah, *see* Jesus Christ

Jesus Christ, a church in his name, 99; approved of tithing, 203; atonement of, 89, 146, 149-51; born of polygamous lineage, 72-73; breaks bonds of death, 26; distinguishing features of the church concerning, 172-73; disruption during death of, 211-12; elder brother, 250-51; Jehovah, 144; mission to dead, 96-97; need of a redeemer, 142, 147-50; quotes Isaiah, 221-22; resurrection of, 94-100; return of, 173, 188-91, 216-17; savior, 148-49; to return as King, 103; title "Son of Man," 135-41

Jesus the Christ, xxvi-xxviii, xxxii, 135, 163-70; letter of appointment on from First Presidency, 163-64; official announcement, 168

John the Revelator, 144, 158, 272-73

Jordan, D. David Starr, 8

"Josephite" church, 52

Josephus, 224

Juvenile Instructor, prints lectures on *Articles of Faith*, 54

K

Keller, Helen, J. E. T. meets, xv

Kennet River, 1

Kingdom and church, selection from *Articles of Faith*, first edition, 66-68

Kingdom of God and Kingdom of Heaven, 150, 171, 175-76, 186-91

Kingdoms, Celestial, Telestial, Terrestrial, *see* progression between the kingdoms

Kolliker, (Prof.), German authority on embryology, 22-23

Koran, 88

L

L.D.S. College, xxii, xxxii

Laban, 221

Lamark (Lamarck), 17, 248

Larson, Stan, introduction to "The Truth, The Way, The Life," by B. H. Roberts, xxx-xxxi, xliv n78,

Latter-day Revelation, prepared by J. E. T., xxx, xliii n75

League of Nations controversy, xviii, xxxv n20

Leah, 71

Lehi, 221, 223

liberty (and freedom), 103-105

Liberty Bonds, 195

Life of Christ, by Frederick Farrar, xxvii, xli n59, 168

"little-great men," 7, 82, 125

Lord Chancellor of England, president of Philosophical Society of Great Britain, 124-25

Lost Tribes, *see* Ten Tribes

Lucifer, *see* Satan

Lund, Anthon H., assists in ordaining J. E. T. an apostle, xxv, 91; replaces A. H. Cannon as member of the reading committee for *Articles of Faith*, 55

Lutheran church, 158

Lyman, F. M., home missionary, 51

Lyman, Francis M., chair of *Articles of Faith* reading committee, xxii, 48, 55; assists in ordaining J. E. T. an apostle, xxv, 91; gives apostolic charge, xxv-xxvi, 91-92

Lyman, Richard R., 8, 170, 239

M

Maeser, Karl, xv; J. E. T., convicted as part of Edmunds-Tucker Act, xx-xxi; member of *Articles of Faith* reading committee, xxii, 48, 55; memorial address regarding, 9; tours LDS school system with, xv

Maeser, Reinhard, on young J. E. T., xv

Malachi, 203, 204

man, 13; a creature of bias, 76; and ape, 246-47; created in image of deity 10; has used superior strength to oppress woman, 131; potential to become like God, 141, 153; reason placed on earth, 131, 142, 145; teach him he evolved from brute he will live like a brute, 84

Manifesto, of Wilford Woodruff, xxi, 74

marriage relation, eternal, 84, 133-32

Martin family, J. E. T. helps recuperate from diphtheria, xxxi-xxxii

Martin, Jesse, patriarch, prophesies of J. E. T. call to apostleship, 40-41, 91

materialist, 210

matter, 63-64

McCune, President, invitation at Free Thought Forum, 8

McKay, David O., agrees with Reed Smoot on League of Nations,

xviii; J. E. T. replaces as head of European mission, xxix

Melchizedek, Abraham paid tithes to, 201-202; priesthood named after, 119; restoration of, 160

memory, library of the mind, 113

meridian of time, 142, 154-55, 174

meteorites, discovery of, 240

Methodist church, 158

"Methods and Motives of Science," talk by J. E. T., 6-7, 77-85

Meyers, Albert, xxviii

Michael, 144

Mill, John Stuart, 5

Mills, John M., 163

Milton, 222-23

miracles, 232; of New Testament, 125

missionaries, 114

Mormon (Book of Mormon leader), not the church of, 99

Mormon church, *see* Church of Jesus Christ of Latter-day Saints

"Mormonism and Science," talk by J. E. T., 8

Moroni, on gifts of the spirit, 231-32; promise of, 219-20

Mosaic Law, Christ fulfilled, 228; on tithe, 202-203

Moses, 154; and Satan, 232-33; had more than one wife, 71, 73; story of Moses and angel, 87-88

Mother in Heaven, 132, 145; church bold enough to declare we have, 84

N

Nathanael, 137-38

Natural Selection, 19, 24

nature, 63-64

priesthood, 155; bestowed on men only, 131-32; definition of, 117

Proctor, (Prof.) R.A., J. E. T. attends lecture by on "Birth and Growth of Worlds," 4

progression between the kingdoms, xxiii, xxxviii n39, 69

progressive religion, 102

prophecy, spirit of, by J. E. T. concerning Ten Tribes, 184; to deny would be false to science, 82

prophet, incorrect to address president as, 119; placed before philosopher, 18

Q

quadrumana, 248

R

Rachel, wife of Jacob, 71

"Ready References," J. E. T. compiles with Joseph Fielding Smith, xxix

reason, human, 65

rebaptism, 49-50

Redeemer, need of, 142, 147-50

Reformation, 157

religion, a support, 256, 260-61

repentance, 112-13, 151

Republican, 261

restoration, 143, 157-61, 272-73

resurrection, 130; analogies of, 95-96; LDS belief in, 94; of Jesus Christ, 94-100

revelation, a religion enriched by new, 98-99; literalness of resurrection known through, 96; modern, 98-99; need for continuous, 101-106, 155

Revelator, 119

Revised Version, quoted, 269

Reynolds, George, member of *Articles of Faith* reading committee, xxii, 47, 48, 55; remarks thanking J. E. T. for teaching theology class, 53

Richards, George, assists in ordaining J. E. T. an apostle, xxv

Richards, Stephen L, agrees with H. J. Grant on League of Nations, xviii, xxxvii n33

Richter, John Paul, "Dream Vision of the Infinite," 253-54

Roberts, Brigham H., evolution controversy, xxx-xxxi, xliii-xliv n76-n79, 236-237, 239; letter to J. E. T. regarding Reed Smoot hearings, xxxviii-xxxix n45; on progression between the kingdoms, xxxviii n39; pamphlet "Succession in the Presidency of the Church," 51-52; talks on League of Nations in Tabernacle, xviii

Rocky Mountains, 182

rose bush, analogy of transplant, 64

Rushton, claims to own seer stones, 45

S

sabbath, 228

sacrament, taking unworthily, 51

Saint, 121

Samuel, prophet, was offspring of polygamous marriage, 72

Satan, 138, 195-96, 232-33, 235; is skillful salesman, 103; son of the morning, 146; war in heaven, 144

Savage, Lucine (Clark), xxiv

scholastic attainment, not necessary to understand gospel, 178

school bully, 33-35

schools, 178

Spencer, Herbert, and "development hypothesis," 10

spiritual gifts, 231-32

stake presidency, concerning church courts, 198

Stephen, 139

"Stimulants and Narcotics," talk by J. E. T., xvii

Story of Mormonism, by J. E. T., xxv

Strauss, on Bathybius, 21

Student's Darwin, by Aveling, 25

"Succession in the Presidency of the Church," by B. H. Roberts, 51-52

Sunday Night Talks by Radio, by J. E. T., xxx

T

Tables for Blowpipe Determination of Minerals, by J. E. T., xxiv

Talmage, Albert, brother of J. E. T., blinded, xv

Talmage, Elsie (Brandley), at J. E. T. bedside at his death, xxxi; daughter of J. E. T., xviii; on her father, xviii-xix

Talmage, George, brother of J. E. T., 61

Talmage, Helen, at J. E. T. bedside at his death, xxxi; daughter of J. E. T., xviii

Talmage, James, death of, xv; paternal grandfather of J. E. T., xiii

Talmage, James E. (J. E. T.):
—Alderman, xvii
—assignment to excommunicate those practicing plural marriage xxi, xxxvii n33
—baptism of xv, xxxiv n7, 1-3
—bicycle story, xxii
—birth of, xiv
—blessings given to, 37-43, 92-93

—blinds brother, xv
—call to the apostleship, xxv-xxvi, 90-93
—changes Fourth Article of Faith, xxiii, 49
—charge of apostasy against, xxv
—children of, xviii
—death of, xxxi
—death of grandfather, xv
—disagrees with mixing politics and religion, xviii
—evolution controversy, xxx-xxxi, xliii n76, n77
—experience with astrology, xiv, 30-36
—experiments with hashish, xvii, 10-11
—fellowships and membership in scientific societies, xxii
—fights Ben, school bully, 33-35
—given a room in Salt Lake temple, xxvi, 164, 165-66
—golfing with Heber J. Grant, xiii
—helps Martin family, xxxi-xxxii
—helps prepare *An Address: The Church of Jesus Christ of Latter-day Saints,* xxv
—helps prepare *The Origin of Man,* xxv, xxix n49, 7
—home dedicated by Joseph F. Smith, xx
—home missionary, xvii, xxxv n16, 45, 51, 52, 54
—injures knee, xxix-xxx
—insomnia, xxxiii, 54
—installs seismograph at University of Utah, xxii
—journal entries regarding *Articles of Faith,* 44-62
—Justice of the Peace, xvii
—League of Nations controversy, xviii

286

—letter of appointment from First Presidency concerning *Articles of Faith*, 46, and *Jesus the Christ*, 163-64

—made deputy U.S. Marshal, xvii

—naturalized, xvii

—not blessed with visual or oracular manifestations, 45-46

—on calling and ordination as an apostle, xxv-xxvi, 90-93

—on evolution, science, and religion, 4-9, 236-40, 241-55

—on happiness, 114-16

—on higher criticism, xxvii, xli n61, 124, 219-20

—on his mission in life, 4

—on marriage relationship, 84

—on modern revelation, 101-106

—on Mother in Heaven, 84, 132, 145

—on polygamy xx-xxi, 71-74

—on priesthood offices and titles, 117-21

—on progression between the kingdoms, xxiii, xxxviii n39, 69

—on resurrection, 94-100

—on science and religion, 4-9, 75-82

—on the Bible, 123-27

—on the eternity of sex roles, 128-34

—on the fall of man, 110-11

—on the Holy Ghost, xxiii, 50-51, 55-56, 65-66

—on the kingdom of God, 66-68, 176-77, 186-91

—on the sacrament, 51

—on the title "Son of Man,' 135-41

—on the Word of Wisdom, xxxii-xxxiii, lviv n83-n86, 109-11

—on tithing, 175, 201-208

—on wealth and poverty, 69-70

—on World War I, xxviii, 39, 183

—ordained a High Priest, xvii

—prepares definitions for *Webster's Dictionary,* xxx

—prepares *Latter-day Revelation,* xxx, xliii n75

—prepares "Ready References" with Joseph Fielding Smith, xxix

—president of L.D.S. College, xxii, xxxii

—president of University of Utah, xxii, 52-53

—prophecy concerning the Ten Tribes, 184

—relieved of duties of teaching theology class, 52-53

—replaces David O. McKay as head of European mission, xxix

—revises Book of Mormon, xxix

—revises Doctrine and Covenants, xxix

—revises Pearl of Great Price, xxiv

—rumors regarding, xxxii-xxxiii

—sells copyright of *Articles of Faith* to the church, 59

—solemnizes marriage of J. Reuben Clark, xxiv, xxxviii n43

—"Son of Man" controversy, xxvii-xxviii, xli-xlii n63, xlii n64, 167

—suggests idea for "triple combination," xxix

—supports Manifesto of Wilford Woodruff, xxi,

—sustains Vision of the Redemption of the Dead, xxix

—talks on radio, xxx

—teaches Pittman shorthand at Lehigh University, xvi

288